Hudson River Watershed

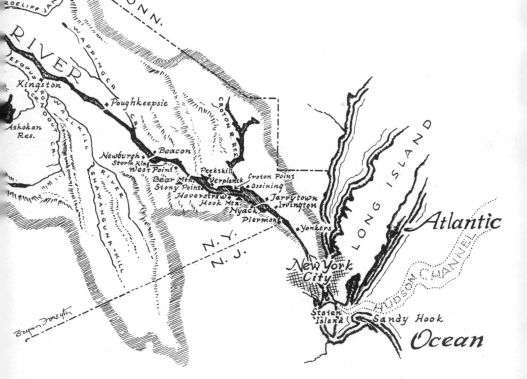

MASS.

CONN.

Hudson

ROELIFF JANSEN

RIVER

ESOPUS

Kingston

ESOPUS CR.

RONDOUT CR.

Ashokan
Res.

WALLKILL

WAPPINGER CR.

Poughkeepsie

RIVER

SHAWANGUNK KILL

Newburgh
Storm King
West Point
Bear Mtn.
Stony Point
Haverstraw
Hook Mtn.
Nyack
Piermont

Beacon

CROTON RES.

Peekskill
Verplanck
Croton Point
Ossining
Tarrytown
Irvington

Yonkers

CROTON RES.

LONG ISLAND

Atlantic

N.Y.
N.J.

New York
City

Staten
Island

HUDSON CHANNEL

Sandy Hook

Ocean

Bryan Forsyth

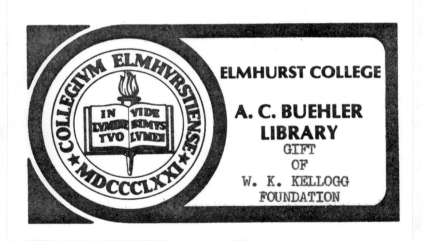

THE
HUDSON RIVER

ROBERT H. BOYLE

THE

HUDSON RIVER

A Natural and Unnatural History

W · W · NORTON & COMPANY · INC

NEW YORK

SBN 393-05379-2

Library of Congress Catalog Card No. 68-10877

Published simultaneously in Canada by
George J. McLeod Limited, Toronto

PRINTED IN THE UNITED STATES OF AMERICA

3 4 5 6 7 8 9 0

To my mother, who first introduced me to the Hudson; to my wife, Jane, who encouraged my explorations; and my children, Stephanie, Peter, and Alexander, who went along, sometimes.

CONTENTS

PREFACE

In essence, this book is an account of the Hudson River, what there is in it, good and bad, and why. In time, the book goes from the beginning of the Hudson seventy-five million years ago to the present day, and in distance it covers the river from its Adirondack Mountain headwaters to its former terminus on the edge of the Continental Shelf. In range of species, it goes from plankton to striped bass to man, whose sometimes unnatural deeds threaten the river with death but whose better spirit is needed for its survival and ultimately his own. To a great extent, I have treated man as a biotic factor, and there is little "history" per se. Readers who are interested in the great and stirring human events that have occurred in the Hudson Valley are advised to consult other books, notably Carl Carmer's *The Hudson*.

There are many persons I wish to thank for their assistance in various ways. The contributions of some are obviously acknowledged in the text, but I would like now to express my thanks and appreciation to Andre Laguerre, Richard W. Johnston, John Tibby, Roy Terrell, Arthur Brawley, Jack Olsen, Gilbert Rogin, Gay Flood, and Christiana Walford of *Sports Illustrated;* Dr. James Alexander (and his wife, Betty) and Dominick Pirone (and his wife, Joan) of Fordham University; Marcia Smith of the Adirondack Museum; Dr. Edgar M. Reilly, Jr., Stanley Smith, John Wilcox, Dr. Donald Collins, and Y. W. Isachsen of the New York State Museum and Science Service; Dr. J. A. Adams of the New York State Agricultural Experiment Station, Highland; Dr. George Bennett of the Illinois Natural History Survey; Dr. C. Lavett Smith, Dr. James Atz, and Howard S. Feinberg of the American Museum of Natural History; Dr. Gwyneth Parry Howells and Dr. T. J. Kneip of New York University; Jack Focht, Cooperative Extension Agent, Rockland County; Dr. Emanuel Sorge of the City University of New York; Dr. Charles Wurster of the State University of New York, Stony Brook; Walter Bogan of the Scientists' Institute for Public Information; and Dr. Lionel A. Walford, John and Roberta Clark, Dave Deuel, Bori Olla, Jack Casey, Bruce Freeman, and Susan Smith, all members, past or present, of the United States Bureau of Sport Fisheries and Wildlife Laboratory at Sandy Hook, New Jersey. The poem "Taxonomic Tragedy" appears through the kind permission of Miss Smith. Thanks are also due to D. W. Bennett and Virginia Steiner of the American Littoral Society. I am indebted to several members of both the New York State conservation and health departments, but to avoid putting them on the spot, I acknowledge their contributions *in petto.*

A number of book specialists were most helpful: Eva, David, and Clarence Gilman of Crompond; Mr. and Mrs. William Embler of Guilderland; Virginia Abelson of Croton-on-Hudson; John Johnson of North Bennington, Vermont; Henry Tripp of New York City; Eric Lundberg of Ashton, Maryland; and Colonel Henry A. Siegel of Goshen, Connecticut.

I would also like to thank Mr. and Mrs. Alfred Forsyth of Chappaqua for many kindnesses, not the least of which is Bryan Forsyth's endpaper map. Others I wish to thank are Richard and Gloria Garrett of Crotonville; Mr. and Mrs. Carl Carmer of Irvington; Susan Reed and William Hoppen of Ardsley; Constantine D'Amato of Rhinebeck; Mrs. Frank J. Clark of Fishers Island;

Richard H. Pough of Pelham; Arthur Glowka of Stamford, Connecticut; Andrew Turchinsky of Yonkers; F. W. Haida of Croton Falls; Rod Vandivert of Islip; Nancy Mathews of Brewster; Richard A. Wolters, James S. Hays, James Canel, Mr. and Mrs. Robert Hofer, Ric Riccardi, Augie Berg, Henry Gourdine, and Tony Morabito of Ossining; Kenneth Gerhardt and James Mowbray of Peekskill; Elgin Ciampi of Tuxedo Park; Lloyd Morgan and William Ewen of Hastings; Raymond Lent and Sonny Mitchell of Verplanck; Charles White of Buchanan; Jesse Brodey of White Plains; Harry and Elsie Darbee of Roscoe; David Sive of Pearl River; Everett Nack of Claverack; Frank Potter of Washington, D.C.; Terry Rotola, Al Butzel, General Malcolm K. Beyer, Seth Rosenbaum, Joe Mintzer, John Wilson, Theodore J. Cornu, Irving Younger, John Cushman, and Thomas F. Moore of New York City; Ted O'Leary of Kansas City, Missouri; Sy Pauls of Fishkill; and Mrs. Adolph Elwyn, Mrs. Willard Brinton, Alwyn Lee, Dan and Norma Salzberg, Jerome Smath, Robert Karas, Wilson Seibert, Richard Wolff, Rodney J. Vermilye, Gabriel Frayne, Dr. Arthur Jensen, Jerome Traum, John Griswold, Robert Hoebermann, Dick and Sophy Boyer, Jane Alspach, Howard Powley, Richie and Pat Ferris, Eugene Price, Ed Hatzmann, Bert Rechtschaffer, Ronald Dagon, Dom and Pete Anfiteatro, Jacquin Sanders, Albert and Rose Granovsky, Frank Zoller, Nick Dini, and Brett Wangler, all of Croton-on-Hudson. Merrill Pollack and Iva Kaplan of W. W. Norton & Co. were of the greatest help in giving advice and direction above and beyond the call of editorial duty.

I would like to thank my wife, Jane, and the children for their understanding during all the difficulties they endured while this book was in progress.

Two brief notes. The opinions in this book are my own and are not to be attributed to any other persons unless they are specifically quoted. I have no wish to play the pedant, but in the interests of accuracy, I have given both the common and scientific names for flora and fauna. As a general rule, the scientific name is used when a species first comes in for major discussion.

THE
HUDSON RIVER

I

THE RIVER

To those who know it, the Hudson River is the most beautiful, messed up, productive, ignored, and surprising piece of water on the face of the earth. There is no other river quite like it, and for some persons, myself included, no other river will do. The Hudson is *the* river.

Such an attitude may seem affected or extravagant. Compared to other American rivers, the Hudson is a relative midget; there are almost eighty rivers that are longer. From its source in the Adirondack Mountains to its mouth at the Battery on the southern tip of Manhattan Island, the Hudson runs only 315 miles. Yet the river has grandeur, and is of just such a size and length as to compel strong sentiments. You feel as though you can come to grips with the Hudson. But then, just when you think you understand the river, perceive its rhythms, and maybe even explain it all to someone else, you discover something new.

Part of the difficulty—and much of the wonder—about the Hudson is caused by its diversity. The river is all sorts of things.

It is trout stream and estuary, water supply and sewer, ship channel and shad river, playground and chamber pot. It is abused, revered, and almost always misunderstood. For instance, in periods of drought there are New Yorkers who bemoan the condition of the river flowing past Manhattan and wonder why the water cannot be cleansed and tapped. But even if the river thereabouts were clean, the water would still be undrinkable because it is salty. What one sees from Manhattan is not so much a river flowing out to sea but the Atlantic Ocean thrusting inland. Because the lower river is polluted, it has become popular to write it off as devoid of life. Any number of politicians and a few biologists have come forward to pronounce publicized benedictions over the Hudson and say loud prayers for its dead. For instance, in October, 1966, the *New York Times,* reporting on a scientific symposium, ran the headline, LIFE ABANDONING POLLUTED HUDSON. The *Times* said that Atlantic salmon, "abundant in colonial times," had disappeared, and that sea sturgeon were a rarity. In point of fact, Atlantic salmon were never native to the river; also, sea sturgeon are exceedingly common. One December day, I was with fishermen who caught so many sturgeon that I was able to pile them around me chest-high in a boat to protect myself from a bitter wind.

The Hudson, then, is not a river to be described in simple black and white terms. For all its proximity to New York City, it is largely an unknown river. It is a very subtle river, a very diverse river, and the main key to its character is the extraordinary variety to be found both in it and along its shores.

Geologically, the Hudson River, like the Grand Canyon, is an open book of the history of the earth, although some of the pages are torn and a few chapters are missing. The river flows through five physiographic provinces—the Canadian Shield, the Folded Appalachians, the Hudson Highlands, the New England Upland, and the New Jersey Lowland—and past a sixth, the Catskills. According to Christopher J. Schuberth, a specialist in the geology of the New York City area and a staff member of the American Museum of Natural History, few rivers in North America traverse "such geological diversity and complexity in such a short length." Each of these provinces has its attractions. Manhattan Island, part of the New England Upland, is the eroded root of a moun-

tain created four hundred million years ago, of which the durable
bedrock of mica schist serves as the foundation for skyscrapers.
"More than 170 mineral varieties have been reported from Manhattan alone," Schuberth reports. "Also, it is probable that no
other area on the face of the earth has been subjected to such extensive artificial removal of rock through engineering enterprises.
Because of this, and because metamorphic and associated igneous
rocks can offer a wide variety of mineralogical associations, the
mineral record of metropolitan New York exceeds that of any
other known area of similar dimension."

The changing landscapes give the Hudson its charm. There are
the soaring cliffs of the Palisades, the slumbering heights of the
Highlands, and the distant vistas of the Catskills. Though the
scenes vary, they have a common theme—a sort of fairy-tale
magic that lingers in the mind from childhood, the notion that
this is the way the world ought to look. It was brought home to
me most vividly one early autumn twilight when I was standing
in the back garden of Boscobel, the magnificently restored
Federal-style mansion near Cold Spring in the Highlands. A sliver
of a crescent moon hung in the southern sky as on a stage set.
Below were the marshes of Constitution Island, and across the
river lights were coming on at West Point. There was the distant,
muted toot of some ancient military air. The hills were a soft purple, and between them the river shimmered like a chain of placid
lakes. There was nothing ungracious as far as the eye could see.
There was a suggestion of wilderness and mystery, but no sense
of intimidation or of being overwhelmed. Everything was to scale
—marshes, spires, river—and man lived in harmony with the
land.

Baedeker himself was entranced by the Hudson. He deemed its
scenery "grander and more inspiring" than that of the Rhine, and
Henry James, a native son returning after years of expatriation,
found so much at which to marvel on "this perpetually interesting
river" that he allowed, "a decent respect for the Hudson would
confine us to use of the boat." On occasion, a lover of the Hudson
will get carried away. In the 1930s, Henry Collins Brown, a resident of Hastings-on-Hudson, sought out possible rivals for comparison. He found the Arno golden because of silt, the Rhine
"marcelled and coiffured no end" and "more like a toy river than

anything else," and the Tiber so low the water seemed "to have gone off on a holiday." Returning home, Brown wrote a book about the Hudson, which he declared to be the most beautiful river in the world. "When I say the most beautiful river in the world, I mean just that," Brown wrote, offering the hope, nonetheless, that his book would "palliate existence" for those who did not live along its banks.

Botanically, the Hudson has great variety. What plant ecologists call the oak-chestnut-hickory forest is the "climax" vegetation, the final steady state plant community, of the Hudson Valley, extending from Manhattan to Glens Falls a distance of two hundred miles. The term oak-chestnut-hickory forest may be misleading in two ways. First, the chestnut trees succumbed to a blight accidentally introduced from Asia at the turn of the last century; also, there are far more species of trees than these. Indeed, there probably are more species of trees in the Hudson Valley than in the British Isles. There are more than a dozen oaks: red (*Quercus rubra*), pin (*Q. palustris*), black (*Q. velutina*), rock chestnut (*Q. prinus*), post or iron (*Q. stellata*), white (*Q. alba*), burr (*Q. macrocarpa*), scarlet (*Q. coccinea*), swamp white (*Q. bicolor*), yellow (*Q. muehlenbergii*), black jack (*Q. marilandica*), scrub (*Q. ilicifolia*), chinquapin (*Q. prinoides*), and willow (*Q. phellos*). There are the hickories: swamp (*Carya cordiformis*), white-heart (*C. tomentosa*), pignut (*C. glabra*), and small-fruited (*C. ovalis*). There are numerous other trees: mountain laurel (*Kalmia latifolia*), hackberry (*Celtis occidentalis*), white ash (*Fraxinus americana*), American beech (*Fagus grandifolia*), red pine (*Pinus resinosa*), pitch pine (*P. rigida*), Arborvitae (*Thuja occidentalis*), red cedar (*Juniperus virginiana*), sweet gum (*Liquidambar styraciflua*), tamarack (*Larix laricina*), sycamore (*Platanus occidentalis*), white elm (*Ulmus americana*), flowering dogwood (*Cornus florida*), tupelo (*Nyssa sylvatica*), mountain magnolia (*Magnolia acuminata*), black willow (*Salix nigra*), sassafras (*Sassafras albidum*), red mulberry (*Morus rubra*), tulip tree (*Liriodendron tulipifera*), black walnut (*Juglans nigra*), butternut (*J. cinerea*), red maple (*Acer rubrum*), sugar maple (*A. saccharum*), witch hazel (*Hamamelis virginiana*), and river birch (*Betula nigra*).

Similarly, there is a wealth of small herbaceous plants. The variety of vegetation may be explained in part by the diversity of habitat offered by the changing topography. Also, the river has a moderating influence on air temperature. In many ways, the Hudson Valley serves as a long, finger-like extension of the south, a kind of chute up which warm air can travel northward. Thus, southern plants normally found in the Carolinas or Virginia, such as prickly pear (*Opuntia humifusa*), grow in parts of the valley. As a rough rule of thumb, Iona Island, forty-five miles north of the Battery, is the dividing line of temperature. "The sea breeze stops here, and its effects are visible upon vegetation," Benson J. Lossing, a nineteenth-century student of the river, observed. "The spring season is two weeks earlier than at Newburgh, only fourteen miles northward, above the Highlands." Nowadays, let a southerly breeze spring up on a still day, and the smog from New York City rolls straight up the river to Iona. The change in the atmospheric conditions of the lower Hudson Valley from good to bad probably occurred sometime around 1900 as the result of an increase in manufacturing plants and the introduction of coal-fired electric power and the automobile, with its internal combustion engine. In 1863 the first telescopic photographs of the moon were taken in Hastings-on-Hudson by Dr. Henry Draper and his father, Dr. John Draper. In a paper submitted to the Smithsonian Institution in 1864, Henry Draper noted that the observatory site had "no offensive manufactories [that] vitiate the atmosphere with smoke. The advantages of the location are very great and often when the valleys round are filled with foggy exhalations, there is a clear sky over the observatory, the mist flowing like a great stream and losing itself in the chasm through which the Hudson here passes."

Within the past twenty to one hundred years, a number of southern animals have established themselves year round in the valley, among them the fence lizard (*Sceloporus undulatus*) and the Carolina wren (*Thryothorus ludovicianus*). Each has found conditions to its liking. The Carolina wren, for instance, has a curiously confined habitat along the face of the Palisades. Sensitive to cold, it is apparently able to get along on the rock ledges warmed by the sun. By contrast, there are northern birds as well, such as the Canada warbler (*Wilsonia canadensis*), which nests in the moist woodlands of the Highlands. For birds, the Hudson

Valley is an interesting transition or "tension" zone.

Above all, there is the Hudson River itself and the unseen life beneath its surface. The Hudson nowadays is really not a single, continuous river but a half dozen or so different bodies of water stitched together. As the river flows from the Adirondacks to the Atlantic, it is by turns a mountain trout stream, a bass and pike river, a canal, a septic tank at Troy and Albany, an estuary, and a seaport. South of the Narrows at the entrance to New York harbor is the sunken channel of an older Hudson. In glacial times, the Continental Shelf was land above sea level, and the Hudson then flowed another 120 miles out to sea. The channel of this old Hudson, which disappeared upon the retreat of the last ice sheet ten to fifteen thousand years ago, may still be discerned on the floor of the shelf by electronic instruments. The channel runs to the edge of the shelf where it widens, deepens, and disappears into the abyss of the vast Hudson Canyon that extends almost halfway to Bermuda.

The Hudson River that most people know is the 154-mile stretch from Manhattan to Troy. Here the lower Hudson is an estuary, an arm of the sea. On occasion, the river also is called a fiord. Superficially, the lower Hudson has all the appearances of a fiord, for it is capacious, deep, and bordered in part by mountains. I was once out on the river with a couple of Norwegian sea captains who were seeing the Hudson for the first time, and they both felt happily at home. But technically speaking, the Hudson is not a fiord because it does not have a shallow sill at the entrance. More properly, the Hudson is a drowned river; after the last glacier melted, rising seawater moved in and flooded the old course of the river. Because of this, the lower Hudson is unusually deep and is suitable for navigation by ocean-going vessels up to Albany.

From Manhattan to Troy, there is no drop at all in the surface elevation of the river, and the ocean tides run all the way to the Federal Lock and Dam at Troy. Aside from the spring runoff from the Adirondacks, which can be so powerful as to smother the tides down to Albany, the lower Hudson has relatively little downstream current, as one would ordinarily think of such a force. A log dropped into the river at Troy would take months to float down to Manhattan. In some stretches, for every eight miles that the current and ebb tide carried the log downriver, the flood tide might shove it back up as much as seven and a half miles. To the Mahican Indians of Henry Hudson's day, the tidal action of the Hudson was a wonder, and they called the river *Muhheakun-nuk*, which means "great waters constantly in motion."

After the spring runoff of fresh water has washed downriver and out to sea, the powerful flood tide helps to make a good stretch of the lower Hudson saline or brackish. Sea water off New York harbor has a salinity of almost thirty parts per thousand, but as this sea water moves into the lower river it becomes more and more diluted with freshwater drainage from the land the further upstream it travels. This intrusion of sea water into the Hudson has not been studied thoroughly and is something of a puzzle. However, the maximum salinities appear to occur between the late summer and early spring, and the salinities are generally a little higher on the bottom of the river than they are at the surface because salt water is heavier than fresh water.

From late summer to early fall, the salinity of the water at the bottom of the Hudson at the Battery is about twenty-three parts per thousand. At Yonkers, seventeen miles upstream, the salinity is fifteen parts per thousand; at Dobbs Ferry, fourteen parts; Croton Point, eight to ten; Bear Mountain, four to five; and West Point, two. The upriver penetration varies. Ordinarily, the "salt line" or "salt wedge," as this phenomenon is called, stops near Newburgh, sixty miles from the Battery. However, in 1966, a drought year, brackishness was detected at high tide at Pough-keepsie, seventy-five miles from the Battery. On other occasions, the salt line may be thrust downstream. For example, in early May of 1968, after the spring runoff, the salt line was moving up-river to Peekskill. Suddenly a torrential storm dumped five inches of rain on the lower Hudson Valley, and the salt line was knocked forty-three miles downriver to the Battery. After the runoff from the storm abated, the salt line began to move upstream once again. Whatever the complexities of the salt line, marine fishes and other creatures from the Atlantic use it to work their way up-river to places where they are not supposed to be found. For in-stance, sea anemones (*Sagartia leucolena*) live on the bottom of the Hudson near the George Washington Bridge.

To be sure, the Hudson is heavily polluted by sewage and

industrial wastes, especially in the vicinities of the Troy-Albany area and Manhattan. But in between those two points, the river seethes with an amazing abundance and variety of aquatic life. It may be that the rocking tidal action, the varying depths, and other forces which are not yet completely understood somehow disperse sewage so that it acts like fertilizer spread on a farmer's field. I do not say this to avoid an honest confrontation of the problems of the river; they are considerable, and I daresay the reader will gag once or twice. Nor do I say this to sanction or excuse pollution: pollution is a menace to public health; it is a deterrent to wholesome use of the river; it is like a pistol pointed at the heart of the Hudson. So far, however, the river has been spared biological annihilation by geographic accident. If New York City had been built fifty miles further up, say where Peekskill or Newburgh are, the Hudson probably would be a dead river. Heavy pollution loads in the narrow Highlands gorge would simply be too much for the river to handle. This is the kind of problem that the Delaware River faces with Philadelphia and Camden and the Potomac has had with Washington.

As of now, the biological productivity of the lower Hudson is staggering. Fishes are there by the millions, with marine and freshwater species often side by side in the same patch of water. All told, the populations of fishes utilizing the lower Hudson for spawning, nursery, or feeding grounds comprise the greatest single wildlife resource in New York State. It is also without question the most neglected resource; at this writing, not one state conservation department biologist is to be found studying it regularly. Besides sea sturgeon, the river is aswarm year-round or seasonally with striped bass, white perch, bluefish, shad, herring, largemouth bass, carp, needlefish, yellow perch, menhaden, golden shiners, darters, carp, tomcod, and sunfish, to cite only some. There is the short-nosed or round-nosed sturgeon, officially classified by the Department of the Interior as "endangered," or close to extinct, in the United States. Perhaps it is extinct elsewhere along the Atlantic Coast, but not only is this fish present in the Hudson, but occasional specimens exceed the published record size in the scientific literature. The lower Hudson also receives an interesting infusion of so-called tropical or subtropical fishes, such as the jack crevalle and the mullet, both ordinarily associated with Florida waters.

In brief, the Hudson estuary is incredibly rich. There are a number of reasons for this, and here, for the moment, I will set aside any effects pollution might have and look at the natural workings of the estuary. For one thing, an estuary receives nutrients washed from the land as a matter of course. Moreover, as Dr. Alistair W. McCrone, a geologist at New York University, has written, "Since the river constantly cuts into such varied terrain, it is not surprising that a large assortment of minerals is present in the bottom sediments. Similarily, its waters contain a great variety of ions derived by solution of these minerals." Among the elements Dr. McCrone detected in the bottom muds are aluminum, antimony, beryllium, boron, calcium, chromium, copper, iron, gallium, lead, magnesium, nickel, scandium, silicon, titanium, vanadium, yttrium, and zirconium. Nothing ever really goes to waste in an estuary. When a plant or animal dies, bacteria, shrimps, crabs, eels, and other scavengers feed upon it and help recycle the nutrients. The rocking action of the tides keeps the lower Hudson stirred like a thick soup. Mixing is very thorough; the bottom water temperature one hundred feet down in the Hudson is rarely a centigrade degree cooler than the surface temperature. In essence, the Hudson estuary is a nutrient trap, a protein plant, a self-perpetuating fertilizer factory. The different habitats of bottom muds, sand, rocks, old shell beds, inshore shallows, tidal creeks, marshes, and plunging holes offer food and hospitality to all sorts of creatures, and because a good portion of the lower Hudson is brackish, it can be visited by marine species that can take diluted sea water or by freshwater species that can tolerate low salinities. For fishes, the lower Hudson is a kind of Times Square. In 1936, the New York State Conservation Department conducted a biological survey of the lower Hudson watershed, and in the published report that followed, a biologist wrote (and these are his italics): *The lower Hudson compares favorably with the richest lakes.*

The Hudson estuary does not stand by itself in splendid or even somewhat tarnished isolation. Along with the Chesapeake Bay system, the Delaware Bay, the wetlands fringing southern Long Island and the Jersey shore, and the Long Island Sound complex, the Hudson helps to make the Continental Shelf of the eastern United States one of the most productive fishing grounds ever known. This is why foreign trawlers are so common a sight off the coast. If I may cite a figure which may cause some biologists to grumble, it is likely that spawning grounds in the Hudson River supply the inshore Atlantic Coast with 10 to 20 per cent of the total run of striped bass during the summer months. According to a biologist friend, whom I will not name to spare him criticism from desk-bound colleagues, the Hudson River now has a population of approximately seventeen million striped bass, give or take a million. In other words, there may be more stripers in the Hudson than there are people in New York State. I often find this a cheering thought.

Besides all the natural variety to be found in the Hudson Valley there is man himself. The valley is a jumble of human activity, from the giant city at the river mouth to Adirondack lumber camps. There are cement plants, farms, pulp mills, parks, monasteries and convents, power plants, vineyards, factories, and great estates along the shores. Morgan, Rockefeller, Gould, Harriman, Astor, and Vanderbilt are among the names of the river rich. There is contrast almost everywhere. Franklin D. Roosevelt lies buried at Hyde Park, while across the river followers of Father Divine encamp. A few miles south on the east shore lies the grave of Teilhard de Chardin, the Jesuit paleontologist and philosopher, and inland, at Millbrook, Dr. Timothy Leary, the grand panjandrum of LSD and founder of the League of Spiritual Discovery, turned on, tuned in, and dropped out, to the dismay of the fox hunting squires of Dutchess County. The Statue of Liberty is off the mouth of the Hudson; thirty miles "up the river" is Sing Sing. A few hundred yards south of the prison are a couple of commercial fishermen who keep their catch alive for sale in the flooded depths of an old silver mine tunneled into a cliff. Outside Peekskill is a quarry that supplied the granite for the Cathedral of St. John the Divine. (I have ignored the no-tresspass signs and gone there to explore. The property is owned now by the Gandhi Foundation, and I do not expect to be ejected physically.) Nearby are a couple of brothers, the Gilmans, who have the finest stock of out-of-print books in the country. They have been buying from estates for almost fifty years, and their treasures fill one garage, a barn, and a house from cellar to attic. A couple of miles away on

Annsville Creek lives Jimmy Mowbray, a one-time pitcher in the Philly farm system who came home ten years ago when his arm went bad. Jimmy sells live bait—there is an enormous sign on the highway saying WORMS, with a red arrow pointing at his house. In the winter, Jimmy hunts and traps along the Hudson, and as he once told me, "Nobody knows the river until they've walked the railroad tracks from Peekskill to Poughkeepsie."

In a word, life along the Hudson is never boring. There is always something new to learn. The river has its surprises. I was reminded of this recently by the death of Billy Wyant, seventy-six, another bait seiner who lived near Jimmy Mowbray along Annsville Creek. Billy was a cantankerous sort who always refused to let me go out to his live bait boxes at the end of his wooden pier. Jimmy happily lets me look at his catch, but Billy was stubborn and never let me have even a peek. In my mind, his boxes harbored unrecorded fishes, and they assumed the importance of the true tabernacle.

Billy cared about the Hudson, he knew a lot about it, and when I sometimes stopped by after visiting Jimmy, I was prepared to endure his crankiness in the hope that I would learn something new. I remember the last time we talked. Billy teetered out of his house, a trailer moored into the side of a hill near an auto junk-yard, and we exchanged trivialities. Then I got going about a strange thing I had seen, a couple of sturgeon that had been caught with rubber bands entangled around them. I have since learned that considering the amount and kinds of refuse thrown into the river, this is not unusual. But Billy suddenly smiled. He drew close, and in a dreamy beery breath he whispered, "Kid, there's a lot of crazy things to be found in the Hudson River."

2

ORIGIN AND
DISCOVERY

The early geologic history of the Hudson River is little known, and even that is a matter of controversy. Possibly the Hudson, or an ancestral stream, dates back seventy-five million years to the Cretaceous Period, when there was a subtle elevation of the eastern seaboard. In the Tertiary Period, which began sixty-five million years ago, continued elevation of the land rejuvenated stream flow, and the Hudson and its tributaries began cutting a valley between the Catskill Mountains on the west and the Taconic Mountains to the east. "The enormous amount of work involved can be grasped if one remembers that the river and its tributaries have not only removed the rock between the tops and bases of these ranges but also the continuation of these formations that once extended farther north and lapped upon the Adirondacks," Dr. Winifred Goldring, state paleontologist, wrote in *Geology of the Coxsackie Quadrangle, New York,* published in 1943.

During the Tertiary, the Hudson also cut into the Highlands, but instead of following its present course from the Tappan Zee south past Manhattan, the river possibly veered to the west, coursing through the Sparkill Gap in the Palisades. Then it ran behind the Palisades down past the vicinities of Paterson and Millburn, New Jersey, and then turned east and emptied into the ocean south of Staten Island. Christopher Schuberth cites good evidence for this in his recent study, *The Geology of New York City and Environs.* Ten to fifteen million years ago, according to Schuberth, a smaller stream probably moved north by headward erosion and then "captured" the Hudson. The course through the Sparkill Gap was abandoned, and the Hudson began flowing south past Manhattan to the sea.

About a million and a half years ago, the ice age began. Possibly four ice sheets advanced and retreated in the region, and each gouged the river valley deeper and deeper. The last ice sheet, the Wisconsin, moved south from Labrador between 75,000 and 115,-000 years ago. It reached its furthest point south in the New York area on Staten Island and Long Island, both largely composed of terminal moraine and glacial outwash. With much of the Northern Hemisphere then locked in ice, the level of the sea was lower, and the Hudson ran for another 120 miles out to sea, carving its way through the terrestrial plain that is now the Continental Shelf.

Mastodons and mammoths roamed the cold, boggy, ice-free land of the shelf. Teeth from these extinct beasts have been dredged from the shelf, and a good number of them have been taken from along the banks of the now-submerged Hudson. As the glacier melted in northward retreat twelve to fifteen thousand years ago, the mammoths and mastodons moved inland up the Hudson Valley. The first mastodon remains found by white settlers in North America were unearthed at Claverack in 1705. In 1706, the remains of another were found in Coxsackie.

As the glacier withdrew from the valley, climatic conditions changed, and so in response did the vegetation and animals. In all likelihood there were, for instance, four stages of plant succession: first tundra, then subarctic dwarf forest, a boreal coniferous forest, and finally the deciduous forest of the present age. Where did the present forest come from? According to Professor E. Lucy Braun of the University of Cincinnati, a reservoir of deciduous trees existed on the Cumberland and Allegheny plateaus all through the ice age. This forest was not disturbed by the glaciers, and as the last ice sheet retreated north, the trees followed. Plants that are relicts of early post-glacial time, so-called alpine plants, such as Greenland sandwort (*Arenaria groenlandica*) and tundra reindeer moss (*Cladonia rangiferina*), can still be found among the peaks of the Highlands, the Catskills and the Adirondacks. It is worth noting here that geologic and climatic evidence would indicate that the Hudson Valley, or much of the Northern Hemisphere, for that matter, is merely between glaciers. We may still be living in the Pleistocene Epoch, and if we are to go by the records of the past, the next glacier should appear perhaps in about ten thousand years. Almost all the plants and animals now in the Hudson Valley, including man himself, have slipped in, so to speak, through this small chink in the enormity of time.

So far as is known, there was no human settlement in the Hudson Valley until about 4000 B.C. In 1960 Louis Brennan, a writer and archeologist in Ossining, discovered an Indian kitchen midden at Croton Point, and oyster shells taken from the site were carbon dated as approximately six thousand years old.

No one can say for certain when the Algonkian Tribes originally appeared in the eastern United States and Canada. The Algonkians, sometimes called the Algonquian or Algonquin, were the "native" aborigines encountered by the first European explorers in the lower Hudson Valley. According to legend, these Indians had come from the west seeking a river that flowed two ways, and they found it in the tidal Hudson. Around 1300 A.D. (the exact date is impossible to ascertain), another group of Indians made their presence felt in central New York State. They were composed of various tribes, and sometime in the 1500s, possibly around 1570, they banded together as the Five Nations, or Confederacy or League of the Iroquois. This supposedly was done in whole or part at the urging of a chief, Ha-yo-went'-ha, who was later transferred and transformed by Henry Wadsworth Longfellow to the middle west as Hiawatha. The Iroquois Confederacy was so well organized as a system of government that it later influenced Benjamin Franklin in his efforts to unite the

American colonies.

The first European to discover the Hudson River, or at least New York harbor, was a Florentine, Giovanni da Verrazano, who was sailing for the French king, Francis I, in 1524. Verrazano called the river by two names, the River of the Steep Hills and the Grand River. He wrote to the king that while exploring the coast,

> we found a very pleasant situation among some steep hills, through which a very large river, deep at its mouth, forced its way to the sea; from the sea to the estuary of the river, any ship heavily laden might pass, with the help of the tide, which rises eight feet. But as we were riding at anchor in a good berth, we would not venture up in our vessel, without a knowledge of the mouth; therefore we took the [small] boat, and entering the river [the Narrows], we found the country on its banks [Brooklyn and Staten Island] well populated, the inhabitants not differing much from the others, being dressed out with the feathers of birds of various colors. They came towards us with evident delight, raising loud shouts of admiration, and showing us where we could most securely land with our boat. We passed up this river, about half a league, when we found it formed a most beautiful lake three leagues in circuit [upper New York Bay], upon which they were rowing thirty or more of their small boats, from one shore to the other, filled with multitudes who came to see us. All of a sudden, as is wont to happen to navigators, a violent contrary wind blew in from the sea, and forced us to return to our ship, greatly regretting to leave this region which seemed so commodious and delightful, and which we supposed must also contain great riches, as the hills showed many indications of minerals.

In the very next year, 1525, Estevan Gómez, a Portuguese sailing for Spain, explored the coast from Rhode Island to Maryland and supposedly made notice of the river. Gómez left a brief legacy: the Spanish named the stretch of coast Tierra de Estevan Gómez and the river was variously called Rio de Gómez, Rio San Antonio, and Rio de Guamas.

In the years that followed, the French may have visited the

Hudson to trade. Two maps showing the river were drawn in Europe in 1556 and 1569. However, these maps and the voyages of Verrazano, Gómez, and the French rank as mere historical curiosities in terms of exploitation and settlement. The true honor for the discovery of the river falls to the navigator after whom it is named, Henry Hudson.

Little is known about Hudson other than that he probably was the grandson of a London alderman who helped found the Muscovy Company, a trading group. In 1607, Hudson sailed an English ship sent forth by the Muscovy Company to Spitzbergen in an attempt to find a northern passage to the "islands of spicery." In 1608, he tried again, this time seeking a northeast passage near Novaya Zemlya off the Russian coast, but he was blocked by ice. In 1609, the Dutch East India Company hired Hudson to find a passage to China, and on April 6 of that year he sailed from Holland aboard the *Half Moon*, a yacht of eighty tons, with a mixed Dutch and English crew. At first, Hudson sailed up the Norwegian coast, but upon encountering ice, he changed course for North America. Captain John Smith had suggested that there might be a northwest passage to China through that land.

Hudson sailed to Nova Scotia, reaching there on July 18, 1609, and then he moved down the Maine coast and around Cape Cod to Chesapeake Bay. Here he turned north and moved along the coast, seeking the passage. On September 4, the *Half Moon* dropped anchor near Staten Island. Hudson stayed there for nine days, trading with the Indians and sending five men in the ship's boat to explore the Narrows, where the men saw the Upper Bay. As they were returning, they were set upon by twenty-six Indians in two canoes, and a seaman, John Colman, was slain by an arrow in his throat. On September 9, a large band of armed Indians came near the *Half Moon* in two canoes, ostensibly to trade. The crew lured two on board and took them as hostages, and there was no trouble. On September 11, Hudson sailed the *Half Moon* through the Narrows and on the next day began exploring the river, anchoring near the north end of Manhattan. On September 13, the ship reached Yonkers, where the crew bought oysters from the Indians, who now seemed friendly. On the 14th, Hudson sailed through the Highlands and anchored near West Point, where the Indian hostages escaped and "called to us in scorne."

He reached the Kingston area on the 15th, the site of the present day city of Hudson on the 16th, and somewhere near Castleton on the 17th. Here the ship lay at anchor on the 18th; the river channel was becoming narrow and difficult to navigate. By this time, Hudson undoubtedly realized that the river was not the northwest passage he was seeking. On the afternoon of the 18th, he visited with the local Indians, and he wrote in his log,

I sailed to the shore, in one of their canoes with the chief of a tribe, consisting of forty men and seventeen women. These I saw there in a house well constructed of oak bark and circular in shape. so that it had the appearance of being built with an arched roof. It contained a great quantity of maize, or Indian corn, and beans of last year's growth, and there lay near the house, for the purpose of drying enough to load three ships, besides what was growing in the fields. On coming into the house, two mats were spread out to sit upon, and some food was immediately served in well-made red wooden bowls; two men were also despatched at once with bows and arrows in quest of game, who soon after brought in a pair of pigeons which they had shot. They likewise killed a fat dog and skinned it in great haste with shells which they had got out of the water. They supposed that I would remain with them for the night, but I returned after a short time on board the ship. The land is the finest for cultivation that I ever in my life set foot upon, and it also abounds in trees of every description. The natives are a very good people, for when they saw I would not remain, they supposed that I was afraid of their bows, and taking their arrows, they broke them in pieces and threw them into the fire.

This is one of the few excerpts from Hudson's log. The principal source of information about the voyage is the journal kept by an officer of the *Half Moon,* Robert Juet of Lime-house, and published in England in 1625. All that remains of Hudson's own observations are brief extracts published by Johan de Laet in Holland in 1625. All the books, documents, and papers of every kind, including, presumably, Hudson's log, belonging to the old East and West India companies have been missing since 1821, when the Dutch government sold the archives at public auction. This loss was discovered by John Romeyn Brodhead of Albany, who was sent to Europe in 1841 by the state legislature to buy or copy documents relating to the colonial settlement of New York. Vexed by Washington Irving's sketches of the Dutch as so many fatheaded louts, the legislature wanted to show that the Dutch really were solid, right-minded folk of whom New Yorkers had a right to be proud. The only trace of Hudson's voyage that Brodhead found was a memorandum in a "ship book" of the East India Company that had accidentally escaped sale, and this merely noted that the yacht *Halve-Maan*, of forty lasts (eighty tons), had been sent "towards the north." Brodhead advertised for the missing documents in the leading Dutch newspapers, and he eventually found one buyer whose collection he examined. As Brodhead reported to the legislature, "Nothing, however, relating to our history was found; and the mortifying conviction is now forced upon us that the papers of the West India Company relating to New Netherland—which, until the year 1821, were easily attainable by the state, and whose destruction has left such a chasm in the original materials for the illustration of our annals—are now irrecoverably lost!"

On the morning of September 19, 1609, the *Half Moon* sailed up to the future site of Albany. The ship stayed there several days, while the mate and a crew rowed upriver in the boat to take soundings. They rowed about twenty miles north, but the river was not navigable and neither was the Mohawk, the mouth of which they must have passed. Aboard the *Half Moon*, Indians visited, bringing grapes, pumpkins, and otter and beaver skins. Hudson purposely got some drunk, to discover, Juet wrote, "whether they had any treacherie in them."

On September 23, Hudson sailed the *Half Moon* back down the river. On the next day, near Castleton, the ship ran aground "on a banke of Oze in the middle of the river, and sate there till the floud." The downriver voyage was uneventful until October 1, when the *Half Moon* anchored at noon near Stony Point. Indians came to visit, and one was shot after he sneaked aboard and stole Juet's "Pillow, and two shirts, and two Bandeleeres." The Indians fled, some in their canoes, others by swimming. "We manned our Boate, and got our things againe," Juet wrote. "Then one of them that swamme got hold our boat, thinking to overthrow it. But our

Cooke tooke a Sword, and cut off one of his hands, and he was drowned."

Hudson weighed anchor and sailed the *Half Moon* downriver. On October 2, the Indians attacked the ship as it sailed past the north end of Manhattan Island. Two canoes full of Indians shot arrows at the stern, and the crew fired back, killing two or three. On shore, about a hundred Indians gathered to shoot arrows. Juet killed two, and the Indians fled into the woods. Another canoe appeared with nine or ten Indians, and four or five of them were killed.

Hudson spent the night in the lee of Stevens Point, Hoboken, where bad weather delayed sailing for a day. On October 4, the *Half Moon* weighed anchor in what Hudson called the "great River of the Mountains" and passed through the Narrows at noon. "Then we tooke in our Boat," wrote Juet, "and set our mayne-sayle and sprit-sayle, and our top-sayles, and steered away East South-east, and South-east by East off into the mayne sea."

Short of stores, the *Half Moon* stopped at Dartmouth in England on November 7, 1609. English authorities ordered Hudson to remain, and the *Half Moon* returned to Holland without him. In the spring of 1610, Hudson, sailing for England, made his fourth and final voyage. Still seeking the passage to China, he sailed *The Discovery* south of Baffin Island and into what is now Hudson's Bay. The crew mutinied, and Hudson, his son, John, and seven others were set adrift in a small boat, never to be seen again. One of the leaders of the mutiny was Robert Juet.

What was the Hudson River Valley like when Hudson sailed up it? How does it differ from the valley of today? Fortunately, it is possible to put together a picture from surviving accounts by early Dutch observers and from research done by present-day scientists. For instance, Ralph H. Smith, an ecologist with the New York State Conservation Department, has delineated the vegetation, even going to the point of locating ancient trees that served as surveyor's benchmarks.

Perhaps the most basic difference between the Hudson Valley, then and now, is the smell. Indeed, this is true of the east coast of the United States. Instead of being laden with the noxious stinks of oil, gas, chemicals, and industrial wastes, the North America of Indian days was so marvelously fragrant the land could be smelled miles out at sea. Columbus and his crew inhaled an off-shore breeze on which "there came so fair and sweet a smell of flowers or trees from the land." Verrazano noticed the trees on the coast, which "for a long distance, exhale the sweetest odors." Raleigh's colonists in Virginia "felt a most dilicate sweete smell, though they saw no land, where ere they long espied." Off Maine, John Winthrop perceived "a smell off the shore like the smell of a garden." Near the Narrows, Hudson's crew smelled the grass and flowers "and very sweet smells came from them." On Manhattan Island, wildflowers were so numerous and fragrant that one Dutch chronicler, Jasper Danckaerts, tells how he and a companion "sometimes encountered such a sweet smell in the air that we stood still, because we did not know what it was we were meeting." In the region of the Hudson Highlands, the trees gave off "strong perfume." Indeed, Adriaen Van der Donck, who wrote the fullest account of the early days, reported, "The air in the New-Netherlands is so dry, sweet and healthy, that we need not wish it were otherwise. In purity, agreeableness, and fineness, it would be folly to seek for an example of it in any other country."

Oak-chestnut-hickory forests extended through the Hudson Valley from Manhattan to Glens Falls, a distance of almost two hundred miles, "the finest oaks for height and thickness that one could ever see," wrote de Laet. In the Catskills, above an elevation of two thousand feet, northern hardwoods, beech, sugar maple, yellow birch, and hemlock grew, whole forests of beech, maple, and hemlock thrived in the Mohawk Valley. The sandy area around Albany normally supported spruce and fir trees, but in the fall, Indians burned over the land for hunting, leaving pitch pine and oak, both resistant to fire. Nowadays, this region is known as the Karner Sand Plains, and it is of interest because it is the home of some rare plants and animals. Here, not long ago, Vladimir Nabokov, the lepidopterist and novelist, discovered a new subspecies of butterfly, *Lycæides melissa samuelis,* commonly known as the Karner Blue. "Karner is the name of a little railway station between Albany and Schenectady," Nabokov says. "People go there on Sundays to picnic, shedding papers and beer cans. Among this, the butterfly."

Hickory trees probably covered Governors Island, called Nut

Island by the Dutch. In the woods of the mainland, Nicolaes Van Wassenaer wrote, "are found all sorts of fruits . . . yea, fruits in great profusion," while the Reverend Johannes Megapolensis, minister at the patroonship of Rensselaerswyck, near Albany, reported that "the ground in the flat land near the rivers is covered with strawberries, which grow here so plentifully in the fields, that one can lie down and eat them."

The Dutch were particularly taken with the change of color of the leaves in the fall. In the cool, moist climate of Europe, leaves do not take on the brilliant scarlets, deep reds, and yellows that they do in the Hudson Valley and elsewhere in the Northeast, and of the autumns, Van der Donck wrote, "more delightful cannot be found on the earth." But as Van der Donck confessed, "I am incompetent to describe the beauties, the grand and sublime works, wherewith Providence has diversified this land." Jacob Steendam, an early settler on Manhattan, wrote:

> This is the land, with milk and honey flowing
> With healing herbs like thistles freely growing
> The place where buds of Aaron's rods are blowing
> O, this is Eden!

Manhattan was more irregular in outline than it is now. The island was indented with bays, creeks, coves, and marshes. Freshwater brooks ran across the island, "pleasant and proper for man and beast to drink, as well as agreeable to behold, affording cool and pleasant resting places." Minetta Brook, which flowed through Washington Square in Manhattan and emptied in the Hudson, was fed by two streams, one arising near Sixth Avenue and Seventeenth Street, the other at Fifth Avenue and Twentieth. Trout were caught in the brook until the late eighteenth century. Paved over nowadays, the water of Minetta Brook surfaces in the lobby fountains of two apartment houses, at 33 Washington Square West and at 2 Fifth Avenue. Another stream emptied into the Hudson at Forty-second Street; it has long been a sewer. Collect Pond, sixty to seventy feet deep, was where the Tombs prison now stands; the pond was drained and filled in the early nineteenth century. According to one story, the gridiron plan of Manhattan was thought up in 1807 by three commissioners who happened to stop near a bank where workmen were screening gravel.

One of the commissioners began drawing a map of the island on the ground with a stick. After he finished, the sun happened to come from behind a cloud, and the shadow of the gravel screen fell across the map. "There is the plan!" a commissioner shouted, and they all agreed.

In the time of the Indians, two creeks ran to the Hudson and East rivers from Collect Pond and a marsh on Canal Street. During heavy rains, the marsh and streams were so swollen that Manhattan was divided in two. The shoreline has changed greatly. Rivington Street marks the northern edge of a former ninety-acre saltmarsh, and curving Pearl Street follows the original shoreline of the East River. The Battery is largely on landfill, and the Hudson once ran where Greenwich Street is today. In 1916, workmen excavating a subway extension at Dey and Greenwich streets ran into the timbers of Captain Adriaen Block's ship, *Tiger,* which had burned by the riverside in November of 1613. Block, who had been trading furs, built a new ship, *Onrust* ("Restless"), from the trees on Manhattan and sailed back to Holland in the spring.

Manhattan had both forests and meadows. Harlem in those days was a meadow. The meadows were probably caused by fires set by the Indians, either to chase out game or to clear land for planting. Left alone, these meadows soon reverted to second-growth forest. The Hudson Valley, then and now, is quick to regenerate forest cover. Once, while exploring a dense woods, Van der Donck found it hard to believe the Indians, who told him they had burned it over twenty years earlier.

There were prodigious quantities of game. "Birds fill also the woods so that men can scarcely go through them for the whistling, the noise and the chattering. Whoever is not lazy can catch them with little difficulty," wrote Van Wassenaer. Isaack de Rasieres, who was a commercial agent in New Netherlands in the 1620s, noted: "Of the birds, there is a kind . . . which we call *maize thieves,* because they do so much damage to the maize. They fly in large flocks, so that they flatten the corn in any place where they alight, just as if cattle had lain there. Sometimes we take them by surprise and fire amongst them with hailshot, immediately that we have made them rise, so that sixty, seventy, and eighty fall at once, which is very pleasant to see." In the spring and fall, the marshes and sky were alive with ducks, geese, swans and shorebirds. The New York area was and still is a great gathering point for birds; there was duck shooting off the Battery until the 1870s. Van der Donck wrote that "the people who reside near the water are frequently disturbed in their rest at night by the noise of the water fowls, particularly by the swans, which in their season are so plenty, that the bays and shores where they resort appear as if they were dressed in white drapery."

There were heath hens, now extinct; ruffed grouse; wild turkeys "which weight from thirty to forty pounds"; and wild pigeons "so numerous that they shut out the sunshine." There were deer, "incredibly numerous" and "as fat as any Holland cow can be"; "multitudes of wolves"; black bear; mink; otter; muskrats; raccoon; and beaver. "We estimate that eighty-thousand beavers are annually killed in this quarter of the country," Van der Donck wrote. The beaver was so valuable that it was drawn into the seal of New Netherland in 1623.

There were also mountain lions, some elk, and, probably rarely, moose. The last mountain lion, or "catamount," in the New York City region is said to have been shot in the Palisades in the 1850s. One settler, David de Vries, wrote: "Nothing is wanted but good marksmen with powder and shot"; while Van der Donck noted: "There are some persons who imagine that the animals of the country will be destroyed in time, but this is an unnecessary anxiety."

The Dutch called the Hudson by various names: the River of Prince Mauritius, the Nassau River, the Manhattan River, and the North River. In early Colonial days, the Dutch claimed the land between the Delaware and Connecticut rivers. The Delaware was known as the South River and the Hudson as the North River, while the Connecticut was called the Fresh River. The name North River still is used in the Manhattan area, but the river officially became the Hudson River after the English seized control in 1664. Whatever the name of the Hudson, Van der Donck wrote, "This river is rich in fishes." The Mohawk had its charms: "The water is as clear as crystal, and as fresh as milk," said the Reverend Megapolensis. The blue-claw crab of the lower Hudson and shore waters was an omen: "In the summer-time crabs come on the flat shores, of very good taste. Their claws are of the color of the flag of our Prince, orange, white and blue, so that the crabs show sufficiently that we ought to people the country, and that it belongs to us," de Vries wrote. There were lobsters, mussels, scallops, clams, and oysters. Gowanus oysters from the East River were up to a foot long and were considered the "best in the country." Within the present harbor area and up the Hudson to Croton Point were 350 square miles of oyster beds, then constituting, according to one modern authority, "more than 50 per cent of the world's available supply of oysters." As late as 1839, these grounds yielded more than a million and a half bushels of oysters a year. The grounds were considered inexhaustible, but they have been rendered useless or annihilated by dredging, filling, silting, overexploitation, and pollution. There are still a few oysters and many, many clams at the mouth of the harbor along the seaward shore of Staten Island, and some of the clams are as "fat as butter." But health authorities have closed the beds because the clams and oysters feed by filtering organisms from the water, and the organisms they retain and concentrate may be harmful to man.

Whales, porpoises, and seals once disported in the waters off Manhattan. Robbins Reef near the Statue of Liberty was a favorite haunt of seals. Occasionally, harbor seals will come down the coast during winter, pass through the Narrows, and swim up the Hudson. In the spring of 1967, a harbor seal ventured as far north as Albany.

Most of all, there were fishes. Up the Hudson, Reverend Megapolensis wrote, "In the spring, in May, the perch are so plenty, that one man with a hook and line will catch in one hour as many as ten or twelve can eat." This still holds true of the white perch in the Hudson. In the East River, there were codfish. The earliest Dutch settlers are said to have known ten species of fishes found in local waters, and thus Van der Donck wrote that "every one was desirous to see the fishes which were caught, for the purpose of discovering whether the same were known to them, and if they did not know a fish, then they gave it a name. First in the fishing season, they caught many shad, which they named *Elft* [eleventh]. Later they caught the striped bass, which they named *Twalft* [twelfth]. Later still they caught the drums which they named *Dertienen* [thirteenth]." De Rasieres described the striped bass as "a sort of white salmon, which is of very good flavor, and quite as large; it has white scales; the heads are so full of fat that in some there are two or three spoonfuls, so that there is good eating for one who is fond of picking heads. It seems that this fish makes them [the Indians] lascivious, for it is often observed that those who have caught any when they have gone fishing, have given them, on their return, to the women, who look for them anxiously. Our people also confirm this." The Dutch also found "a great plenty of sturgeon" in the Hudson, fish "which we Christians do not like, but the Indians eat them greedily."

There were no salmon in the Hudson. The Atlantic salmon (*Salmo salar*) was never native to the Hudson watershed. I stress this because the attractive myth persists that the Hudson was a great salmon river and that when it is cleansed of pollution the salmon will be "restored." This notion that the Hudson had salmon appears fairly often and is stated by various authorities. Theodore Gordon, the Catskill recluse who introduced dry fly fishing to the United States in the 1890s, believed that the Hudson was a salmon river, and the late Professor Paul R. Needham, the great authority on trout, wrote in his estimable study, *Trout Streams*, that large numbers of salmon used to be taken in the Hudson.

This erroneous belief got its start with Juet and Hudson, who both mentioned salmon. They undoubtedly mistook striped bass for salmon, for no other early Dutch observer ever made any mention of salmon in the Hudson. In all likelihood, the Connecticut River, to which the Dutch laid claim, marked the southernmost edge of the salmon range, while the Hudson is the most northerly major spawning ground for striped bass on the Atlantic Coast of the United States. Salmon persisted in the Connecticut into the early 1800s' when the construction of high dams prevented them from reaching their spawning grounds. That salmon were absent from the Hudson is borne out by other accounts. In 1682, the Scottish proprietors of New Jersey noted: "The Bay also, and Hudson's River are plentifully stored with sturgeons, great bass and other scale fish and shell fish as oysters, &c., and are easy to take." A history of New Jersey published in 1765 mentioned the fish in the Delaware and Hudson rivers: "The most noted are sturgeon, rock, cod, sheepshead, horse mackeral, blackfish, sea bass, flounders, shad, herring, munchers, trout, pike, perch, red perch, sunfish and many inferior sort." In 1771, the Colonial government of New York passed "An Act to prevent the taking and destruction of salmon in the Hudson River." This is sometimes cited as proof of salmon in the river, but perusal of the act reveals that the government was considering stocking salmon in the Hudson and wished them protected.

Samuel Williams, in *The Natural and Civil History of Vermont* (1774), wrote: "In the spring, about the 25th of April, these fish [salmon] begin to pass up the Connecticut River and proceed to the higher branches. . . . None of them are ever found to the south or west of the Connecticut River."

Still, the myth of salmon persisted. In 1810, Dr. Samuel Latham Mitchill, the pioneer icthyologist of New York, wrote: "Now, with all this information relative to the several sorts of fish, that have frequented the Hudson, since the possession of its banks by European immigrants, there are no regular notices of *salmon*. Neither a swimming-course, nor a breeding-place has been detected. It is, therefore, a fair presumption, that these fishes never found within its water sufficient inducement to visit them in great numbers, or at regular times, and that those which have been taken are merely strays or wanderers."

In 1815, no less a personage than De Witt Clinton took up the question of salmon in the Hudson. Besides being an adept politician, Clinton was a first-rate naturalist who knew the river well. In 1824, he described a new species of minnow, the spot-tail shiner, which he discovered in the river and is thus named *Notropis hudsonius*. In his "Introductory Discourse" before the Literary and Philosophical Society of New York, Clinton said, "Hudson certainly did not intend the common salmon. I believe the fish he meant is our rock fish or streaked [striped] bass, which comes into the river about that time, in great numbers."

Only on the rarest of occasions have salmon ever been caught in the Hudson, and these without question were strays. In 1840, an eight-pound salmon was taken near Troy, and in 1930, an angler reported catching a fifteen-pounder near Kingston. It is true that salmon have been planted in the Hudson. For instance, between 1882 and 1888, when fish stocking was the rage, a total of 2,091,723 Atlantic salmon fry were planted in the Adirondack headwaters of the Hudson. Of these, perhaps only 1,000 were later taken as adults upon their return to the river from the sea. The Hudson, in sum, appears to lack whatever salmon need for success, both now and in the days of the Indians.

Along the Hudson and in most of the northeast, the Indians belonged to the Algonkian or Algonquian stock, a widely distributed linguistic family. A separate family, the Iroquois, controlled the Mohawk River. Several words from the Algonkian language, *papoose, squaw, wampum,* and *wigwam,* were used so widely by the early settlers that present-day Americans have come to think of them as used by Indians everywhere. *Wampum* is a shortened version of *wampumpeak,* meaning "strings of white shell beads," which were used for both ornamental purposes and currency. Basically, there were two kinds of wampum both usually made from the hard-shell clam. There were white beads and purple beads, the latter made from the dark portion of the shell and considered more valuable. When the great Linnaeus, the father of systematic classification, learned that the hard-shell clam was used for money, he gave the clam the specific scientific name *mercenaria.*

The Dutch capitalized on the idea of using wampum as the principal medium of exchange for beaver skins and other furs. Indeed, wampum was manufactured in New Netherland, and following complaints about unfinished and counterfeit wampum, an ordinance passed in 1650 made it illegal to sell wampum made of "stone, bone, glass, muscle-shells [*sic*], horn, yea, even of wood and broken beads." As late as 1880, residents of Bergen County, New Jersey, were manufacturing wampum for western traders.

Within the Hudson Valley, the Algonkians were formed into three loose confederacies: the Mahican, which occupied both sides of the river south of Albany; the Delaware, on the west shore south from present-day Catskill into New Jersey; and the Wappinger, which ran from Poughkeepsie south to Manhattan. The Montauk confederation ruled Long Island. Within each confederation were tribes. The Wappinger confederation, for example, included the Wappinger, Nochpeem, Kitchawank, Sintsink (popularly Sing Sing and meaning, prophetically, in view of the prison, "stone upon stone"), Pacham, Wecquaesgeek, Siwanoy, and Manhattan tribes.

Modern-day excavation of campsites and burial grounds indicate heavy Algonkian settlement along the Hudson. Dr. William Ritchie of the New York State Museum says: "It is impossible satisfactorily to estimate the size of the Indian population of the eastern New York-southern New England area at any period in prehistoric or early historic times." Another authority, James Mooney of the Bureau of American Ethnology in the Smithsonian Institution, estimated that in 1600 there were about 3,000 Mahicans; 4,750 Wappingers, including those in Connecticut; 8,000 Delawares, and 6,000 Montauks, including the Canarsees in Brooklyn.

In many places, the Indian names remain. Thus Manhattan, "the island"; Schenectady, from the Iroquois *Ska-neh-ta-de*, originally applied to the Albany area and meaning "beyond the opening" or "beyond the pine trees," probably in reference to the Karner sand plains: Cohoes, "canoe falling"; Copake, "snake pond"; Taconic, "full of timber"; Mattewan, probably "good furs"; Poughkeepsie, possibly "safe harbor"; Wassaic, "rocky place," from *gussuk*, rock, and *ick*, place; Wicopee, "end of the land"; Coxsackie, possibly "owl hoot" or "place of wild geese"; Canarsie, "at the boundary or fence"; Tuxedo, possibly "lake of clear, flowing water"; Hoosac or Hoosick, "place of stones"; Schodack, "place of fire," because this island in the Hudson was the traditional Mahican capitol and site of the council fire; Hackensack, "lowland"; Tappan, "cold springs"; Kayaderosseras, "lake country"; Sacandaga, "marsh" or "much water"; Esopus, probably "river"; Mohonk, either from *mohewoneck*, "racoon skin coat," or *mohan*, "to eat solid food"; Ashokan, "to cross the creek"; Armonk, possibly from *amochk*, "beaver"; Chappaqua, possibly "well-watered place"; Mount Kisco, from *kishkituck*, "land on the edge of a creek," undoubtedly in reference to the nearby Croton River; Kitchawan, aboriginal name for the Croton River, "large and swift current"; Croton, from *kenotin;* "wind" or "tempest," and Muscoot, "place of rushes."

Along the Hudson, Indians camped mainly at the mouths of streams that emptied into the river, or along bays and coves. The living at such sites was extremely easy; there was an abundance of fish, game, and plant food. "Famine they do not fear," Van der

Donck observed. In fact, the river Indians could afford to be gourmets, and they were especially fond of oysters, which they ate in incredible numbers. There are kitchen middens along the Hudson where the shells are piled to a depth of a dozen feet or more.

The favorite fish was the striped bass. The Indian spring began with fishing for stripers, caught in nets made from swamp milkweed, "Indian hemp." De Vries wrote:

Striped bass are caught in large quantities and dried by the Indians,—for at this time [April and May] the squaws are engaged in sowing the maize, and cultivating the land, and the men go afishing in order to assist their wives a little by their draughts of fish. Sometimes they catch them with seines from seventy to eighty fathoms in length, which they braid themselves, and on which, in place of lead, they hang stones, and instead of corks which we put on to float them, they fasten small sticks an ell in length, round, and sharp at the end. Over the purse, they have a figure made of wood, resembling the devil, and when the fish swim into the net and comes to the purse, so that the figure begins to move, they then begin to cry out and call upon the *mannetoe*, that is, the devil, to give them many fish. They catch great quantities of this fish; which they also catch in little set nets, six or seven fathoms long, braided like a herring net. They set them on sticks in the river, one and one-half fathoms deep.

In October, after the corn was picked and dried, the Indian women put the grain in rush baskets, which they buried in the earth. They then accompanied their husbands and children to hunt deer, leaving the old people at home to guard the grain. "In December, they return home," de Rasieres wrote, "and the flesh which they have not been able to eat while fresh, they smoke on the way, and bring it back with them. They come home as fat as moles." According to de Vries, the Indians often hunted deer by driving them into the Hudson. The Indians would form a long line and beat their way toward the river, making "a noise as if they were wolves, by which many deer are devoured." As the Indians drew closer to the river, they would close ranks so that the deer could not escape their arrows. Those deer that dove into the Hudson were snared and drowned by Indians waiting in canoes. Sometimes, on land, the Indians drove the deer into enclosures. The name of Pound Ridge in Westchester County is derived from this practice.

The land to the west of Albany was under the domination of the Iroquois, the League of Five Nations or tribes. The total population of these tribes was around fifty-five hundred, a figure given by both Mooney and Ritchie. The five tribes spread across the state, from near Albany to the Genesee River, a distance of 150 miles, and they were, in order from east to west, the Mohawks, Oneidas, Onondagas, Cayugas, and Senecas. The name *Iroquois* itself was not used by these tribes; *Iroquois* is an Algonkian word meaning "real adders," a term indicative of the hostility between the two peoples. The name the Iroquois used for themselves was *Ogwanonhsioni,* meaning "long house builders." Indeed, the Iroquois called their land the "Long House," since the boundaries of their territory across the state resembled that form of dwelling.

The Mohawks near Albany were the "guardians of the eastern door" to the Long House. They were fierce and aggressive, very much unlike the placid Hudson Valley Algonkians, upon whom they later preyed. At one time, the Mohawks forced the Delawares to lay down their arms and dress as squaws, and it was not unusual for a lone Mohawk to venture down the Hudson to demand tribute from a tribe. According to one authority, Alanson Skinner, the Iroquois boasted that "when their messengers failed to return, so swift, sure and terrible was the reckoning, that when one fell ill in an Algonkin village, his enemies nursed him and cared for him until he grew well, rather than face ruin if he did not go back."

The Dutch were quick to learn of the Mohawks' reputation. In 1626, the Dutch commander at Fort Orange, now Albany, and six of his men joined some Mahicans to fight the Mohawks. The Mohawks killed the commander and three of his men, "among the latter was Tymen Bouwsenz, whom they devoured, after having well roasted him." The Mohawks, incidentally, called themselves *Kanyengehaga,* "people of the place of flint"; Mohawk was a name applied by their enemies, meaning "those who eat people." In any event, the Dutch were quick to make peace with the Mohawks and stood aloof as the Mahicans were driven into Connecticut. The Dutch even looked the other way when the Mohawks held a European captive. In 1643, a party of Mohawks arrived near Albany to fish in the Hudson, bringing with them Father Isaac Jogues, a French Jesuit, whom they had tortured severely and whom they planned to roast alive after the fishing was done. Jogues was able to flee by swimming to a Dutch ship, but arrangements for the escape were clandestine, for the Dutch had no wish to rile the Mohawks.

The Algonkian Indians down along the Hudson had less luck with the Dutch; they were too easygoing. The Dutch found them "quite modest, without guile and inexperienced," and noted their great love for their children: "they are fond of them beyond measure." By European standards, the squaws were promiscuous, "and our Dutchmen run after them very much," noted the Reverend Megapolensis. As time went on, the Dutch treated the Indians badly, even killing in their sleep women and children who had sought refuge from the Mohawks. Indian resentment grew, and de Vries, who was otherwise fair, wrote of the west-shore tribes, "Their disposition is bad. They are very revengeful, resembling the Italians." Before the century was done, the Algonkian tribes of the Hudson Valley were shattered and broken, and of them barely a trace remains. In 1664, the Mohawks forced the Mahicans to move their council fire from Schodack Island in the river to what is now Stockbridge, Massachusetts. A few Mahicans lingered on in the Hudson Valley, but they disappeared around the early 1800s; others moved to Pennsylvania, where they lost their tribal identity. Most of the Mahicans who had settled in Stockbridge moved west in the mid-nineteenth century and joined with the Munsees, a Delaware tribe, on a reservation near Green Bay, Wisconsin.

Nowadays, the last of the Mahicans in the East are to be found near New London, Connecticut, where their forefathers moved from Stockbridge to mingle with their kinsmen, the Mohegans. Two Mohegans who claim Mahican ancestry are a brother and sister, Harold and Gladys Tantaquidgeon, proprietors of the

Tantaquidgeon Indian Museum in Uncasville, Connecticut. Miss Tantaquidgeon says: "It is part of the legend of our family that our people originally came from the northwest around the Hudson River. In round numbers, there still are about 175 of us living in this part of Connecticut."

3

THE
HAND OF MAN

After the return of the *Half Moon* to Holland, individual Dutch traders began to visit New Netherland, as the land that Hudson had discovered came to be known. The States General of Holland gave control of trade to the United Netherlands Company in 1614 and then to the newly formed West India Company in 1621. From the beginning, furs were the major interest of the Dutch, and beaver, otter, mink, and muskrat skins were soon going to Holland in great numbers.

The Dutch did not begin serious settlement until 1623, and they were fortunate that they did not lose the colony to the English, who regarded the coast as theirs because of voyages dating back to John Cabot. In point of fact, the Pilgrims planned to settle along Hudson's River, but a storm at sea drove them to Plymouth in 1620. Dutch settlement was slow. The company offered each settler a *bouwerie*, a farm, but few Dutchman had reason to leave the pleasant life at home. In 1629, in a misguided effort to spur colonization, the West India Company drew up a charter of Privileges and Exemptions under the terms of which the company allowed any member to buy enormous tracts of land from the Indians along the bank of any navigable river. These tracts could extend for sixteen miles on one shore or eight miles on both shores, and they could run as far inland "as the situation of the occupiers will permit." The only requirement was that the purchaser, styled a *patroon*, should establish on his land a colony of at least fifty persons within four years. Manhattan Island and Fort Orange, reserved for the company, were exempt from claim.

A patroon had considerable powers. He was able to "administer civil and criminal justice, in person, or by deputy, within his colonie, to appoint local officers and magistrates; to erect courts . . . ; to keep a gallows, if such were required." A patroon had the right of trade in everything but furs, which were reserved for the company. Several patroonships were soon established along the Hudson. In 1630, Michael Pauw bought what is now Jersey City and the whole of Staten Island, calling it Pavonia, a Latinized version of his name. In that same year, Killian Van Rensselaer, an Amsterdam diamond merchant, had an agent start buying land near Fort Orange, and by 1637, Van Rensselaer was in control of a patroonship, Rensselaerswyck, comprising nearly seven hundred square miles on both banks of the Hudson. In 1646, Adriaen Van der Donck, who has been quoted previously, purchased a patroonship north of Manhattan. A member of the gentry in Holland, Van der Donck was called by the title of *Jonkheer*, young heir, and from this the name Yonkers derives. Nearby, Jonas Bronck settled on five hundred acres of land that are now part of the Bronx.

Rensselaerswyck was the only successful patroonship, but when the English took over New Netherland in 1664, they allowed manors to be established on similar lines. In 1668, Robert Livingston purchased 160,000 acres in what is now Columbia County; in 1680, Frederick Philipse acquired large holdings in southern Westchester, and in 1697, Colonel Stephanus Van Cortlandt bought northern Westchester. In terms of generating settlement, the patroonships and manors were doomed to failure. At Rensselaerswyck, a tenant had to pay rent of five hundred guilders (two hundred dollars) a year, give three days' annual service with his horse and wagon, keep up roads, split and deliver two fathoms of firewood, and deliver a "quit rent" of two bushels of wheat, two pairs of fowl, and twenty-five pounds of butter. In 1701, the Earl of Bellemont, governor of New York, observed that Livingston "has on his great grant of sixteen miles long and twenty-four broad but four or five cottages, as I am told—men live in vassalage under him, and work for him, and are too poor to be farmers, having not the wherewithal to buy cattle to start a farm."

Peter Kalm, a Swedish botanist and student of Linnaeus, visited the Hudson Valley in 1749 and on his journey upriver noted the scarcity of settlement. The feelings between landlord and tenants were often strong, and they lasted for years. In the early nineteenth century, Martin Van Buren got his start in politics by battling the Van Rensselaers and Livingstons. In essence, the semifeudal system of patroonships and manors remained in force until an armed revolt by farmers in Columbia County in the 1840s. Whatever the injustices of the system, and there were many, the net effect was that the Hudson was lightly settled for more than two centuries, and as a result the river was spared much indiscriminate abuse.

Of course, there was some settlement under Dutch and English rule. Farmers raised potatoes, corn, barley, oats, wheat, and flax, and Kalm reported that the wheat flour from the valley "is reckoned the best in all North America." Timber was cut and exported. Albany shipped vast quantities of white pine downriver. Sawmills and gristmills sprang up on tributary streams, or "kills" as the Dutch called them. For instance, Peekskill was named for the stream explored by Jan Peek, an early trader who mistook it for the main stem of the Hudson. The Dutch called the Catskill Mountains the Katzberg, the mountains where bobcats and lynx abounded. The major stream that flowed east toward the Hudson was called the Katz Kill, now, redundantly, Catskill Creek.

Roads along the Hudson were poor, and the river itself served as the main highway. Both passengers and produce were carried up and down the river by so-called Hudson River sloops. These broad-bottomed ships, obviously patterned after canal craft in

Holland, were used on the river for more than three hundred years, until the 1890s, when they were rendered uneconomical by steam-powered tugs pulling barges.* A typical river sloop was sixty-five to seventy-five feet long and had a capacity of one hundred tons. "Frequently the bottom consists of white oak, and the sides of red cedar, because the latter withstands decay much longer than the former," Kalm wrote after a trip to Albany aboard a sloop. "The red cedar is likewise apt to split when it hits against anything which the keel of the boat sometimes strikes. Therefore people choose white oak for the bottom, as being the softer wood, and not splitting so easily. The bottom, being continually under water, is not so much exposed to weathering and holds out longer."

The sloops had one mast placed well forward, a large mainsail to catch the fickle breezes, a small jib, and sometimes a topsail. The use of the centerboard was developed on these sloops. They had high quarterdecks, a relic of the poops of medieval ships, and the vessels were painted in gaudy colors. The sloops were eminently seaworthy; between 1785 and 1787, Captain Stewart Dean of Albany sailed the sloop *Experiment* around Cape Horn to Canton to make the first direct voyage from the United States to China. On the Hudson, passengers could promenade or dance on deck, and a trip from New York to Albany occasioned as much excitement as a voyage to Europe. Sometimes, it seemed to take as long. Alexander Hamilton is said to have written the first paper in *The Federalist* while a passenger on a windless voyage along the Hudson.

The duration of a trip depended upon a combination of winds and tide. The sloop *Caroline* once sailed the sixty miles from Manhattan to Fishkill in five hours. Then again, the same trip sometimes took four or five days. When wind and tide were unfavorable, there was nothing to do but drop anchor. The tide in the Hudson has its vagaries. In some places, the flood tide will "make" almost an hour earlier on one shore than the other, and in certain parts the ebb will "hang" longer. The winds offered a problem, particularly the northwest wind that roars through

---

* A replica of a Hudson River sloop was under construction in a Maine shipyard in early 1969. Named *Clearwater*, the vessel was scheduled to be sailing the Hudson as a floating museum by fall, 1969.

"Mother Cronk's Cove," the gap between Storm King and Crow's Nest mountains at the north gate of the Highlands. There, in 1824, the sloop *Neptune* capsized and thirty-five persons drowned.

To the Dutch, the perilous stretch of the river through the Highlands was known as Martyr's Reach. All in all, the Dutch divided the Hudson into fourteen reaches, distances that could be seen point to point as one sailed between New York City and Albany. The first was the great Chip Rock reach along the Palisades; the early Dutch called the Palisades the Great Chip. It was followed by the Tappan Zee and Haverstraw Bay reaches. Between the Zee and the Bay on the west shore is Verdrietege Hook, or Hook Mountain. Verdrietege is the Dutch for tedious, and the mountain was thus named by skippers impatiently waiting for a good wind. Similarly, the hilly knob named Pyngyp, several miles up river, supposedly comes from a Dutch sailor's expression for the cracking sound of a boom coming around on a tack. As the Hudson twisted through the Highlands, there was Seylmaker's Reach, Crescent Reach, Hoge's, and Martyr's or Vorsen's. Lange Rak or Long Reach ran from Wappinger Creek to Crum Elbow. Fisher's Reach extended to Esopus; Claverack, Backerak, Playsier, Vaste, and Hunter's reaches followed.

The early Dutch skippers, faced with the unpredictable dangers of the river, endowed much of the land with stories. The myths and legends of the Hudson owe their popularity to Washington Irving, but it may be that the stories he wrote were being told when, as a youngster of seventeen, he sailed up to Albany in a sloop. According to one nineteenth-century critic, Thomas Wentworth Higginson, "It was not Irving who invested the Hudson with romance, but the Hudson that inspired Irving. When in 1786, Mrs. Josiah Quincy, then a young girl, sailed upon that river in a sloop, she wrote: 'Our captain had a legend for every scene, whether supernatural or traditional or of actual occurrence during the war, and not a mountain reared its head unconnected with some marvelous story.' Irving was but then three years old, yet Ichabod Crane and Rip Van Winkle or their prototypes were already on the spot waiting for biographers. . . . What was needed was self-confidence and a strong literary desire to take the materials at hand."

In some of Irving's tales, the natural history of the river and the

Hudson Valley occupies a prominent place, such as the explanation that the numerous thunderstorms are caused by Hendrick Hudson's crew bowling in the mountains. Then there appear to be connections between the river stories and German legend, such as Rip Van Winkle and the long sleep of Frederick Barbarossa. In the early 1700s, Palatine Germans from the Rhine country settled West Camp, Newburgh, Germantown, and Rhinebeck. All told, the British shipped two thousand Palatine Germans to the valley, the largest single group to settle in Colonial days, to make tar, turpentine, and resin for the navy. After discovering for themselves the hardships of the patroonships and manors, many of the Germans moved out of the valley to settle elsewhere. Still they left a legacy larger than the names of river villages. One youngster, John Peter Zenger, later did much to establish freedom of the press by besting English libel law in court, and others bequeathed a rich body of folklore.

The imagination of the Dutch settlers must have been stirred by the river and its hills. A modern historian, M. W. Goodwin, in *Dutch and English on the Hudson*, has written:

> We may find it hard to reconcile the reputation of the Dutch as a phlegmatic and unimaginative people with the fact that they and their children endowed the Hudson with more glamour, more of the supernatural and of elfin lore than haunts any other waterway in America. Does the explanation perhaps lie in the fact that the Dutch colonists, coming from a small country situated on a level plain where the landscape was open as far as the eye could see, and left no room for mystery, were suddenly transplanted to a region shut in between overhanging cliffs where lighting flashed and thunder rolled from mountain wall to mountain wall, where thick forests obscured the view, and strange aboriginal savages hid in the underbush? Was it not the sense of wonder springing from this change in their accustomed surroundings that peopled the dim depths of the *hinterland* with shapes of elf and goblin, of demons and superhuman presences?

While life in the hinterland remained quiet, the city at the mouth of the river was growing, more in significance than in size. Under the Dutch, New Amsterdam never had a population larger than fifteen hundred, but it was remarkably polyglot. After fleeing down the Hudson from the Mohawks, Isaac Jogues wrote in 1646: "On the island of Manhate, and its environs, there may well be four or five hundred men of different sects and nation: the Director General told me that there were men of eighteen different languages. . . . No religion is publicly exercised but the Calvinist, and orders are to admit none but Calvinists, but this is not observed; for besides the Calvinists there are in the colony Catholics, English Puritans, Lutherans, Anabaptists, here called Mnistes, etc." The West India Company made Manhattan the center for trade in New Netherland, and the advantages and location of the harbor made it a focal point up and down the coast. An anonymous visitor, possibly a spy for the English, wrote in 1661 about Manhattan:

From Long island they have beef, pork, wheat, butter, some tobacco, wampen and peage [wampumpeak, wampum]. From New England beef, sheep, wheat, flower, bisket, malt, fish, butter, cider-apples, iron, tar, wampen and peage.

From Virginia, store of tobacco, oxhides, dried, some beef, pork and fruit, and for payment give Holland and other linnen, canvage [canvas], tape, thrid, cordage, brasse, Hading cloth, stuffs, stockings, spices, fruit, all sorts of iron work, wine, Brandy, Annis, salt, and all usefull manufactures.

The town is seated between New England and Virginia, commodiously for trades, and that is their chief employment, for they plant and sow litle.

From Amsterdam came each year 7 or 8 big ships with passengers and all sorts of goods, and they lade back beaver and other skins, dry oxhides and Virginia tobacco. Tis said that each year is carried from thence about 20000 sterl. value in beaver skins only.

When the English seized New Amsterdam in 1664, the name was changed to New York and the North River finally became the Hudson. To the English, the Dutch were known by the nickname of "Jankees," a derisive combination of John and cheese pronounced *Yankees*. Calling Dutchmen Jankees was like calling an Irishman a Harp or a German a Kraut. In *The American Language*, H. L. Mencken asks: "But how did this nickname for Dutchmen ever come to be applied to Englishmen, and particularly to the people of New England, male and female alike? To this day no satisfactory answer has been made. All that may be said with any certainty is that it was already in use by 1765 [in New England] as a term of derision, and that by 1775 the Yankees began to take pride in it." I suspect that there is a satisfactory answer to Mencken's question, and that the answer is this: in 1757, during the French and Indian War, a Dr. Shuckburgh, a British Army surgeon stationed at Fort Cralo in Rensellaer on the Hudson, wrote the song "Yankee Doodle" to ridicule the Colonial militia. Many of the militia were from New England, and I assume that they carried the song back home where they started calling one another Yankees.

Under English rule, many of the Dutch persisted in staying among themselves. Dutch was spoken in Albany until the Revolution, and Franklin D. Roosevelt told Carl Carmer that Dutch was still spoken in isolated communities when he was born in 1882. Over the years any number of Dutch words passed into English, among them *stoop, waffle, cookie,* and *coleslaw.*

With the English in charge, New York grew in importance as a trading center. Indeed, the city so thrived on trade that at first pirates actually were welcomed. The pirates were not above carrying on business in local waters; an Albany report of 1696 states "pirates in great numbers infest the Hudson River at its mouth and waylay vessels on their way to Albany, speeding out from behind coves and from behind islands and again returning to the rocky shores, or ascending the mountains along the river to conceal their plunder." Piracy off the coast became so great a scandal that New Yorkers formed a company to buy a ship equipped with thirty-six guns to drive pirates off the seas. One of the shareholders in the company was Robert Livingston, and the man the company picked to captain the ship was a resident of Liberty Street, William Kidd, whose crew was supposedly composed in the main of Hudson River men who came from the vicinity of Livingston Manor. The scandal became even greater when Kidd himself turned pirate. He was eventually captured and executed. According to legends, part of Kidd's treasure from a Moorish ship, *Quedah Merchant,* is sunk in the Hudson off Jones Point opposite Peekskill, where the crew, returning home, scuttled the prize during a storm. At one point in the nineteenth century, a promoter raised twenty-two thousand dollars to build a coffer dam and pumping station to retrieve the treasure, but nothing was ever found, not even the promoter, who apparently ran off with most of the money.

At the time of the American Revolution, life along the Hudson was bucolic. However, by its very geographical position, the river became the pivot upon which British grand strategy turned. They aimed to seize the Hudson and thus divide the rebelling colonies in two. In this they failed. They occupied Manhattan for the duration of the war, and they made a few forays upriver, burning Kingston in 1777, but they never were able to assume control of the Hudson. From the beginning, Washington appreciated the value of the Highlands, and work was commenced on forts on Constitution Island, at West Point, and elsewhere. The greatest battle of the war, in fact, what is perhaps the most significant battle in American history, took place on the Hudson near Saratoga in 1777. Here General John Burgoyne and his army of ten thousand men were defeated on October 7, when General Benedict Arnold, who later attempted to betray West Point, led three regiments into the center of the British line and broke it. Burgoyne withdrew, but victory was not possible, and on October 14 he sent an aide, Major Kingston, to negotiate a cessation of hostilities. Before discussing terms, the major "expatiated with taste and eloquence on the beautiful scenery of the Hudson's river and the charms of the season."

During the Revolution, the Iroquois supported the British against the Americans, who were called the *Was-to-heh-no*, "people of Boston." (The name was used until the 1900s.) After the war, the Iroquois, who had become the Six Nations in the early 1700s by taking in the Tuscororas, lost most of their lands, and they are now settled on reservations in New York State and Canada. As a result of a savage American campaign against the Senecas during the Revolution, George Washington is still called *Honandaganius*, "destroyer of towns," as are all the presidents who have followed him.

After the Revolution, the population of the Hudson Valley grew rapidly. In 1771, New York City had a population of only 21,862; by 1820, it had grown to 123,705, by far the largest in the nation. Further up the Hudson, Yankees moved in from New England. The city of Hudson was founded in 1783 by Nantucket whaling men seeking protection from the ravages of British ships, and within three years Hudson was the home port of twenty-five vessels and had its own shipbuilding yards. Poughkeepsie, too, became a port for Yankee whalers, and Yankee merchants' founded Troy to rival Albany as a center of commerce. A Troy meatpacker, Samuel Wilson, supplied the army during the war of 1812 and stamped government consignments "U. S." One of his workmen said the initials stood for "Uncle Sam." The joke spread, and the symbol of Uncle Sam came into national existence.

One of the earliest industries was iron mining. In 1751, the Sterling mine and furnace opened in Orange County, and it was here that a giant chain, with each link weighing about 150 pounds, was forged to protect the Hudson during the Revolution. The fifteen-hundred-foot chain was stretched from West Point to Constitution Island to stop British ships from moving upriver. In the years that followed other iron deposits were mined.

Limestone was required for the making of iron, and soon it was being used for cement as well. About 1820, the manufacture of natural cement began at Rosendale in Ulster County. The Rosendale cement was of excellent quality, and was used in the construction of the Brooklyn Bridge and the base of the Statue of Liberty, but it lost out to Portland cement, also made in the Hudson Valley, because it took much longer to dry. The deposits of clay gave rise to a thriving brick industry along the Hudson. The hills were also quarried for traprock and sandstone. Although there is some specialized mining—the plains near Albany yield a fine molding sand, and outside Peekskill is one of the few emery mines in the world—the Hudson Valley has traditionally supplied the materials which New York City consumes in its never-ending cycle of rebuilding.

In the early nineteenth century, several developments were of profound importance to the Hudson Valley, The first of these was the practical demonstration of the steamboat by Robert Fulton. On August 7 and 8, 1807, the steamboat *Clermont*, named after the river estate of Robert Livingston, Fulton's backer, steamed from New York to Albany in twenty-eight hours and forty-five minutes. Belching smoke and fire from her stack, the *Clermont* was such a strange sight that a farmer said he had "seen the devil going up the river in a sawmill." Fulton failed in his attempt to have a monopoly on river traffic, and the steamboat competition grew so fierce that the ships evolved into floating palaces and the fare between New York and Albany on occasion dropped from seven or eight dollars to twenty-five cents.

Rival steamboat lines tried to establish supremacy by speed, and racing was common on the river. In 1845, the steamer *Swallow* was racing two other boats downriver near Hudson when she ran head-on into a rocky island, which became known as Swallow Rock. She broke up and caught fire, and at least fifty of her three hundred passengers perished. In 1852, the *Henry Clay* was racing downriver near Yonkers when she caught fire. The captain ran her on shore, but more than sixty persons died, among them Maria Hawthorne, sister of the novelist, who was returning home to Salem, on a roundabout route from Saratoga in order to enjoy the beauties of the river.

The most famous race—inspired by a one-thousand-dollar bet —occurred in 1847 between the *Cornelius Vanderbilt,* owned by Commodore Vanderbilt, a former Staten Island ferryman, and the *Oregon,* belonging to George Law. The race was from the Battery to Sing Sing and back. Vanderbilt was at the wheel of his own boat. The race was close until Vanderbilt miscalculated the turn at Sing Sing. The *Oregon* ran out of fuel downriver, but the Captain ordered the chairs, benches, berths, and any other woodwork that would burn thrown into the furnaces, and the gutted steamer won by twelve hundred feet. The greatest boat on the river was the *Mary Powell.* Three hundred feet long, trim, graceful, and beautifully kept by one family, the Andersons, for almost sixty years, the *Mary Powell* was the acknowledged queen of the river. She began service from Roundout Creek, Kingston, to New York City in 1861, and for many years she was the fastest boat on the Hudson. She never had a serious accident, and she never lost a passenger. To many oldtimers on the Hudson, the sight of this great sidewheeler moving along the river was the most magnificent spectacle they ever saw. Toward the end of her days, the *Mary Powell* was sold to the Day Line, and then she was finally sold to a junk dealer and dismantled. Today the only vestige of the river traffic of olden times is the Day Line's *Alexander Hamilton,* built in 1922, the only sidewheeler still in service in American coastal waters.

A second development was the opening of the Erie and Champlain canals. The idea of a canal linking the Hudson with the Great Lakes dates back to 1785, but it took the push and drive of De Witt Clinton, chairman of a canal commission, to get the Erie and Champlain Canals authorized by the legislature. Work on both started in 1817. The Champlain canal, only sixty-four miles long from Fort Edward on the Hudson to Whitehall, New York, was completed first. The Erie Canal was a far more ambitious undertaking, involving three thousand men with picks and shovels, five hundred horses, and two hundred yoke of oxen. On July 4, 1817, shortly after Clinton had become governor, he dug the first spadeful of dirt at Rome. The first task was to complete the middle section of the canal linking the Mohawk and Seneca rivers. All told, the Erie was 363 miles long, and it had eighty-three regular locks. Near Buffalo, special locks had to be built to raise the water level sixty feet in a two-mile stretch, and a 750-foot aqueduct carried the canal over the Genessee River.

The Erie was completed in late 1825. On October 26 of that year, the canalboat *Seneca Chief* began a triumphant journey from Buffalo pulled by four gray horses. It was followed by another boat, fittingly called *Noah's Ark,* which carried two eagles, a bear, two fawns, a variety of other animals and birds, and several species of fish. At Albany, the steamboat *Chancellor Livingston* took the *Seneca Chief* in tow for the trip downriver. Upon arrival in New York, the boats proceeded toward Sandy Hook, where Governor Clinton, in symbolic ceremony, poured a keg of Lake Erie water into the Atlantic. As an added touch, Clinton's fellow naturalist, Dr. Samuel Latham Mitchill, poured in water from the Mississippi, Thames, Nile, Seine, Danube, Rhine, Amazon, Orinoco, Ganges, Indus, Gambia, Columbia, and La Plata rivers.

The way to the Middle West was open; the Appalachians had been outflanked. Shipping time from Buffalo to Manhattan was cut from twenty to eight days, and the freight rate dropped from one hundred dollars to five dollars a ton. The canal, which had cost more than seventeen million dollars to build, soon collected more than one million dollars a year in tolls. Canal towns, with names proudly bespeaking navigation—Middleport, Gasport, Lockport, Weedsport, and Brockport—sprouted, and New York City prospered.

Then there was the development of the railroads. The first railroad incorporated in the United States was the Mohawk and Hudson, chartered by the state in 1826. It began operation in 1831 and ran from Albany to Schenectady. The line was the genesis of the New York Central. Railroads were slow in coming to eastern New York because of opposition from canal and steamboat interests. The Hudson River route to Albany from New York City was not completed until 1851.

As New York City grew, it outraced its supply of water. Ever since it was first settled, the city had depended on wells, but as early as 1748 water had become so bad that even horses refused to drink it. In 1799, the state legislature granted a charter to the Manhattan Company to supply water for the city, but the Manhattan Company was little more than a device by which Aaron Burr could get into the banking business. In 1828, fires ravaged Manhattan, and in 1832, thirty-five hundred people died from cholera. As a result, the city decided to go thirty miles north to dam and tap the Croton River, a large tributary of the Hudson. In 1842, the Croton dam and aqueduct were finished, and although the supply was supposed to be adequate for a century, more water was needed within twenty years' time. Over the years, New York City has constantly reached upstate for water. The original Croton Reservoir has been much enlarged, and there are numerous other reservoirs in northern Westchester and Putnam counties. In 1907, the city began developing reservoirs in the Catskills, and streams there which formerly flowed to the Hudson or Delaware have been impounded.

At the same time that the railroad, steamboats, and canal system were opening up the Hudson Valley, the river was receiving national attention from writers, artists, and aesthetes, and the case may be made that the valley, more than any other locale, inspired a new American attitude toward nature. Washington Irving was merely one of a number of nineteenth-century writers who sang the praises of the river. Among the others were James Kirke Paulding, John Bigelow, and Nathaniel Parker Willis, whose works are now stuck in the attic of literature. Willis was a dandified sort, "an anticipation of Oscar Wilde," Oliver Wendell Holmes said, and he bought a retreat, Idlewild, near Cornwall, where his pen "capered nimbly away" in homage to the Hudson. In the words of a friendly critic, Edgar Mayhew Bacon, at Idlewild Willis "cultivated the acquaintance of trees and wild flowers, protected the birds and evinced a kindly fellowship for the frogs." Willis disliked the name Butter Hill, from the Dutch Boeter Berg, and fought a successful campaign to change the name of the mountain to Storm King. It is easy to mock Willis as some pressed flower in the pages of history, but he was among the first of American writers to foster an appreciation for the land. As Bacon wrote, "To a generation whose eyes had not been educated to see, and who generally understood that the country was designed by Providence as the place in which to raise corn and potatoes, his letters were a revelation."

William Cullen Bryant urged Americans to forego visits abroad to see "the Western shore of the Hudson," as "worthy of a pilgrimage across the Atlantic as the Alps themselves." At Newburgh, a gardener's son, Andrew Jackson Downing, became the father of landscape gardening in America. His first book, *A Treatise on the Theory and Practice of Landscape Gardening Adapted to North America,* published when he was twenty-six, made him famous. Courted by the river gentry to design estates, he laid out the grounds for the White House and the Capitol. Something of a snob, Downing nonetheless campaigned for public parks, and his arguments helped prepare the way for Central Park in New York, which was designed by his pupil, Frederick Law Olmsted. Downing drowned in the Hudson in 1852, trying to rescue a fellow passenger from the wreckage of the *Henry Clay.*

During the early nineteenth century, the Hudson inspired America's first own school of artists, the Hudson River School. The leading figure was Thomas Cole, born in England in 1801 in the center of smokey, industrialized Lancaster. His father had failed in business as a woolen merchant, and young Cole had to work for a calico designer. He found the work repugnant and daydreamed of wilderness America. In 1818, the Cole family emigrated to Philadelphia and then moved to Ohio. Cole began doing portraits and wandering the countryside. He became interested in landscapes, and in 1825 he traveled up the Hudson River. There, as he saw the Catskills "at a pleasing distance," was the country of his boyhood dreams. Never one to paint at the scene— "I must wait for time to throw a veil over the common details," he wrote—Cole hurried back to New York and turned out three landscapes which were bought almost as soon as they were shown.

Cole settled in the village of Catskill, where his home and studio still stand. "The painter of American scenery has indeed privileges superior to any other; and nature here is new to art," he declared. Cole and the other members of the Hudson River School changed the conception of the landscape. Man did not dominate the paintings. Indeed, man was often absent, and when he did appear he was a small detail, the equal, not the master, of a dog or deer. In essence, man was one with the environment; he was part of the land, living with it in peace, not ravaging it.

Cole had more grandiose plans than being "a mere leaf painter." He painted giant canvases, such as the *Course of Empire* and *Voyage of Life* series. Here he failed. As James Thomas Flexner, the critic, has written of *The Voyage of Life* "The landscapes are not up to Cole's usual standard; the rocks are cardboard; the storms, fustian; the angel, a winged togaed cliché; and Everyman has become that pointless character, Nobody." Angrily, Cole returned to his Catskill landscapes. "I am not the painter I would have been had taste been higher," he lamented. Nonetheless, the Hudson gave him succor and inspiration. On a trip to Europe, Cole found the natural scenery there could not equal what he knew at home, and "although there is a peculiar softness and beauty in Italian skies, our skies are far more gorgeous." The Rhine was "infinitely inferior to the Hudson in natural magnificence and grandeur." In much the same spirit, Cole's friend, Asher B. Durand, wrote home: ". . . for real and unalloyed enjoyment of scenery, the rocks, trees and green meadows of Hoboken will have a charm that all Switzerland cannot boast."

More spectacular than Cole was his pupil, Frederick E. Church, the son of a wealthy Hartford businessman, the only pupil Cole ever deigned to take. Church made his home near Mount Merino, three miles south of Hudson, where, after a trip to the Near East, he built a castle in a style that he called "personal Persian." Increasingly bothered by rheumatism that interfered with his painting, he busied himself making his estate, Olana, into a work of landscape art. The view from the house is one of the best of the Hudson and the Catskills. "About an hour this side of Albany is the Center of the World—I own it," he declared.

The sense of being at the center of the world—this has always been part of the lure of the Hudson. John Burroughs, the naturalist, felt it. In the essay "The Sharp Lookout" he wrote:

> I sit here amid the junipers of the Hudson, with purpose every year to go to Florida or to the West Indies or to the Pacific Coast, yet the seasons pass and I am still loitering, with a half-defined suspicion, perhaps, that, if I remain quiet and keep a sharp lookout, these countries will come to me. I may stick it out yet and not miss much after all. The great trouble is for Mohammed to know when the mountain really comes to him. Sometimes a rabbit or a jay or a little warbler brings the woods to my door. A loon on the river, and the Canada lakes are here; the sea gulls and the fish hawk bring the sea; the call of the wild gander at night, what does it suggest? and the eagle flapping by, or floating along on a raft of ice, does he not bring the mountain?

For all the rhapsodizing, there were still other changes at work. The coming of the steamboat and railroad, the development of the canal system, and the building of reservoirs had their effects, subtle and otherwise, on the ecology of the Hudson Valley. The use of steamboats encouraged the cutting of trees for fuel. As early as 1825, the thirteen steamers on the Hudson and the ferries in the harbor used one hundred thousand cords of wood in the eight months of the year that the river was free of ice. Wood was cut on the top of the Palisades and slid down the cliffs to deep water. Thus the name High Gutter Point on the New York–New Jersey state line. In time, the steamers turned to coal, and nowadays coal clinkers are to be found on the bottom of the river. Iron furnaces consumed enormous amounts of charcoal, and the brick kilns relied on cordwood. Neither industry demanded particularly good wood, and the end result was that much of the valley was clear cut every thirty or forty years. Other timber was cut for telegraph and telephone poles, posts, railroad ties, and building lumber. In the Catskills, mile upon mile of hemlocks were left to die after being stripped of their bark for tanning, and as the hemlocks vanished between 1830 and 1870, the color of the mountains changed from a very dark blue to the soft green of hardwoods. Other lands, of course, were cleared for farms. Much of the forest cover has since returned because of a decline in agriculture, but contrary to popular belief, there are no virgin forests between New York and Albany. In the 1930s, Rogers McVaugh, a plant ecologist, investigated the flora of Columbia County, and he found that what had been taken for virgin forests were in actuality mature second-growth forests that began growing in the early 1700s after the original trees had been cut.

Changing land practices prompted the spread of some native animals. The cottontail rabbit (*Syvilagus floridanus*) originally was not found north of the New York City area; the Dutch name for rabbit was *coney,* hence Coney Island. But in the early nineteenth century, the cottontail rabbit literally followed the cabbage patches up the Hudson Valley, reaching Albany in 1850. The bobwhite quail (*Colinus virginianus*) did much the same, but now, for various reasons, including the decline in agriculture, it has retreated down the valley and is found in Westchester. The prolific rabbit, however, has not only hung on upriver but has penetrated north into Canada.

The opening of the canal system caused an agricultural upheaval in the valley. Catskill lost its position as a wheat and flour market, while Rochester on Lake Ontario boomed. In 1812, Rochester had a population of fifteen; by 1840, the population was twenty thousand and Rochester was the leading flour-milling center in the country. The Hudson Valley was finished as a wheat producer, and farmers had to turn to other crops. Andrew Jackson Downing and his brother, Charles, pioneered in efforts to replace wheat with specialty crops—apples, pears, plums, melons, and grapes—and this heritage still persists, with apples from the valley shipped abroad to Britain and Sweden. The leading vegetable crop is corn, grown on ten thousand acres of the old floodplains of the tributary Esopus and Walkill. The cool weather allows farmers to produce excellent corn, U. S. Fancy grade, in volume from the middle of July to the beginning of October, and it is shipped as far as Texas, Florida, and Europe. In the old days, the floodplains of the Walkill were celebrated for their abundance of woodcock (*Philohela minor*).

The opening of the Erie and Champlain canals allowed several fishes not native to the Hudson Watershed to gain entrance. De Witt Clinton, keen naturalist that he was, suspected that this would happen, and in 1820, he wrote: "I expect great changes from the junction of the western and eastern waters on the subject of fish. Already several have penetrated the canal at Rome into the Mohawk river."

The most notable species to get into the Hudson through the canals were the smallmouth bass (*Micropterus dolomieui*) and largemouth bass (*M. salmoides*). Prior to the completion of the canals, the smallmouth and largemouth had been found in the western part of the state, in waters draining into the Great Lakes. They were probably present also in Lake Champlain, but not elsewhere in New England. The canals offered both fish a way to the Hudson, and they swam in and flourished.

The smallmouth is primarily a creature of streams and large, cold, rocky lakes, while the largemouth is fond of quiet backwaters in rivers, streams, and ponds. In the Hudson watershed both species found sufficient variety, and their presence made an impact. The smallmouth doubtless drove trout from portions of some streams. Moreover, the smallmouth, revered by some anglers as "pound for pound, inch for inch, the gamest fish that swims," was stocked in any number of Adirondack lakes, where the native trout suddenly found themselves under seige. The largemouth probably did less damage; the damage had already been done to brook trout by farmers who dammed up streams for mills or ice ponds. Such ponds, usually shallow and warmed by the sun, were unsuitable for trout, but the tough largemouths are able to endure water temperatures into the nineties. Similarly, many of the trout streams dammed for city reservoirs are now bass lakes.

Once bass were established in the Hudson Valley, their popularity grew, and it is interesting to trace their movements into New England, which Louis Agassiz called a "zoological island" because of its sparse fish fauna. In 1850, Samuel Tisdale of East Wareham, Massachusetts, brought twenty-seven live bass, species not given, from Saratoga Lake and put them into a pond near his home. From there bass were taken and stocked in twenty-five other ponds. In 1867, descendants from Tisdale's plantings were stocked in a lake in New Hampshire. As early as 1852, bass from a pond in Dutchess County were introduced into a lake in Litchfield County, Connecticut, and by 1867, bass were stocked in lakes and ponds throughout that state. In 1869, officials of the state of Maine and the Oquossoc Angling Association procured "a quantity of black bass" from Newburgh on the Hudson, and stocked various waters where the bass soon were reported "to have increased largely in numbers." Nowadays, Maine is celebrated for its excellent smallmouth bass fishing.

New York's position as a port made it a place of entry for many inadvertent pests. One of the first to arrive was the Hessian fly (*Phytophaga destructor*), a scourge of wheat, which came over during the Revolution in the straw bedding of Hessian mercenaries who landed at New York. The so-called German cockroach (*Blattella germanica*) first became obvious in 1842 when Manhattan began receiving water from the Croton Aqueduct. The cockroach was then nicknamed the Croton bug, and it apparently underwent a population explosion, utilizing the new maze of wet pipes throughout the city somewhat like cockroach superhighways.

The Central railroad tracks that skirt the river from New York to Albany have been cursed by many persons for denying access to the river, but they have not been without some small beneficial influence. The blocks of stone used for the roadbed serve as a refuge for small fish and invertebrates, and in some cases the causeways have turned bays into productive coves and marshes. This is the case, for instance, with the extensive river marshes north and south of both Tivoli and Hudson; all four of these bays were open water until the late nineteenth century.

Foreign weeds are numerous on the railroad rights of way along the river and around old docks. The troublesome "Stockport weed" (*Galium mollugo*) is believed to have come by ship, and the "bird-foot trefoil" (*Lotus corniculatus*) probably came in ballast. The bird-foot trefoil has value as forage, and it is now planted and cut as hay. The pesty knapweed (*Centaurea jacea*) may have come by rail, and the same holds true of its relative

Centaurea maculosa distinguished by its pinkish-purple flowers along roadsides.

The harmful purple loosestrife (*Lythrum salicaria*), which takes root in marshes and dries them up, came as seeds entangled in wool wastes unloaded at a Newburgh factory. According to Stanley Smith, the erudite curator of botany at the New York State Museum, Japanese lady's thumb (*Persicaria caespitosa*), arrived in Albany in rice straw packed around china, circus wagons from the Middle West brought in tumbleweed (*Cycloloma atriplicifolium*), and botanists at the state museum have discovered a smut (*Ustilago commelinae*), hitherto known only from the Yalu River in Korea, on both banks of the Hudson from Manhattan north to the mouth of the Sacandaga River.

Then again, escapes from gardens have resulted in the establishment of any number of foreign plants and flowers which many persons regard as native, such as the dandelion (*Taraxacum officinale*), the common daisy (*Chrysanthemum leucanthemum*), catnip (*Nepeta cataria*), peppermint (*Mentha piperita*), spearmint (*M. spicata*), multiflora rose (*Rosa multiflora*), Queen Anne's lace (*Daucus carota*), the wineberry (*Rubus phoenicolasius*), the common orange daylily (*Hemerocallis fulva*), the iris that is the *fleur-de-lis* of France (*Iris pseudacorus*), and sweet woodruff (*Asperula odorata*), used to make May wine. According to Morris K. Jacobson and William K. Emerson, authorities on shells, the common cellar snail of Europe (*Oxychilus cellarius*) is well established in the Hudson Valley. They report it in the city as "inhabitating dank spots in old basements where it is not above hiding near barrels of pickles, wine, potatoes, and other stored foods," and fine, large specimens live under loose boulders in the highway cut near Annsville Creek, Peekskill, a favorite collecting ground. Another successful immigrant is the Chinese mystery snail (*Viviparus malleatus*), which probably gained entry with exotic water plants. It has been found in the Hudson near Saratoga and in the tributary Saw Mill River in Westchester. A native freshwater mollusk that was not recognized as a different species until 1934 is the Hudson rams horn (*Promenetus hudsonicus*), first taken from a small swamp near the Poughkeepsie Rural Cemetery.

There were, of course some purposeful introductions of flora and fauna. The ring-necked pheasant (*Phasianus colchicus*) was brought to New York during colonial times but did not thrive. Before the 1900s, it was re-introduced from China and England, and it has since given joy. Other exotics have caused trouble. The pestiferous English sparrow (*Passer domesticus*) is not native to the United States. Its initial introduction to this continent came in 1852, when fifty birds were let loose in the Narrows from the steamship *Europa*. In 1890, Eugene Schieffelin, a New York drug manufacturer and a misguided Shakespeare enthusiast, introduced starlings (*Sturnus vulgaris*) to North America. Schieffelin wished to see every species of bird mentioned by Shakespeare living in the United States. He released the starlings in Central Park, and they first nested beneath the eaves of the northeast wing of the American Museum of Natural History. From there the pests began spreading up the Hudson Valley, reaching Ossining by 1899, and then moved across the continent, arriving at Juneau, Alaska, in 1952. Both the starling and sparrow are particularly annoying in that they are aggressive birds and harass native species, notably the bluebird (*Sialia sialis*).

But for all the introductions of exotics, the clearing of forests, the damming of tributary streams, the development of manufacturing, the spread of settlement, and the spiralling of pollution, the Hudson River Valley has held up surprisingly well. This is not to say that all is well. Each stretch of the Hudson has its own serious problems, its own character, its own delights, and I shall examine these stretches now, starting in the Adirondacks and following the Hudson downstream.

4

THE ADIRONDACK
HEADWATERS

The highest source of the Hudson River is a two-acre pond, Lake Tear of the Clouds, 4,293 feet up on the southwest slope of Mount Marcy in the Adirondacks. The pond was discovered in 1872 by Verplanck Colvin, Adirondack explorer and enthusiast, who described it as "a minute, unpretending tear of the clouds, as it were, a lonely pool, shivering in the breezes of the mountains, and sending its limpid surplus through Feldspar Brook and to the Opalescent River, the wellspring of the Hudson."

Mount Marcy, which reaches 5,344 feet, is the highest mountain in New York State; it lies in the High Peak region of the Adirondacks, the great divide between the Hudson and St. Lawrence watersheds. In some places, a difference of only an inch or two in the slope of the land determines toward which river water will flow. Near Lake Avalanche, which was thought to be the highest source of the Hudson until Lake Tear was discovered, water drips down a cliff from a spring, and drops that splatter to the south go to the Hudson, those to the north to the St. Lawrence.

Geologically, the Adirondacks are of great interest. They are not part of the Appalachian system but a southward extension of the Canadian shield which includes the Laurentians. The ancestral Adirondacks go back to the Precambrian era of more than one billion years ago, when they were part of a large chain of mountains that thrust as high, perhaps, as the Himalayas of the present. In time, they were worn down and covered by the sea. After the sea retreated mountains rose again, and this time they were cut to low relief. The region was elevated in the Tertiary Period, and severe erosion shaped the Adirondacks into roughly the form they have today. Rock debris from the mountains was carried to sea and deposited on the continental shelf. The glaciers covered the Adirondacks and ground the high peaks down to their ancient roots. The summit of Mount Marcy is composed of anorthosite, a very durable rock resistant to erosion.

The lower slopes of Marcy and the banks of the upper Hudson are covered by a deciduous hardwood forest of beech, birch, and maple, interspersed with red spruce (*Picea rubens*), hemlock (*Tsuga canadensis*), white pine (*Pinus strobus*), and balsam fir (*Abies balsamea*). The cool, moist forest floor is spattered with mosses, ferns, and wildflowers—bunchberry (*Cornus canadensis*), large-leaved goldenrod (*Solidago macrophylla*), and wood sorrel (*Oxalis acetosella*). Further up the mountain, the hardwoods thin out, and red spruce and balsam fir become dominant. Near the elevation of Lake Tear, the red spruce disappears, and several hundred feet higher, the balsam fir vanishes and a dwarf fir forest appears. On the bald summit, plants cling to cracks and fissures in the hard rock. Many are alpine plants, remnants of glacial times, such as Labrador tea (*Ledum groenlandicum*), three-toothed cinquefoil (*Potentilla tridentata*), boreal bentgrass (*Agrostis borealis*), and Lapland rosebay (*Rhododendron lapponicum*). It is not unusual to find pockets of snow on the peak in July.

The Marcy region has long attracted naturalists and scientists as well as outdoor enthusiasts. Theodore Roosevelt was having lunch near Lake Tear when he received word from a messenger that President McKinley had taken a turn for the worse in Buffalo. In the summer of 1905, Elon Howard Eaton of the New York State Museum spent six weeks studying the birds of the region, and he found one hundred species nesting within ten miles of the mountain. Of these, thirty-two belonged to the Canadian fauna and the remainder belonged to the Alleghenian or were of general distribution in eastern North America. In 1920, the Ecological Society of America published a report on Marcy compiled by Barrington Moore, chairman of the society's Committee on Cooperation, Norman Taylor of the Brooklyn Botanic Garden, Drs. C. C. Adams and T. L. Hankinson of the New York State College of Forestry at Syracuse University, and Professor George P. Burns of the University of Vermont. Although they took due note of insects and mammals ("About a dozen mouse traps let out for two nights in this low tree growth resulted in getting one red-backed mouse in a dense thicket of conifers near Station *d* . . . "), their main interest was the timberline. They noted that of seventy-three plants reported from the alpine zone in 1891 by Charles H. Peck, the state botanist, twenty-one appeared to be missing,

> or at least not seen by us. Of 7 species not reported by Peck and which apparently have come in since 1879 or later, it is significant that none of these are true alpines and 4 are certainly encroachments from lower down the mountain. Only 23 species are true alpines, and at least 30 have apparently come up through the timber line from the forest below, dwarfed in stature and changed in color, but still flowering and fruiting. Not one case of invasion from the alpine zone into the fir forest below was found. The evidence of the plants shows that the alpine forms are not spreading downward and may be even be vanishing while the lowland forms are pushing upward, indicating that the northward migration which followed the retreat of the ice sheet is still going on.

There are botanists who disagree; they say that the alpine plants reported as missing are present. In any event, in 1957, Howard E. Woodin, an ecologist at Middlebury College, led a party to the top of Marcy to construct a permanent vegetation transect above the timber line. He noted the precise location of alpine plants and drove steel eyebolts into the rock to serve as benchmarks. In a paper in *Ecology*, Woodin wrote that he hoped his work would permit future investigators to learn whether the timber line was moving up and down the mountain. He suggested that periodic checks be made every ten years, and by 1987, perhaps, ecologists could determine climatic change.

In 1961, Professor Edwin H. Ketchledge of the College of Forestry at Syracuse, a veteran of the High Peak region, resurveyed Woodin's transect on Marcy, carefully noting the bryophytes, mosses, and lichens. These would be of more critical importance than the plants previously noted, because the mosses, for instance, are the controlling plants, building up the soil in which others take root. Professor Ketchledge feels that it would take 50 to 150 years to determine the degree of climate change because any differences noted over a shorter span might reflect the results of one very severe winter and not the long-range view. But, sad to say, it is highly unlikely that any ecologist will ever be able to make such determinations on Marcy or elsewhere in the Adirondacks. The plant life is being trampled under by an increasing number of people, so much so that Professor Ketchledge is now doing a study on trail erosion and site deterioration for the U.S. Forest Service, which is concerned because the impact of people on plant life has become a problem elsewhere in the northeast as well.

Lake Tear has a peculiarity of its own: it has no fishes. Nor are there fishes in Feldspar Brook, which flows down Marcy from the pond. Indeed, there are said to have been no fish in the Opalescent River above Hanging Spear Falls until brook trout were stocked. Apparently the slopes of these streams are too steep to support adequate aquatic insect life; furthermore, the spring thaw subjects the streams to heavy scouring.

The Hudson does not become the Hudson in name until about ten miles away from Lake Tear. Here, oddly, the Opalescent River, bringing water from the highest source, joins what is called the Hudson River, a stream coming from Henderson and Sanford Lakes. The region here is forested except near the town of Tahawus, where the National Lead Company operates an open-pit titanium mine and mill. Iron was first discovered there in

1826, when an Indian guided a party of white men led by David Henderson for half a dollar and tobacco. They found a rich, fifty-foot vein of iron ore and eventually bought 105,000 acres from the state. Mining operations began several years later, and one of those who became involved was Joseph Dixon, later dubbed Graphite Dixon when he set up graphite works at Ticonderoga. Dixon built a smelting furnace at Jersey City to make steel, and the mine prospered until the mid-1850s, when the cost of transporting the ore to Jersey City made competition with imported Scotch pig iron unprofitable. From time to time, there was talk of reopening the mine, but an "impurity" in the ore, titantium, made operations unfeasible, and the mine was closed. It remained closed until the start of World War II, when imports of titanium from India, used to make pigments, ceased. Investigation then revealed that the old iron mine up on the Hudson, with its impurities, was potentially the greatest source of titanium in the United States. In 1941, the National Lead Company began operations, and titanium from the mine is now also used to make synthetic gems for the optical and electric industries.

The upper Hudson is a magnificent-looking trout stream. I say *looking* because the river appears to have some drawbacks, which I shall touch on presently. In any event, it is a wild and often turbulent stream, and during the spring a white-water canoe race is held between the settlements of North River and North Creek. In many places, the Hudson is inaccessible by car, and people must hike in. The forested banks, rocky shores, and sandbars of the river are thus spared the normal load of litter. For the angler, there are trout. The brook trout (*Salvelinus fontinalis*) is native to the upper Hudson. The rainbow (*Salmo gairdneri*) and brown trout (*S. trutta*) are imports to the Hudson, the rainbow from the West Coast and the brown from Germany and the British Isles. Both these fishes can stand higher water temperatures than the brook trout—the brown, for instance, can survive in water of 81° F., while a temperature of 75° F. is fatal to the brook—and they were first stocked in the east in the late nineteenth century, when the forest cover was cut and water temperatures raised.

To many anglers the brook trout holds first place in esteem; its specific name, *fontinalis* is a joy, for *fontinalis* means "living in springs." Brook trout are beautiful fish; unfortunately, they are somewhat "dumb," and intensive angling can strip a stream of its breeding population. By contrast, brown trout are full of guile, so much so that when they were first stocked they aroused the enmity of American anglers, who complained the fish were difficult to catch. Browns also have the nasty habit of being cannibalistic, even to the point of devouring their own kind. However, brown trout can be the dry-fly fish par excellence, and inasmuch as they sometimes grow to enormous size, the species has become a prize in its own right.

In certain stretches of the upper Hudson, particularly down towards Warrensburg, there are the so-called "warmwater" fishes, such as northern pike (*Esox lucius*), chain pickerel (*E. niger*), and sunfish, and the smallmouth and largemouth bass that swam into the Hudson upon the completion of the Erie and Champlain canals. The countless lakes, ponds, and streams drained by the upper Hudson contain other species, notably the yellow perch (*Perca flavescens*), an alien to the Adirondacks which has proven most destructive in trout lakes. In Thirteenth Lake, which drains into the Hudson, the State Conservation Department has stocked "Sam Browns," so called because they are a hatchery cross between male Atlantic salmon and female brown trout. Like most hybrids, these fish grow quickly. Four-inch Sam Browns have gotten up to eight pounds in two years, and, blessing of blessing, there is some evidence that they thrive on yellow perch. So far, none of the Sam Browns has been found in the river. The upper Hudson watershed also harbors a few species of fishes that are, like the alpine plants on the summit of Marcy, glacial relicts. Among these are the slimy sculpin (*Cottus cognatus*), the finescaled sucker (*Catostomus catostomus*), and the round whitefish (*Prosopium cylindraceum*).

There are innumerable places an angler can go on the upper Hudson, but according to a fishing friend, Ken Gerhardt of Peekskill, who has been poking about the river for twenty years, the best stretch is the west-east run between the mouths of the Indian and Boreas Rivers. Here the Hudson is truly wild, as wild as one will find in the East, anyway, churning over rapids and gliding into deep pools, as at Blue Ledge, where a cliff towers above the riverside. Here there are brown and rainbow trout and smallmouth bass.

To the fly fisherman, the aquatic insects of the upper Hudson are of the greatest importance. In fact, a couple of insect species, the black flies and punkies, are, in their terrestrial stage, often of concern. When I said previously that the upper Hudson had some drawbacks, I had black flies and punkies in mind.

Black flies belong to the order Diptera, which means they are true flies, having only one pair of wings as adults. So much for systematics. Black flies are also the scourge of the upper Hudson; they are *the* pest of the Adirondacks. They bite freely and leave large welts that can be painful for several days, and by comparison they make mosquitoes a pleasure. In other parts of North America, black flies are reported as having bitten horses, cattle, and sheep to death. Black flies are small and chunky, about one-eighth of an inch long, and they have big, round eyes. They attack silently and swiftly, sometimes squeezing inside clothing to bite. The shortness of their mouth parts probably prompts the flies to seek out the thinner part of the skin. They have a distinct preference for the back of the neck, the ears, the eyelids, the inner wrist and ankles, and they will go through hair to the scalp. They pay no attention to swats and slaps. The bite itself does not hurt, but pain begins soon afterward. Blood may flow, and the worst thing that a person can do is to scratch the bite, prompting a pus infection and prolonged itching. Scratching may also bring about a streptococcal infection with serious consequences.

Specifically, there are two species of black flies on the upper Hudson that are a problem. Both are at their peak in the late spring and early summer, when trout fishing is at its best. The first to appear is *Prosimulium hirtipes*. The adults lay eggs in gelatinous masses in the river, and the eggs hatch out as larvae. The larvae look like small black worms, and they live in the rapids, attached to stones, sticks, or other debris by a silk secretion. They are said to need a strong current of at least two-thirds of a mile an hour to live. There is no need for the larvae to move because food in the form of microscopic plants and animal life is constantly washed to them by the current. At the same time, the black fly larvae have value as food for young trout. When the larvae are completely grown, they spin cocoons, emerge as adults, rise to the surface, and run across the water to dry their wings on land. On the upper Hudson, *P. hirtipes* usually begins emerging from mid- to late May, depending upon the weather. For the first week they do not bite; then they set to with a vengeance.

The second species is *Simulium venustum,* which emerges from late May to early July. It is not the eager biter that *P. hirtipes* is, but it can be an awful plague nonetheless. Flies of this second species are nicknamed "polo ponies" because of the white bands on their legs. When old-time Adirondack guides saw polo ponies, they used to say the black fly season was about over. They did not realize the polo ponies were a second species; they thought that the flies which had been biting them were growing old, Gerhardt says he is able to avoid trouble by taking an antihistamine prescribed by his physician. He gets bitten, but the bites do not itch. Insect repellents are good up to a point; sweating makes them ineffective.

Besides black flies, there are pestiferous punkies, which also belong to the order Diptera. These minute creatures are the smallest flies that bite, and in the Adirondacks they are variously known as "no-see-ums," midges, and gnats. The most widespread species of punkie in the Adirondacks is a shiny, dirty-brown little creature with the scientific name of *Culicoides biguttatus.* The larvae are important food for small fish.

Pests aside, the aquatic insects of importance to fly fishermen and fish on the upper Hudson are, in order of ascending importance:

HELLGRAMITES, the larvae of the dobsonflies, which belong to the order Neuroptera, the nerve-winged insects. They are common in the upper Hudson, where the fierce larvae, up to three inches long, feed on other aquatic insects. Gerhardt has noted three different periods of emergence, at the tag ends of May, June and July.

STONEFLIES, of the order Plecoptera. The larvae or nymphs live mainly in the riffles. Common genera are *Pteronarcys,* vegetarians usually found in leaves piled up by the current, and *Perla,* black and yellow nymphs which prey on other insects. Stonefly nymphs may be confused with mayfly nymphs, but the stoneflies always have their gills on the underside of the body and two claws instead of one on each foot. Adult stoneflies are poor fliers and prefer to clamber about on the underside of leaves near the river. When at rest, the adult folds its four wings flat back over the body which gives the impression that it has only one wing.

CADDISFLIES, of the order Trichoptera. The adults resemble moths, to which they may be related. Like the caterpillars of some moths, most caddisfly larvae—called caddisworms by fishermen—are able to spin silk, which they use to construct a case which serves as their house in the water. Depending on species, larvae live in cylindrical bark houses, in log cabins of twigs, or in sand cottages. In the West, some even live in houses of gold dust. Larvae are a very important food for trout, which eat them case and all.

MAYFLIES, of the order Ephemeroptera. The ordinal name refers to the flies' fleeting life as adults. Adults usually live less than one day, flying only to mate and never eating. To the dry-fly fisherman, mayflies are of supreme importance.

Mayfly larvae or nymphs are elongate and have three tails (rarely two, as do stonefly nymphs) and seven pairs of leaf-like or tube-like gills on the abdomen. Depending upon species, the nymphs are swimmers, burrowers, sprawlers, or climbers. For the most part, they are herbivorous, feeding on algae and decaying vegetation.

Starting in the spring, mayflies emerge from the river as flying adults at different times of the year, depending upon their species. When mayflies emerge in large numbers, causing what anglers call a "hatch," trout feed voraciously. According to Gerhardt, the important species of mayflies on the upper Hudson are, in order of emergence:

The QUILL GORDON. This is the name anglers use for a couple of two-tailed species that usually emerge during the first week of May. They are often thought to be *Iron fraudator* or *Epeorus pleuralis,* but the first man to tie the dry-fly imitation, Theodore Gordon, had no particular species in mind.

The HENDRICKSON, *Ephemerella invaria* or *E. subvaria.* These are small flies, from seven to nine millimeters long, with three tails. They emerge during the last two weeks in May on the Upper Hudson. The dry-fly imitation was first tied by Roy Steenrod in the Catskills and named in honor of a well-known angler, A. E. Hendrickson. The original Hendrickson dry fly was actually a representation of the "subimago," or what anglers call a dun, of the female fly. When a mayfly nymph completes its molt, the winged subimago form emerges, flies from the surface of the water, and rests on land, where it sheds its outer skin and then becomes an "imago" or true adult. The subimago has a softer, duller look than the imago, and the wings are opaque. Mayflies are the only insects which undergo a molt after developing flying wings.

The AMERICAN MARCH BROWN, *Stenonema vicarium*. It emerges in the upper Hudson in late May or early June. A large fly with mottled brownish wings, it often has difficulty arising from the water. Named after the British mayfly, March brown, which is a different species, *Rhithrogena haarupi*.

GREEN DRAKE, *Ephemera guttulata*. This species emerges from about June 7 through to June 21. In the subimago stage, this large mayfly is known to anglers as the green drake; as an imago, it is known as the coffin fly.

CAHILLS, *Stenonema ithaca* and *S. canadense*. These emerge in late June on the river. The common name, so a pretty story has it, comes from a Dublin fly tier who, after tying a fly, would "put it to a customer's ear and inquire if he heard it buzz." Actually, Cahills are named for their originator, Dan Cahill, of Port Jervis, New York, a brakeman on the Erie Railroad during the 1880s.

A good number of the brown trout in the upper Hudson are thin, elongate fish, dubbed "slinks" by fishermen. Apparently trout in the river do not fatten out until they are eighteen to twenty inches long. Gerhardt says: "A sixteen-inch fish from the upper Hudson weighs about a pound, as much as an eleven-inch trout from the Delaware." When an upper Hudson brown does reach eighteen or twenty inches, it begins to add poundage, probably because it can now feast on other fish in the river, particularly large chubs. Five-, six-, and seven-pound browns are not uncommon.

Why are so many of the brown trout slinks? The cause appears to be limited production of insects in the upper Hudson that results from a scarcity of basic nutrients. Minerals taken from the soil are washed into the river, and in the glacially scoured Adirondacks the soil is largely derived from the underlying igneous rocks, mostly quartz and feldspar, which decompose into infertile sands. Also, the Adirondacks have cold weather, high rainfall, and coniferous forests. The humus created under such conditions is acid, and this does not encourage an abundance of aquatic life.

In short, the upper river is somewhat sterile, but this sterility gives the Hudson here one of its greatest charms, clarity. The bottom is visible twenty or thirty feet down. "The upper Hudson is a two-out-of-ten-times river," Gerhardt says. "Eight times you won't catch a fish, but the other two times can be great. I know the Delaware can be great, but I prefer to fish the upper Hudson. I'm in love with it. There is its remoteness; it's seeing a river where the water never colors. It's a lot of things. It's like falling in love with a girl and marrying her."

Until little more than one hundred years ago, the upper Hudson and Adirondacks were largely unexplored and unexploited. Even Indians were scarce, especially during the harsh winter. The name Adirondacks itself is a contemptuous Iroquois word meaning "tree-eaters," which the Iroquois applied to their enemy, the Algonkians, who sometimes came south from Canada to hunt.

Lumbering was the entering wedge into the Adirondacks, and the lumbermen came from the south by way of the Hudson from Glens Falls, Sandy Hill, and Fort Edward. In 1763, Abraham Wing built a sawmill at Glens Falls. A famous cavern underneath the falls is described in *The Last of the Mohicans* by James Fenimore Cooper; there Hawkeye, Uncas, and three other persons hid from Montcalm and his horde of French and Indians. By the early 1800s, the stand of trees in the area was depleted, but two brothers, Alanson and Norman Fox, moved further into the Adirondacks, where they began driving single logs down the Schroon River and the Hudson to Glens Falls. Rafting logs is an old practice, but, surprisingly, no one except the Fox brothers had ever before driven single logs down a river. Their method was so successful as to be revolutionary, and in short order various Adirondack Rivers were officially declared public highways by the state legislature. Lumbermen flocked to the harvest in earnest, and Glens Falls literally became a boomtown. In 1849, the Hudson River Boom Association, composed of cooperative lumbermen, began building the Big Boom in the Big Bend of the Hudson just above Glens Falls. The boom was made of heavy timbers connected by chains. It caught the logs coming down from upriver, and at times logs would be backed up for two or three miles behind the boom. In the spring of 1859, the Big Boom snapped. At least half a million logs went hurtling down the Hudson, and thousands of logs were strewn on the banks of the river as far south as Troy.

Lumber companies used a marking hammer to brand their own logs with a distinctive design before they were sent downstream. Thus,

Bradley & Underwood	DU
A. N. Cheney	 ☼
Finch, Pruyn & Co.	 *ℒ*
George H. Freeman	☐
International Paper	�)(
Morgan & McEchron	OK
Orson Richards	 ∞
Union Bag and Paper	✚

By 1850, New York led all the states in the amount of lumber cut—1.6 billion board feet, one-fifth of the total cut in the entire country. At first only pine, hemlock, and spruce were cut in the Adirondacks, and of these only the largest, for building materials. Hardwoods such as ash, cherry, maple, birch, and beech were spared because the logs did not float easily. In the late 1860s, a method of making ground pulp with chemicals made the smaller softwoods fair game, and stretches of the Adirondacks were scalped of poplar, spruce, pine, and hemlock. Logging railroads penetrated into the mountains, hardwoods were cut, and the destruction was such that by the 1880s, the ravage in the Adirondacks had become a scandal.

Behind the lumbermen came hunters, anglers, and tourists. The fish and game were even more vulnerable than the virgin forests. One of the first animals to disappear was the largest, the moose (*Alces alces*). As Madison Grant, a turn-of-the-century chronicler, remarked, "The history of the moose in the Adirondacks has a melancholy interest." By the 1850s, moose were so decimated that sight of one was a rarity. In 1859, none other than the governor of the state, Horatio Seymour, thought he had shot the last one when he killed a fine bull near West Canada Creek. The honor was not his. Several moose were shot in 1860, and the coup de grâce was administered the next year on the Marion River. A guide named Palmer was canoeing a party downstream when they spied the animal. The sportsmen fired to no avail, but Palmer took deliberate aim and brought the moose down. It was a cow moose, the last of the native moose in the state. In 1951 there was considerable excitement when a moose showed up at a golf course near Troy, then galloped off to parts unknown. The guess was that it had not come down from the Adirondacks but had somehow straggled across country from northern New Hampshire or Maine.

The person most responsible for the popularity of the Adirondacks was the Reverend William Murray, the young pastor of the fashionable Park Street Congregational Church in Boston. Others had written about the mountains, but Murray's book, *Adventures in the Wilderness,* became the rage. It appeared in April, 1869, and that summer, the rush to the Adirondacks was literally on. Unfortunately for the public, Murray had laid it on. He wrote of landing two huge trout with one cast of his rod, and declared: "With a guide who knows his business I would undertake to feed a party of twenty the season through and seldom should they sit down to a dinner lacking trout and venison." Anglers discovered that trout simply were not there in the numbers that Murray proclaimed. Other vacationers were aghast at what Murray had called "unscarred" forests. "In the Adirondack wilderness the lumberman has never been," Murray wrote. For such excesses, Murray was branded a liar, and the tourists who read his book and came were called "Murray's fools."

In fairness to Murray, it might well have been that when he first stumbled into the Adirondack wilds, large trout were not unusual, but such fish were the result of a long, natural process; they were the end product, the best, in a sense, of ten thousand undisturbed years. Unsophisticated, they undoubtedly were easy prey to the angler's flies, spoons, and worms. Given intensive fishing and given the disturbances—the upsets soon wrought by man, such as rapacious logging and all its attendant ecological evils, and the careless introduction of competitive black bass ordered by Governor Seymour in 1862—and given also the marvelously clear but nutrient-deficient waters of the Adirondacks, it is little wonder that native trout fishing there declined.

Despite Murray's exaggerations, the tourists came to the Adirondacks, and between 1869 and 1875, the number of hotels increased from about fifty to more than two hundred. The spell, the lure, of the North Woods was permanently cast in the American character. Here was the place to get away from it all, to commune with nature "undisturbed." One of the most famous visitors was Winslow Homer, the artist, who with his brother, Charles, was a member of the North Woods Club on the upper Hudson near Blue Ledge. Passionately committed to both nature and fishing, Homer painted some of his most glorious watercolors— *Casting in the Falls, Leaping Trout, Boy Fishing,* and *Mink Pond* —on the upper Hudson. As Lloyd Goodrich, his biographer wrote, "Homer's Adirondack phase was a new departure in American watercolor painting. . . . Nothing like the freedom and brilliancy of these works had been seen before in this country."

One of Homer's most famous watercolors is entitled *Adirondack Guide*. The subject is unknown, so far as I can determine, but judging from the matted beard and old clothes it might have been Orson Schofield Phelps, better known as "Old Mountain" Phelps, who in 1849 blazed the first trail to Mount Marcy, his favorite peak. Unwashed and unsung, Phelps became famous in 1878, when Charles Dudley Warner, a friend of Mark Twain, published an essay about Phelps, "The Primitive Man," in *The Atlantic*. From then on Phelps relished playing the character; he apparently smelled like one, too. He eschewed baths, exclaiming, "I don't believe in the eternal sozzlin'!" and on another occasion, he remarked, "Soap is a thing that I hain't no kinder use for." As Warner wrote, "His clothes seemed to have been put on him once for all, like the bark of a tree, a long time ago."

The old-time Adirondack guides have long since passed away —Phelps died in 1905 at the age of eighty-five—but they did leave one contribution, the magnificent Adirondack guide boat, the answer of the mountains to the Hudson River sloop downstream. Best described as a canoe built like a rowboat and exceptionally stormworthy, a guide boat measured up to sixteen feet in length, weighed seventy-five pounds, and could be easily portaged around rapids or from lake to lake. Guides made the joints from spruce roots, and the flush planking was of pine or cedar. Several thousand brass screws and copper nails held the guide boat together, and after the boat was varnished several times, these fittings served as gleaming decorations.

In good part, the demise of the old-time Adirondack guides has been blamed on the rich, who are said to have spoiled them. In the Gilded Age following the Civil War, the Adirondacks served many millionaires as a retreat from the boredom of banking or the intricacies of Wall Street. In much the same manner that the gentry of the lower Hudson of a previous generation sought surcease in decorative villas and ornamented cottages, the rich of the 1880s and 1890s searched for peace in the Adirondacks amid opulent log cabins, stone fireplaces, stuffed deer heads, and the call of the loon. The Adirondacks became the playpen, the sandbox of the rich, their hunting and fishing ground. No matter the original motives, the no-trespass signs, backed up by guides and private wardens on patrol, helped to protect the ecological integrity of the mountains. By 1892, the State Forest Commission estimated that a quarter of the Adirondacks was held as private preserves by individual owners, associations, and clubs. Some of the well-to-do angered the natives with their ways—after the murder of Orlando Dexter, heir to the American News Company, in 1903, the high-handed William Rockefeller went into the mountains surrounded by private detectives—but there can be little doubt that a number of the rich or their offspring understood the ways of the wild and educated the public in the value of wilderness resources. Young Teddy Roosevelt studying the birds of Franklin County; Robert Marshall, climber of Adirondack peaks and founder of the Wilderness Society; Harold K. Hochschild, author of *Township 34*, one of the great studies of the mountains, and benefactor of the superb Adirondack Museum at Blue Mountain, are among the men who found the lesson and taught it to others.

In the Gilded Age, opulent camps followed one upon another. Not all the "camps" were within the Hudson watershed, but the most lavish was—Fox-Lair, the estate of Richard Hudnut on the east branch of the tributary Sacandaga River. A pharmacist turned purveyor of perfumes, Hudnut bought twelve hundred acres around the turn of the century and built an enormous chateau, 215 feet long, overlooking the river. He added a number of outbuildings, stables, servants' quarters, and a golf course. The furniture for Fox-Lair came from France, as did the elegant chef. All told, Hudnut spent about one million dollars. One of his more celebrated visitors was Rudolph Valentino, husband and dancing partner of Natasha Rambova, daughter of Hudnut's second wife. In 1942, the Police Athletic League (PAL) of New York purchased Fox-Lair and since then has run it as a camp for New York City youngsters.

One of the most avid Adirondack enthusiasts was an Albany youngster named Verplanck Colvin. When only 18, he started mapping the area, and thanks to his persistent lobbying, the state legislature in 1872 appointed him superintendent of a topographical survey of the mountains. The state had fallen heir to the unclaimed crown lands in the Adirondacks at the end of the American Revolution, and although great tracts had been sold by the 1870s, the state still retained considerable acreage. Despite the advance of the lumbermen and the swelling numbers of tourists, the Adirondacks were not completely explored, and there were far-sighted persons who were interested in making a great preserve out of the state lands.

For twenty-eight years, Colvin kept at his work, clambering up and down the mountains in the severest weather, making triangulation observations with theodolite and transit. He left only to return to Albany to write voluminous reports in diary form for the legislature. In his passion to map the Adirondacks, Colvin went without food ("supperless we made a bivouac under a sheltering ledge, where a bright fire was our only compensation for the labor of the day"), endured discomfort ("The snow entered our clothing despite all care, and it was impossible to prevent frequent falls over hidden rocks and tree trunks"), and drove himself and his guides ever onward ("At length the guides proposed to camp, as night had nearly settled down, but my pedometer had not yet recorded the ten miles at which I had estimated the distance").

He was absolutely enamored of the Adirondacks, and in one of his reports to the legislature, he wrote:

> Elsewhere are mountains more stupendous, more icy and more drear, but none look down upon a grander landscape, in rich autumn time; more brightly gemmed or jeweled with innumerable lakes, or crystal pools, or wild with savage chasms, or dread passes; none show a denser or more vast appearance of primeval forest stretched over range on range to the far horizon, where the sea of mountains fades away into a dim, vaporous uncertainty.
>
> A region of mystery, over which none can gaze without a strange thrill of interest and of wonder at what may be hidden in that vast area of forest, covering all things with its deep repose. It is not the deer of which we think, treading the deep rich moss among the stately tamaracks; nor the bear, luxuriating in the berry patches on the mountain sides; nor the panther or the wolf in their lonely and desolate wilds seeking their feast of blood: we gaze downward from the mountain height on thousands upon thousands of square miles of wilderness, which was always one—since forest it became—and which hides to-day, as it has hidden for so many ages, the secrets of form, and soil, and rock, and history, on which we ponder. Huge are these almost undecipherable pages of the world's annals; enormous and difficult to read; yet there are marks and traces here and there which tell in a brief, irregular and fragmentary way—to those able to decipher such inscriptions—the prehistoric growth of continents; the origin of rivers; the spread of vegetable and animal life, and the approach of man.

Given his love for the Adirondacks, Colvin was among the first to urge the establishment of an Adirondack preserve, but in his later years he grew dotty. He quit state service, took his records with him, and talked of building a railroad right through the mountains he had sought to save. He died in 1920, and on his deathbed he autographed his paddle, which had dipped into 250 unexplored lakes in one year, and gave it to his first assistant.

Fortunately, Colvin's good works bore fruit while he was busy mapping the mountains. In 1885, the legislature created by statutory law the forest preserve on state lands in both the Adirondacks and Catskills, and ever since 1895, state forest preserve lands in both regions have been protected by the "Forever Wild" clause in the State Constitution. This article prohibits the timber to be sold, removed, or destroyed, and except for the construction of public campsites and trails, these forest preserve lands are safe from the lumberman's axe. As a result, they serve as unique recreation areas and help to protect vital watersheds from abuse or despoliation. Constitutional protection is most important; it guards state lands from being subjected to change by caprice. A statutory law may be thrown out as unconstitutional by the courts, or it may be amended or repealed by a session of the legislature, which is often subjected to intense lobbying by special interests, but a constitutional change requires approval by two different legislatures and then by statewide referendum.

In 1892, the state legislature created the so-called Adirondack Park and in 1904 the Catskill Park. Some persons confuse the parks with the forest preserve lands, but the parks are larger entities, including both private property and most but not all of the forest preserve lands. The private lands contain cities, golf courses, harvestable forests, resorts, factories, and farms. In the main, private owners may do as they wish with their lands inside the "Blue Line"—so called because the boundaries of both parks are drawn in that color on state maps—though they are subject to certain restrictions. For instance, advertising signs may be erected only on the actual site of the business concerned. In size, the Adirondack Park exceeds New Jersey, totalling almost 6 million acres, of which 2.4 million acres are uncuttable forest preserve and 3.2 million privately held. The Catskill Park covers 576,000 acres, of which 240,000 are forest preserve.

Within the Blue Line boundary of the Adirondack Park, state and private acreage are interspersed in crazy-quilt fashion. The largest roadless forest-preserve holding is perhaps the choicest, 180,000 acres encompassing Mount Marcy and the High Peak region. In the years that have followed the establishment of the forest preserve, the once-depleted North Woods have started to come back, and within them roam the fisher (*Martes pennanti pennanti*), a rare member of the marten family, and black bear

(*Ursus americanus*). During the summer, bears are common at Adirondack garbage dumps, and at night, anxious tourists often drive from one dump to another to watch bears forage for dinner. No gray wolves (*Canis lupus*) survive in the Adirondacks, but there are coyotes (*C. latrans*) and "coy dogs," hybrids between the coyote and the domestic dog. There may even be mountain lions (*Felis concolor*), although none has been positively identified by Dr. Edgar M. Reilly, Jr., curator of Zoology at the New York State Museum in Albany.

There are a good many beavers (*Castor canadensis*), not just in the Adirondacks but down along the Hudson Valley too. Of all the mammals of New York, the beaver has the most checkered history. Beavers, of course, were the main object of the Dutch fur trade. They were trapped by the hundreds of thousands and their pelts shipped to Europe for the making of hats. Around 1800, there were two developments that all but killed off the beaver for good: first, Indian trappers discovered they could use castoreum, a secretion found in two sacs below the pubis of the beaver, as scent to attract the animals, and second, the steel trap came into use. By this time the Indians, who had previously rarely ventured into the Adirondacks, were trapping in the mountains, and by 1820 perhaps only one thousand beavers were left there. The species undoubtedly would have been wiped out had it not been for another development around 1820: the hatters of Europe found that they could make a better hat from the fur of the South American copyu or nutria, an animal like a a muskrat. Pressure on the beaver eased, although trapping continued. By 1840, the beaver was rare. There were perhaps three hundred left in New York State, all in the Adirondacks. In the winter of 1894–1895, according to the count of Harry Radford, an Adirondack enthusiast second only to Murray and Colvin, the beaver population sank to the desperate low of not more than five or ten, and trapping was finally prohibited. Between 1901 and 1907, the meager population was augmented with thirty-four stocked beavers, some coming from as far away as Yellowstone National Park.

Since then, the beaver population of the Adirondacks has grown, and in the Hudson Valley beaver are found as far south as Peekskill in Westchester County, where they are reported in marshy Gregory Pond not far from a discount store near Peekskill, and I have lately heard reports of them inhabiting streams tributary to the Croton Reservoir.

According to Dr. Reilly, two "types" of beavers now live in the Hudson Valley. The first type is the beaver that immediately comes to mind: the builder of dams in streams. The second type is not a dam builder but a dweller in quiet waters of a stream or a pond. To keep up the franchise of being a beaver, this type cuts and piles a few sticks near its lodge, but does not otherwise interfere with the course of flowing water. "These bank builders have been less hunted and less bothered," Ed Reilly says, "and they have been able to survive. The other type has been shot by farmers or homeowners, and you don't find as many of them."

5

CARP,
DRAGONFLIES,
AND THE
ALBANY POOL

The character and appearance of the Hudson change entirely when the river leaves the foothills of the Adirondacks at Fort Edward, the head of navigation. Locks and dams now choke the flow and turn the river into a forty-mile chain of sluggish lakes. From Fort Edward down to Troy, the river serves mainly as a highway for pleasure boats and self-propelled barges shuttling in and out of the Champlain and New York State Barge canals, the latter the descendant of the old Erie.

Superficially, the Hudson here has its charms. Melon fields and pastures line the banks, and cows wade belly-deep from shore. On windless days, the river lies flat and glassy, and mirrored trees seem to lead double lives. The canal locks are neatly kept, bordered by mown lawns and clipped shrubbery, and the atmosphere is vaguely European, reminiscent perhaps of the Thames or the Loire.

Ecologically, the canalized Hudson is sort of an entity unto itself, a world apart from its rushing Adirondack parent and sealed off by the locks and dams from the estuary to the south. Before the construction of a dam at Troy in 1826, fishes from the Atlantic used to make their way upstream as far north as Glens Falls, a journey of 209 miles. Shad were found in tributaries of the upper Hudson River, such as the Battenkill and Kayaderosseras Creek, and they even ventured into Saratoga Lake. In colonial times, sturgeon were abundant in this stretch of the Hudson. "We saw them all day long leaping high up into the air, especially in the evening," Peter Kalm, the naturalist, wrote while on his way north to French Canada in 1749. "Our guides and the people who lived hereabouts, asserted that they never see any sturgeons in winter time, because these fish go into the sea late in autumn, but come up again in spring and stay in the river all summer." Striped bass, too, came in numbers, and were caught under the Cohoes Falls of the Mohawk. Nowadays, a stray striper or shad may work its way through the lock system, but they are markedly rare above Troy. The most conspicuous fishes are strangers—black bass, previously discussed, and carp (*Cyprinus carpio*), the most unwanted fish in the Hudson and a species with a horror story all its own.

Originally native to Asia, carp were brought in the late Middle Ages to Europe, where they found favor as a food fish. In the early nineteenth century, a Mr. Henry Robinson of Newburgh, New York, imported carp from France and kept them in ponds. In 1831, he began putting anywhere from one to two dozen a year into the Hudson. With obvious pleasure, he wrote to James DeKay, then state zoologist: "They have increased so much that our fishermen frequently take them in their nets. They are larger than those in my ponds." DeKay was pleased at the news and invited "other patriotic individuals to make similar experiments with other species, which are limited now to the other side of the

Atlantic." The state legislature passed a law protecting carp from capture for a five-year period.

In the 1870s, the old United States Fish Commission, the forerunner of the present U.S. Fish and Wildlife Service, imported carp from Europe and bred them in pools in Washington, D.C. Carp were deemed wonderful fish to raise for food, and politicians came to regard the stock of Fish Commission carp as favors to bestow on constituents. In 1883, 298 out of 301 congressional districts received a total of more than a quarter of a million live carp. They were stocked in ponds and dammed-up streams the country over, and from there they escaped into other waters during spring floods. Americans were quickly disillusioned. Carp were not tasty, they were not game, and they roiled the water while feeding on the bottom, making it difficult for gamefish to see their prey or hatch their eggs. Carp even drove away ducks by uprooting wild rice and wild celery. They have remained a major problem to this day. It is fruitless to try to remove carp from a lake or pond by netting. They are wary fish, hardy fish, and those that escape, even if only a few, quickly set off a new population explosion.

In recent years, Howard A. Loeb and William H. Kelly, research biologists at the New York State Fish Laboratory in DeBruce, tried to find a selective poison that would eradicate carp. Working on carp seined from the barge canal, Loeb and Kelly force-fed their captives a total of 1,496 different poisons, including Warfarin (which is deadly stuff on rats), DDT, and arsenic trioxide. But the carp survived, with the great majority of lethal compounds producing only, to the distress of the biologists, "the vaguest of symptoms." Now Loeb is experimenting on carp and other fishes with LSD and other derivatives of d-lycergic acid. When one of these drugs is released into a test tank, the fishes bob to the surface, swim backwards, and go into a kind of stupor for hours. The initial laboratory results appear promising, but far more research needs to be done. How long would the effect of the drugs persist in water? How would they affect vegetation and invertebrates or other animals, including man himself? Ideally, a harmless drug that caused fishes to surface for an hour or two and had no side effects would be of the greatest value. Not only could carp and other trash be culled and the desirable species left, but, moreover, the drug could possibly be used for selective harvesting at sea.

In the meanwhile, there seems to be only one way to get along with carp, and that is to fish for them. In the 1930s, a Jewish skipper used to cruise the Hudson in a boat with a freshwater live well. He would buy carp from commercial fishermen, fill up the well, and head for the kosher markets in New York City, where the carp were used in making gefüllte fish. Following complaints about oil pollution in the Hudson and a resultant off-taste in the fish, kosher dealers began obtaining their carp from the Middle West. On occasion, Orthodox Jews or old-country Germans and Poles angle for carp along the Hudson or tributary streams. The usual bait is a doughball made from corn meal, stiffened with cotton flavored with maple or strawberry syrup or some other tasty substance, and kneaded around a small treble hook. Rye bread and kernels of corn have been known to work. In the late spring, when the carp are spawning, they lose some of their shyness, to the advantage of one of my friends, Ric Riccardi of Ossining, who stalks the river flats with a bow and arrow. On a good day, Riccardi will take several hundred pounds of carp. The fish in the Hudson reach enormous size; I have a scar on my wrist from being stabbed by the dorsal fin of a forty-pounder I once seined and grappled with at Croton. I know a commercial fisherman, Ace Lent of Verplanck, who netted one weighing about sixty or seventy pounds. The carp butted Ace below the belt, and in great temper, he took it back home and hanged it from a nearby tree.

It may well be that American anglers are missing fine sport by ignoring carp. In the British Isles, carp fishing has an extraordinary number of devotees, and Bernard Venables, an English angling writer, once told me that the man who catches a ten-pound carp is a hero. He takes the live fish home in a wet burlap bag, puts it in a tub of water, and calls in his pals, who doff their caps in awe. The angler then puts the carp back in the bag, takes the fish to where it was caught, and releases it. The record carp in Britain, weighing forty-four pounds, was caught by Richard Walker, another angling writer. It was regarded as so amazing that it was given to the London Zoo Aquarium, where it is still alive and well and the subject of great admiration. When I told Venables about the carp in the Hudson, he was so flabbergasted I had the feeling that, with proper promotion, the river could become the number one attraction in the United States for British tourists.

In the canalized Hudson, especially where the river slows, the aquatic insects differ from those in the rushing river of the Adirondacks. There are, in certain clean coves and backwaters, a profusion of dragonflies and damselflies, which belong to the order Odonata. Dragonflies spend the greater part of their lives, up to a year or more, living underwater as nymphs—stocky, somewhat ugly creatures that literally move by jet propulsion, expelling water from their backsides. Depending upon the species, dragonfly nymphs clamber along submerged weeds while others sprawl on the bottom camouflaged by mud and debris. The nymphs feed by ambushing lesser insects, crustaceans, and sometimes, it is held, small fish as well. I once observed one in an aquarium tank punch a hole in the belly of a tropical fish, a swordtail. The nymph seizes its prey with a pinching lower lip that can shoot out faster than the eye can see. Despite their glowering faces, threatening gestures, and reputation for sewing up ears, adult dragonflies are of no harm to man, but some of the nymphs, which may grow an inch or more in length, have a fierce bite that can puncture the skin.

When the time for the transformation into the adult form is at hand, the nymph heads toward shore and climbs upon a weed or rock, where it splits its skin down the back. These cast skins, or exuviae, can sometimes be found on bushes, tree trunks, or fenceposts along the river, held in place by empty gripping claws. With pulsing, sometimes convulsive movements, the winged adult gradually rents its nymphal casing, and weak and woozy it totters into the first state of terrestrial existence. As blood surges through the intricate network of veins, the compacted wings slowly unfold and stiffen in the sunlight. In several hours, the dragonfly is ready to embark on its adult life, which may last only a month. During this brief time it will mate, lay eggs, and start the cycle anew. Along with the cockroach, the dragonfly is one of the oldest insects extant. Dragonflies go back to the Carboniferous period of 250 million years ago, and fossils with two-foot wingspreads have been unearthed.

Among the more conspicuous species in the Hudson Valley are

Libellula pulchella, a large, brownish dragonfly nicknamed the "ten spot" because of the dark splotches on its wings; *Tetragoneuria cynosura,* a yellowish insect fond of sunlit glades; *Plathemis lydia,* which has an unmistakable chalky white body and black barred wings; *Perithemis tenera,* a small (three-quarter-inch), weak flier with a stubby, reddish body and amber wings; *Sympetrum rubincundulum,* the bright red dragonfly of the early autumn; and *Anax junius,* the big blue-green darner with a splotch of gold. *A. junius* is ordinarily the largest dragonfly to be found soaring near the quiet stretches of the Hudson or around the edges of lakes in the watershed. Its wing span measures from four to five inches, and it is a strong flier with very keen sight. Its name literally means "King of June." Like a number of other dragonflies, the male *A. junius* has his own territory around a pond, and he patrols it regularly like a cop on a beat, foraging on luckless midges, mosquitoes, and moths. In turn, *A. junius* and other dragonflies are one of the favorite foods of largemouth bass.

For years, it was believed that dragonflies perished upon the advent of cold weather, but there are authorities who now hold that certain species, especially *L. pulchella* and *A. junius,* live on and migrate south in the fall, following rivers or the coast like ducks and geese. Indeed, the Federation of Ontario Naturalists has begun trapping dragonflies in Japanese mist nets ordinarily used to capture birds and fixing a small, harmless, printed adhesive label to the wings. I have yet to see a flock of dragonflies migrating south along the Hudson, but they have been seen flying in numbers along the Connecticut and Jersey shores.

Dragonflies and damselflies have a certain practical value, as do canaries in a coal mine. Both dragonflies and damselflies are somewhat fussy insects and lay their eggs in water that they deem clean. Their presence indicates, by rough rule of thumb, whether or not water is badly polluted. Alas, the canalized Hudson probably does not have as many dragonflies as it did in times past. This stretch of the river has been greatly despoiled and disfigured by pollution, much of which is from pulp and paper mills grinding up Adirondack wood for greeting cards, stationery, cartons, and, fittingly, toilet paper. The pollution starts while the river is still in the Adirondacks. At Corinth, a plant of the International Paper Company sucks up eighteen million gallons of river water a day and in return spews raw pulp and paper wastes back into the Hudson through an open ditch and two outfall troughs. This pattern is repeated time and again downriver by different companies: in Glens Falls, Finch, Pruyn & Co.; in South Glens Falls, Patrician Paper; in Queensbury, Hercules Incorporated, which adds a note of color by discharging pigment effluent; in Moreau, Arkell & Smiths; and in Fort Edward, Scott Paper, and down at Mechanicville, West Virginia Pulp and Paper. There is sewage, too, from municipalities and smaller companies, and raw plating wastes from two General Electric factories, but what one notices, what one sees, what strikes one dumb, are the thick, gray mats of pulp wastes bobbing along the surface of the Hudson like so many shredded mattresses. At Fort Edward, the river looks grisly; the mats seem thick enough to walk upon.

The mats drift downstream, where they sink and pile up against the dams. In some places, the wastes are ten to twenty feet thick. They stay until they decompose. Instead of dragonflies or fishes—and here I exempt the stray carp or sucker—one may find the strange creatures that biologists call "index organisms" because they are the telltale signs of gross pollution. There are sludge worms (*Tubifex tubifex*), which dwell upright in the sludge in stationary tubes that are half burrow and half chimney, leeches (*Glossiphonia complanata* and *Helobdella stagnalis*), and rattail maggots. The last are the larvae of syrphus flies, which as adults are bright and handsome insects that resemble bees and feed, in the manner of reformed sinners, upon the nectar of flowers.

At Cohoes, wastes from the Mohawk and the barge canal enter, and the Hudson becomes filthier. An "open sewer" is the phrase most often used to describe stretches of the battered Mohawk, the major tributary of the Hudson. The city of Utica does not treat any sewage at all but pours it into the Mohawk. Other communities, such as Johnstown and Gloversville, tannery towns with factories that discharge enormous amounts of hair, grease, blood, and acids, do the same to a Mohawk tributary, Cayadutta Creek, one of the filthiest streams in the state. Between Fort Edward and the Troy dam, the Hudson receives the raw wastes from the equivalent of six hundred thousand people.

Below the dam at Troy, open sewers from that city face upon the river like so many giant backsides. Herring gulls dip and dart for morsels washing out, and boatmen hurry by, but not so quickly as to kick up spray. Albany, Rensselaer, Watervliet, and Green Island add their own raw contributions to the river. Without question, this stretch of the river is the most polluted part of the Hudson, exceeding even New York City in concentrated filth. Indeed, the river here can be so awesomely foul that it is a source of wonder to sanitary engineers, and in the trade they speak of the place, almost fondly, as the "the Albany Pool." The pool is not too bad during the winter and early spring; cold water holds more dissolved oxygen than does warm water, and fishes are able to move in. There are sturgeon and striped bass and occasional shad which buck up against the Troy dam with ancestral fury, while the spring runoff from the Adirondacks thunders downstream. But then the runoff slows, and death comes to the Albany Pool with the first hot spell, as it did, for instance, on the weekend of June 9, 1967. Alewives (*Alosa pseudoharengus*), a species of herring, had run up from the sea into the pool in enormous numbers. The runoff suddenly slowed, and the weather turned very hot. The thick deposits of sludge on the bottom of the pool began "working," and the rotten egg stink of hydrogen sulphide pervaded the air. The bacteria decomposing the sludge multiplied and consumed the dissolved oxygen in the river water. Milling desperately, the alewives were asphyxiated, and a million of them turned belly up and made the Hudson silver with their glistening bodies.

In the summer, the Hudson River is essentially devoid of dissolved oxygen for a distance of perhaps twenty to thirty miles south of the Troy Dam. The raw sewage which pours into the pool contains enormous amounts of bacteria from human intestinal tracts. Among these bacteria may be certain pathogenic organisms which cause typhoid fever, diarrhea, or infectious hepatitis. The filth is incredible; during a state hearing on the problems of the pool, a press report had it that men "grit their teeth and women left the room."

In determining water quality, health authorities generally do not try to isolate the pathogenic organisms causing human disease. They could spend their professional careers cataloguing the bacteria from one sewer outlet alone, and so instead they make "density counts" of the coliform bacteria which emanate from human feces. Coliform bacteria are easy to detect, and although they are usually harmless in themselves, their relative density in a given volume of water is a good indication of the likely presence of other, definitely harmful, bacteria. For water to be fit for swimming, health authorities generally agree that the coliform density should not exceed one thousand in one hundred milliliters of water, about one-fifth of a pint. In the jargon of official reports, the formula for this ratio is written as 1,000/100 ml. Yet in the heart of the Albany Pool, federal health authorities have found peak densities of more than 50,000/100 ml. At the Rensselaer water-intake pipe—and until 1968 the Albany Pool served as Rensselaer's reservoir for drinking water—coliform densities have exceeded 15,000/100 ml.

Even since the early 1900s, the pollution in the Albany Pool has been lamented and bewailed, but no serious attempt at corrective action was taken until 1965, when voters approved a $1 billion bond issue to clean up the waters of the state. In the hullabaloo to carry the bond issue, the Hudson was declared the prime target, and the issue passed by a four-to-one majority, the greatest in the history of the state on any issue. Now, under plans drawn up by the State Water Resources Commission and approved by the Federal Water Pollution Control Administration, the waters of the Hudson have been given standards from the harbor to the Adirondacks. The Albany Pool, for instance, has been classified as grade C water, which means that it should be elevated to a standard able to support aquatic life. Instead of having zero milligrams of dissolved oxygen in each liter of water at any time of the year, the pool is required to have five milligrams of dissolved oxygen for each liter. Moreover, no wastes injurious to fishes are to be poured into the pool. In sum, the cities, towns, and villages currently making the pool a horror are to install sewage treatment plants, and industries must cease releasing harmful wastes.

Class C is the minimum standard set for any stretch of the Hudson, and the Albany Pool is the only one graded so low. For instance, between the New York-New Jersey State Line and the Bear Mountain Bridge the Hudson is classed SB, tidal salt water suitable for swimming and fishing. From Bear Mountain Bridge north to Chelsea the same standard applies. From Chelsea north to the southern end of Esopus Island, the river is classed A; it must be suitable for drinking purposes. From Esopus Island to the south end of Houghtaling Island, the lower boundary of the Albany Pool, the river is graded B, fit for swimming and fishing.

Originally, the state was to have cleaned up the Hudson by 1970. Now the target date is 1972. Speaking frankly, one state official said, "I think everything will be under construction by 1972, and by 1973 or 1974, the majority of the pollution will be under control. There may be delays. Reports are not reviewed as promptly as they should be in the Health Department. Sometimes engineers inadvertently omit data, and they have to go back again. There are some plants with definite treatment problems. There have been some worthwhile delays, in a sense, where we have decided on joint projects. Then there is the problem of rising construction costs. Hoosick Falls Village asked for bids, and the bids were 50 per cent over the estimate. Now they have to readvertise. And then a few companies have dragged their feet."

In all likelihood, pollution of the Hudson will not be ended until 1975 *at the earliest.* I cannot be more optimistic because of the past performance of antipollution authorities. It is worth noting at this point that much, if not all, of the industrial pollution of the Hudson and Mohawk rivers has been illegal for years. In 1888, the Congress of the United States passed the New York Harbor Act, which made illegal "the placing, discharging, or depositing, by any process or in any manner, of refuse, dirt, ashes, cinders, mud, sand, dredgings, sludge, acid, or any other matter of any kind, other than that flowing from streets, sewers, and passing therefrom in a liquid state, in the tidal waters of the harbor of New York, or its adjacent or tributary waters, or those of Long Island Sound." In 1899, the Congress passed the Federal Refuse Act, which made illegal the dumping of similar refuse into any navigable waters of the United States. Both laws provide that a convicted violator may be punished by a fine, of not less than $250 or more than $2,500, and/or imprisonment, from thirty days to one year. Interestingly, both laws provide that half the amount of the fine decided by the court shall be paid as a reward to the person who reported the violator. The New York State Fish and Game Law handbook, Section 180, Paragraph 1, reads: "No dyestuffs, coal tar, refuse from a gas house, cheese factory, creamery, condensery or canning factory, sawdust, shavings, tanbark, lime, acid or other deleterious or poisonous substance shall be thrown or allowed to run into any waters, either private or public, in quantities injurious to fish life inhabiting those waters or injurious to the propagation of fish therein." Paragraph three, same section, specifically notes, "Oil, acid, sludge, cinders or ashes from a vessel of any type shall not be thrown, dumped or allowed by any person into the waters of the Hudson or Mohawk rivers."

Bureaucratic indifference to the river has been the order of the day, even when gross violations take place on the federal level. There are times when the United States Army Corps of Engineers will claim jurisdiction over the Hudson at least as far north as Fort Edward, the head of navigation. The supervisor of New York harbor, a regular army officer assigned to regional headquarters in Manhattan, is supposed to enforce the New York Harbor Act and the Federal Refuse Acts. Yet, to cite only one case of gross pollution, the Penn Central (formerly New York Central) Diesel and Electric Shops at Harmon, thirty-four miles north of the Battery and clearly within the legal jurisdiction of the Corps, has been pouring oil wastes into the Hudson for years. The oil gushes from a pipe which is three feet in diameter and bears the date of 1929. It empties into the Hudson on the south side of Croton Point adjacent to the mouth of the Croton River. The oil discharges have been so heavy that ducks have drowned there. It takes only a few drops of oil to destroy the natural waterproofing of the feathers. Moreover, and most unfortunately, ducks and other birds may be attracted to the slick during rough weather because oil calms choppy waters. Fish and crabs caught in the area are deemed inedible. In September, 1965, Dr. James Alexander, a chemical oceanographer at Fordham University, and I were out on the river—ironically, while a much publicized federal conference on Hudson pollution was being held at, of all places, the Waldorf-Astoria Hotel—when an oil slick from the Central pipe covered an area three to four miles long and one half to two miles wide. I was afraid to smoke; the river appeared to be a fire hazard. In 1966, a recently formed organization, the Hudson River Fishermen's Association, began phoning complaints to the Corps of Engineers about the Central's constant discharge of oil in violation of federal law. The Corps sent an inspector to check on each complaint, but the discharge of oil did not stop. I am one of the directors of the Hudson River Fishermen's Association, and in June, 1967, while completing research on New York Harbor for this book, I visited Corps headquarters in Manhattan. After passing through a couple of different offices concerned with dredging and similar engineering happenings, I was taken to the office charged with anti-pollution enforcement. The subject of the New York Harbor Act came up during our discussion, and the reigning civilian bureaucrat in charge said that the corps had had some difficulty in handling this law until an act of Congress changed things in 1952. Until then, the supervisor of the harbor had been a Navy line officer. I let this pass and purposely made no mention of the Federal Refuse Act of 1899, which specifically charged the Corps with enforcement. When I asked what happened to violators of federal law, the bureaucrat allowed that the Corps permitted "three or four violations, maybe five" to pile up before sending the case to court. From personal experience on the Hudson, I knew only too well that three or four violations, maybe five, would be reported to the Corps by only a few persistent citizens, such as members of the Hudson River Fishermen's Association. After a few more minutes of nonsense, I could no longer contain myself, and I asked about the constant oil discharge from the Central shops at Harmon. Why, I asked, did not the Corps enforce the law? Why weren't the responsible officials of the Central, or any other illegal polluters, for that matter, cited, charged, tried in court, fined, and sentenced? The bureaucrat replied: "We're dealing with top officials in industry, and you just don't go around treating these people like that." I said that I believed in equality before the law, to which the bureaucrat responded, "Hey, have you been writing to Congressman Ottinger?" Representative Richard Ottinger, whose district in Westchester and Putnam counties borders the river, is a well-known defender of the Hudson against defilement. Mention of his name —Ottinger has been critical of the Corps—caused the interview to fizzle, but I must note here that the Corps spokesman was loath throughout to give me information about the names of, locations of, and judgments made against polluters the Corps had supposedly bagged on its own. I was variously told that I would have to get any information, which is supposed to be a matter of public record, from the Admiralty and Shipping Section of the Department of Justice, or the Eastern District Federal Court in Brooklyn, or the Federal District Court of New Jersey in Newark, or the U. S. Attorney in Newark, or the U. S. Attorney in the Southern District of New York, or maybe from the U. S. Attorney in the Northern District in Albany.

I left thoroughly angry, but another director of the Hudson River Fishermen's Association, Arthur Glowka, an Eastern Airlines pilot and an occasional contributor to *Field and Stream, Outdoor Life,* and *Sports Afield,* immediately took it upon himself to investigate the Corps' ways and means of enforcing federal laws under its jurisdiction. Art Glowka has a persistence and an equanimity of soul that cannot be rivaled by a Buddhist monk, and for many months he began appearing in Corps headquarters asking about polluters. He made no mention whatsoever of his directorship in the HRFA; he simply presented himself as a concerned private citizen. He had such endurance that he has even managed to meet the Army officer in charge, an encounter that registers in my mind as being as significant as the moment when Stanley finally found Livingston. Unfortunately, Glowka's meeting was not so fruitful. His Livingston sort of refused to admit anything. Glowka was told, for instance, that all Corps data on polluters is stored on tape. When he suggested that retrieval of such data would answer his questions quickly—after all, that is why the government uses computer systems—there was much hemming and hawing but no retrieval of data. When Glowka was informed that he could not get any information about polluters without approval from Corps headquarters in Washington, Glowka cheerfully left the office saying, "Okay, I'll write to Washington, and I'll use your name." Within a half hour, Glowka's phone was ringing, with the Corps official saying he need not write to Washington. When, on another occasion, Glowka was told the Corps could not release information he had requested, he appeared in the Manhattan headquarters with a copy of the Freedom of Information Act passed by Congress. There was a hurried, muted buzzing in the back quarters of the office, and Glowka was told the Corps would have to check with its counsel.

Glowka finally got the information he requested after writing to the White House.

I do not mean to cite the Corps of Engineers alone; the New York State Health Department, the Conservation Department, the Water Resources Commission, the Interstate Sanitation Commission (established in 1936 by New York, New Jersey, and Connecticut to clean up the waters of the greater New York area, including the Hudson up to the Bear Mountain Bridge), and the Federal Water Pollution Control Administration all have been lax, if not negligent.

For instance, early in 1967, I got in touch with the Federal Water Pollution Control Administration office in charge of the Hudson River and Lake Champlain. This office happens to be off in Metuchen, New Jersey, which made me pessimistic at the start about the FWPCA's knowledge of the Hudson, but even so I made the call to complain about a couple of polluters of the river, including the Central. The official who answered allowed as how he sure was interested in knowing about polluters. However, he said this in such a fashion as to prompt my asking whether he would take action to end the violations. No, he said, he would not. He did not think that the FWPCA had any authority in the matter, but the next time the Secretary of the Interior called a conference on pollution of the Hudson, he, the official in Metuchen, would like to be able to go to the files and pull out a list of violators. I gave him a succinct goodby and rang off.

About a year later, another official of the FWPCA office in Metuchen arrived in person in Ossining to complain to Richard Garrett, president of the Hudson River Fishermen's Association, about a letter that Garrett had written to Representative Ottinger characterizing the FWPCA, on the basis of the incident related above, as "worthless." Garrett had the official call me, and I said that as far as I was concerned the FWPCA was indeed worthless. Garrett and a friend, Augie Berg, then took the visiting official to look at the oil gushing from the Central pipe. Upon arrival, they could smell the mess a hundred yards away. "Is that oil?" the official asked, to which Berg replied. "It ain't perfume, buddy." They all looked at the oil coming from the pipe, and the official flung his arms into the air in dismay. "You win! You win!" he yelled.

Garrett said, "What do you mean we win? The oil's coming out."
The official looked at Garrett and Berg and asked, "Who are you
people?" Garrett answered, "We're just people." The official promised he would have inspectors up within a week to take action,
and he asked Garrett to phone him at once about any other polluters. The inspectors never came, and whenever Garrett called,
the official was never available. His secretary variously reported
that he was "in conference" or traveling. Garrett left his number
each time, but the official never called back.

What can be done? There are several things.

For one, there is public pressure, and Art Glowka has thought
of a very effective way to mount public interest in stopping pollution. He designed pre-paid "Bag-A-Polluter" postcards. The cards
note the New York Harbor Act of 1888, and point out that the
person who reports a convicted violator may collect up to $1,250
as a reward. The cards have a simple entry form where a person
can write in the name of the polluter, kind of pollution, time and
date, and any adverse effects noted. The Hudson River Fishermen's Association has printed ten thousand Bag-A-Polluter cards
and given them out free up and down the Hudson Valley. All a
person needs to do is spot a polluter, fill out the card, and put it
in the mail to the HRFA which then complains to appropriate
authorities. If the pollution continues, the cards serve as evidence
for inquiring reporters who want to know about problems of the
river. Newspaper and magazine articles in turn generate more
pressure. By way of example, for years the Hudson Wire Company was one of the most noxious polluters of the river in the
Ossining area. The company discharged acids directly into a tributary, Kill Brook, and eyewitnesses reported it to the HRFA.
Stories about the HRFA program and the Hudson Wire Company pollution appeared in the New York *Daily News* and local
papers, and they were most helpful. Not long afterwards, the
company announced it was going to stop polluting.

There is one other thing that can be done to stop illegal polluters. Laws and courts do exist, and as Victor Yannacone, attorney for the Environmental Defense Fund has put it, "Only in a
courtroom can a scientist present his evidence, free from harass-
ment by politicians. And only in a courtroom can bureaucratic

hogwash be tested in the crucible of cross examination." With such thoughts in mind, in June, 1968, Representative Ottinger, the HRFA and several of its officers and directors, Richie Garrett, Dr. James Alexander, Dominick Pirone, and myself, filed a suit in federal court against the Penn Central, the Secretary of the Army, and the Corps of Engineers for the railroad's discharge of oil into the Hudson. The suit was prepared by Ottinger and David Sive, an attorney who is chairman of the Atlantic Chapter of the Sierra Club. It may well be that our suit will be thrown out of court for technical reasons, but the exposure it makes of inaction will, hopefully, prompt an end to this and other abuses of the river by polluters who should have been compelled to stop years ago by state and federal officials asleep on the public payroll.

Besides pollution by municipalities and industry, there is the threat posed by pesticides that wash into the river. Of especial concern are the chlorinated hydrocarbons, DDT, dieldrin, endrin, and heptachlor. It takes at least a decade for these compounds to decompose, and they are highly poisonous to a broad spectrum of living organisms. They can be spread by wind and water, and organisms can absorb them from the environment. Once in the food chain, these compounds can move up and become concentrated in great amounts in animals at the top of the food pyramid.

No one knows for sure what effects the chlorinated hydrocarbons have had on all the life in the Hudson Valley, but some damage appears to have occurred. Ed Reilly, at the State Museum, has noted a decline in the number of certain amphibians, a class of animals particularly vulnerable to pesticides because they do a certain amount of breathing through their skin. For instance, twenty years ago Jefferson's salamander (*Ambystoma jeffersonianum*) was common. Now Reilly has to search all day to find one. Certain birds of prey also have suffered an alarming decline along the Hudson. The osprey or fish hawk (*Pandion haliaetus*) is a marked rarity, and the bald eagle (*Haliaeetus leucocephalus*), which used to give such joy to river watchers, is now very scarce. Fifteen or twenty years ago, it was common to see as many as a half dozen eagles at one time riding the ice floes in early spring. Nowadays an observer is fortunate to see one or two in the course of a year. The same is true of the peregrine falcon or duck hawk

(*Falco peregrinus*) which nested on the cliffs of the Palisades, and often pursued pigeons around Manhattan skyscrapers. Because of DDT, no nesting pair of duck hawks has been seen in the northeastern United States, much less along the Hudson, since 1960.

6

THE MID-HUDSON

Between Albany and Newburgh, the Hudson flows for more than seventy miles between rolling countryside. Several cities dot the shores—Hudson, Poughkeepsie, Saugerties, and Kingston—but the visual impression that one receives, if one heeds Henry James and travels by boat, is of great stretches of largely unspoiled riverside. Willows and ash trees bend over the banks as if in a nineteenth-century landscape, and along the flats herons stand motionless, awaiting prey. The smaller villages have a certain charm. New Baltimore remains quaintly archaic. In 1939 it served as a locale for the producers of the film *Little Old New York*, who wanted to photograph the Hudson Valley as it was in 1807. Similarly, in 1968, the producers of *Hello, Dolly!* chose Garrison, further down in the Highlands, to serve as Yonkers of the 1890s.

Interspersed along the west shore of the river are giant cement plants and brickyards. The cement plants, spewing forth volumes of dust, bring one back abruptly to the present day. Most of the brickyards have gone out of business, victims of the age of steel and glass construction. The old sheds rot in the sun, but their heritage persists: tidal action has eroded the discarded and broken bricks into miles of beaches of fine red dust. A number of west-shore villages south of Albany appear hard put. For-sale signs on river properties are common. Until the turn of the century, these villages prospered from such local industries as brickmaking, shipbuilding, and ice cutting. Ice from the Hudson used to be shipped as far as the West Indies, but refrigeration put an end to this business. For a while, many of the abandoned icehouses were used for raising mushrooms. Growing trays were stacked from the floor to the ceiling, and when supply exceeded demand and the market price dropped, a slight draft of chill air over the trays slowed production satisfactorily.

Life on the east shore is somewhat grander. Between Hudson and Hyde Park lie the great estates that formed "Millionaire's Row" and gave Edith Wharton inspiration. Many of the mansions are still occupied, mostly, it would seem, by determined ladies who emerge in June, just as the green drake mayflies hatch on the upper river, to attend the annual meeting of the Hudson River Conservation Society. Other mansions are now owned by religious orders, and still others are kept as historic houses. The National Park Service runs the Roosevelt home at Hyde Park and the nearby Frederick Vanderbilt mansion, while the state maintains the Ogden Mills chateau and estate at Staatsburg and Frederick Church's castle, Olana, south of Hudson.

Not far from Hudson, in the foothills of the Taconic range, there lives a curious collection of people known locally as Bushwhackers or Pondshiners. Their origin as a sociological island is anyone's guess. Maybe they were just isolated over the years. It has been suggested, perhaps romantically, that they may be the descendants of tenants who took to the hills after the anti-rent wars on the manors in the 1840s.

When Carl Carmer was doing research in the 1930s for his book *The Hudson*, he learned that the Pondshiners, who often bear the family names of Proper, Hotaling, and Simmons, believed in witches and spells. Indeed, one witch was then causing great trouble, and when Carmer asked some Pondshiners why they did not have her arrested, one replied, "Twouldn't do no good. You have to kill a witch to get rid of her and none o' them state troopers has got anything but lead bullets. It takes a silver bullet to kill a witch."

From what I have been able to gather, the witching days are over. Pondshiners usually support themselves by making baskets. I know of one, a sturdily built woman in her thirties, who not only makes baskets but also fells the oak, ash, and hickory trees needed for the strips, handles, and frame. Making a basket is a laborious procedure; to start, she has to peel the bark off a log and then pound the wood until the growth rings are loosened. She then uses a knife to cut off strips of the desired length. When not making baskets, she cuts hardwoods, which she trucks to a veneer factory across the river.

The Pondshiners are not the only isolated groups in or near the Hudson Valley. Further up the Hudson near Glens Falls are the so-called Van Guilders. Blond and blue-eyed, they are said to be descended from Dutch settlers who ran away from the patroonship of Rensselaerswyck. On the east shore behind Kingston are the so-called Eagle Nesters, who have an admixture of Negro and Indian ancestry, while further south in the Ramapo Mountains on the New York-New Jersey state line, the Jackson Whites carry on. They are so named because they are descended in part from three boatloads of women brought to Manhattan from Britain and the West Indies during the Revolution by an entrepreneur named Jackson. The women entertained British troops, but at the conclusion of the war they were driven from the city and fled to the Ramapos, where they settled down in the woods with runaway Hessian mercenaries and Tuscarora Indians who had dropped out of the long trek from North Carolina to upstate New York to join the Iroquois.

The Catskill Mountains are the dominant features of the landscape of the mid-Hudson region. From the east shore, there are superb views across the river of the plum-colored mountains. The Indians called the Catskills *On-ti-o-ras,* "mountains of the sky," because from far off they looked like dark clouds along the horizon. The views from the Catskills themselves are superb. The finest is from the top of South Mountain, where the old Catskill Mountain House used to stand. During the nineteenth century, seeing the view from the Mountain House was a must for foreign travelers, and James Fenimore Cooper had Hawkeye describe the scene as beholding "all creation . . . the river in sight for seventy miles under my feet, looking like a curled shaving, though it was eight miles to its banks."

Unlike the Adirondacks, which are composed of igneous rock, the Catskills are sedimentary in origin. Four hundred million years ago, the sea covered the land where the Catskills are now. Then the sea retreated, a plateau arose, and in the passing years water and wind carved the mountains, exposing the mollusk fossils embedded in their flanks. In 1920, the workers digging the foundation for the Gilboa Dam on Schoharie Creek, which flows north into the Mohawk, uncovered remains of the oldest forest yet found in the world. The forest grew in the Devonian period 370 million years ago, and apparently all the trees were of a single kind, *Aneurophyton,* which had a swollen base, grew to a height of forty feet, and was topped by fernlike fronds. Several of the most important Catskill streams have been dammed to supply New York City with water. Reservoirs in the Catskills were supposed to assure the city of water for years, but in 1966, following a long-term drought, the reservoirs ran low and the city constructed a plant to draw water from the Hudson at Chelsea, south of Poughkeepsie. The river water hereabouts has surprising clarity and given extensive treatment it is fit to drink; Poughkeepsie uses the Hudson for its supply.

From the Troy Dam down to the city of Hudson, a distance of some thirty miles, the river is laced with sandbars, islands, and marshes. These have been formed by natural sediments which settle out in the tide water after having been carried downstream from the Adirondacks. Castleton, fifteen miles south of Troy, was the site of the so-called Overslaugh Bar, which was a hindrance to navigation well into the nineteenth century. In the 1860s, the state and federal governments embarked upon a long term project of dredging the bar, deepening the main channel, and constructing dikes along the islands and banks of the river.

In the 1960s, the Army Corps of Engineers dredged the ship channel to Albany to a depth of thirty-four feet and a width of four hundred. During the dredging, the river was so laden with silt that it was the color and consistency of gravy. Great amounts of the spoil were simply dumped on flats and islands, and so now near Castleton there are Sahara deserts of silt three stories high with dead tree branches poking through. Even a dredge operator I met was angry. "I hate to do it," he said. "I'm a duck hunter myself, but you can't fight the government." Once, when I was in a badgering mood I asked a Corps official where the spoil was placed. "In disposal areas," he said. I asked, "Such as where?" He replied, "Oh, for example, there was an unused [sic] little stream, so we dumped there." The Corps is now studying a proposal to deepen the channel to thirty-seven feet and widen it to six hundred, because river pilots are supposedly "not happy going at night."

During the summer months, when the salt line begins to work its way north, some unusual marine animals may venture upstream for a considerable distance. In 1932, an angler reported catching a barndoor skate (*Raja laevis*) at North Albany; the fish is preserved in the state museum. In the fall of 1936, mammalian dolphins (*Delphinus delphis*) swam up river. The carcass of one was found near Albany, and that of another near Highland, across from Poughkeepsie. They died after their skins blistered in the fresh water. Until the 1850s and 1860s, dolphins and porpoises were regular summer visitors in the Hudson up to Peekskill.

For the most part, the fishes to be found in the mid-Hudson are suckers, carp, shiners, killifish, catfish, bullheads, black bass of both species, northern pike, pickerel, crappies, yellow perch, and white perch. Mixed in with them are anadromous fishes, which live in salt water but spawn in fresh, such as shad and herring, striped bass, sea sturgeon, and tomcod.

Historically, shad have been the most important commercial fish in the Hudson, and the Hudson in turn has ranked as one of the most productive shad rivers in North America. There are several different species of shad that frequent the rivers of North America, but the species in the Hudson, the American shad (*Alosa sapidissima*), is the most desirable. In fact, its scientific name means "shad most delicious."

Each spring, mature shad, born in the Hudson four to five years earlier, return from the Atlantic to spawn on the river flats that run northward from Kingston to Coxsackie. The commercial season extends from March 15 to June 1, but the fish usually do not arrive until about the first week in April. They seem to come in waves, and the appearance of the largest shad, known as "lilac" shad because of the lilacs then in bloom, signals the end of the run. Female lilac shad weigh as much as ten or twelve pounds. As the shad work their way upriver, fishermen set to the harvest with gill nets affixed to stakes or drifted with the tide. The shad swim into the nets head first, and when they attempt to withdraw, their gill covers catch on the mesh. In order to allow some fish to get upriver to spawn, the state conservation department requires that all nets be taken from the river from Friday to Sunday mornings. The fishing lasts about six weeks, with the female or roe shad commanding the higher price because of the eggs, a great delicacy. At riverside, a roe shad usually sells for a dollar, while the male or buck shad costs a quarter. There are some gourmets who consider the male better eating; not only is the flesh tastier, but the testes are excellent when poached.

Upon reaching Kingston and points north, the shad begin to spawn. Depending on age, a female carries between 116,000 and 468,000 eggs, and, according to those who have observed spawning on other rivers, the female mates with a single male, usually between sunset and midnight. Both swim near the surface, splashing vigorously. After they spawn, they are very emaciated as they make their way downriver again to sea. Spent shad, called "backers" or "downrunners," are sometimes caught, but they are commercially worthless.

The fertilized eggs roll about the bottom of the Hudson, where they may be suffocated by silt washed down by heavy rains or by dredging, or eaten by predators. Catfish and eels are very fond of the eggs; in fact, eels often attack female shad caught in nets, ripping open the belly to get at the roe. Hatching takes anywhere from six to ten days, depending on temperature. Upon hatching, the shad larvae are about ten millimeters long, and for a week or two they nourish themselves on their yolk sacs. Unlike their parents, juvenile shad have teeth; they stay upriver during the summer months, nosing about in the depths of the river or in coves and marshes for small crustaceans, insect larvae, and other tidbits. The coves and marshes are not only rich feeding grounds but, being shallow, offer places of refuge from larger predators, such as striped bass. When the state maintained hatcheries, special care had to be taken to prevent eels from entering rearing ponds through water pipes to get at the young shad. The mortality among shad eggs and juveniles is extremely high; perhaps only one adult survives to reach market for every hundred thousand eggs fertilized.

Upon the approach of cool weather in September, the young shad begin working their way down the Hudson to the Atlantic. The young shad often swim near the surface, and their rippling passage downstream has been likened to a gentle spatter of raindrops. By the time they reach the harbor mouth in October and November, they are from three to five inches long and prepared to cope with life in the ocean until they return to the Hudson to spawn four or five years later.

Tagging studies indicate that at sea the shad move north to the Gulf of Maine, where they mingle in the summer and fall with shad from the Connecticut and Delaware rivers and Chesapeake Bay. They apparently feed on small crustaceans, such as inch-long mysid shrimp. No one knows for certain where they spend the winter, but they probably move south along the Continental Shelf and as spring approaches they head inshore. In the early spring, there are great numbers of shad in the Delaware Bay, but probably only half of them are Delaware River fish. The other half seem to be migrants heading for more northern rivers, such as the Hudson and the Connecticut.

Over the years, the catch of Hudson shad has had violent ups and downs. In colonial days, shad were extremely abundant. In the mid 1800s, records show the fishery in relative decline. Then, toward the end of the nineteenth century, shad again became abundant; in 1889, the catch from the Hudson was 4,332,000 pounds, the all-time record. The future appeared excellent, but the fish went into a decline, and by 1916, the catch was a meager 40,173 pounds, the worst on record. In 1919, the catch was up to 374,974 pounds, but then it dropped to 94,369 pounds in 1924. During the late 1920s and early 30s, it began to edge upward, and suddenly, in 1936, the catch was way up again, 2,467,900 pounds. For the next twenty-three years, with two exceptions, the annual catch was at least 1,000,000 pounds. In 1942, 4,253,528 pounds were caught, the highest number for this century. In 1960, the catch began to skid, and it is now down to about 100,000 pounds annually.

Fishermen and biologists have put forward any number of theories for these baffling fluctuations. One explanation is that shad populations are cyclical, and that the swings are normal and to be expected. Then, too, pollution, ship traffic, and other factors have been blamed. In the late 1940s, the United States Fish and Wildlife Service assigned a biologist, Gerald B. Talbot, to look into the problems affecting Hudson River shad. Talbot, now director of the U. S. Bureau of Sport Fisheries and Wildlife Laboratory in Tiburon, California, did a detailed study, "Factors Associated with Fluctuations in Abundance of Hudson River Shad," in which he examined just about every possibility. He looked into stream flow and found no correlation between it and the size of the catch. "Tidal action, particularly during low flows, has more effect on the river velocity than does runoff," he noted. A comparison of water temperatures over the years revealed nothing statistically significant. Ship traffic, although a mechanical hazard to nets, was not detrimental to the run, and dredging operations of that day had "no measurable adverse effect." (I say "of that day" because the Corps of Engineers had yet to dredge the thirty-four-foot-deep ship channel to Albany.)

Until 1935, the state operated shad hatcheries and stocked the Hudson with young. Some fishermen insisted the closing of the hatcheries caused the catch to dwindle. But catches, in fact, improved afterwards. Talbot did an extensive analysis and concluded that "the number of eggs that it has been possible to obtain for hatchery operations is only an extremely small fraction of the amount spawned naturally, and the increased survival rate, if any, resulting from current shad-hatchery practices has not produced, and cannot be expected to produce, an increase in shad production."

Pollution played an uncertain role. As early as 1906, pollution in the Albany Pool was a problem; at that time a state report noted, "Formerly, shad were caught up to the Troy Dam. . . . It would seem as if, year after year, the run of fish was retarded by an invisible line which annually stretched further and further down the river and beyond which the fish would not pass. . . . At present, the fish do not seem to run much above Hudson." Even so, downriver at the Battery, Talbot found "no correlation between average oxygen content of the water . . . and shad production during the period between 1915 and 1951. Any effect that pollution in this area has had on the runs of shad may well have been uniform since about 1919, as there appears to be little over-all change in water quality, as measured by oxygen content since that time."

Talbot believed the principal factor causing the fluctuation of the shad catch was the number of fish allowed to escape upriver to spawn. Recaptures of tagged fish demonstrated that too many spawners were being netted on their way upriver, and Talbot suggested that overfishing be curbed by closing more days to netting. He calculated that the size of the run each year was dependent on the amount of fish that had escaped the nets during the previous five years, four years, and one year, and by using a mathematical formula, he found it would be possible to "predict the size of the shad run one year in advance within desired confidence limits." Unfortunately, nothing was done; Talbot's findings were assigned to bureaucratic limbo. Ironically, shad might return to the Hudson in abundance because so many fishermen have given up in disgust; thus the shad population might have time to rebuild, as it has in the past.

No matter what factor or combination of factors has prompted the current decline of the shad, the descendants of Hudson River fish carry on elsewhere. Back in the nineteenth century, when stocking exotics such as carp was the rage, Seth Green, a New York pioneer of pisciculture, became the first person to hatch shad artificially, and he established a state hatchery at Castleton on the Hudson. In 1871, the state of California asked New York authorities for permission to stock shad from the Hudson in the Sacramento River. At the time, Californians feared that immigrant Chinese, who were very fond of fish, would seine the Sacramento clean. New York agreed, and on June 19, 1871, Green began an epic rail journey west. He wrote:

> I started at 6 a. m. from my hatching establishment ten miles below Albany, on the Hudson River, with twelve thousand young shad in four eight-gallon milk-cans. They had been hatched the night before at the establishment under charge of the New York commissioners. I arrived at Rochester at 10 p. m. and changed the water, substituting that from the

Genesee River, without injury to the fish. I arrived at Cleveland at 7:45 next morning: put two hundred shad in Lake Erie, and changed the water again. The fish were then fresh and lively, without any signs of sickness. I again changed the water at Toledo, and when I arrived at Chicago at 7 p. m. the fish were still in good order. Here I first tried the water from the city water-works, but found there was too much oil in it; so I went to the lake. Having tasted the water and found that it would answer, I put two hundred fish in Lake Michigan, and on June 21 started with cans newly filled, at 10:45 a. m., for California. I carried an extra can of water, for before me was a long stretch of almost arid land; still I was fortunate enough to find some places between Chicago and Omaha where I could get a few pails of water and make a partial change. The fish were still in good order when we arrived at Omaha; but there I could not find any water in which they would live five minutes. The way I tested the water was by filling a tumbler and putting a few fish in it; it was easy to tell at once, by the behavior of the fry, whether the water agreed with them or not. . . . From Omaha I did not find any good water for four hundred miles, and the only way I kept my charges alive was by drawing the water out of the cans into pails, and pouring it from one pail into another until purified; this process being assisted by my getting a little ice-water from the car-tanks.

June 22. Bad water all day, with the thermometer 100 degrees in the shade from 9 a. m. to 4 p. m. I used ice-water the entire day, a very little at a time, and had hard work to keep the temperature of the water below 82 degrees. I began to feel blue, and doubtful of the result. The fish suffered considerably, but the weather began to be cold toward night, and I got the temperature of the water down to 75 degrees at 9 p. m., the fish recovering a little.

June 23. I arrived at Laramie River at 5 p. m. and got a good change of water; fish doing well, and I began once more to feel hopeful and encouraged. We had a frost that night, and next morning at 7 I changed water at Green River, where it was in proper condition. At 2 p. m. I got another change from a stream in which there were trout, and again at Ogden, where I put two hundred fish in the river.

June 25. The water was changed at the Humboldt River; the water was good and continued good all the rest of the way.

June 26. I arrived at Sacramento and took the fish up the river two hundred and seventy-five miles from Sacramento, in company with Messrs. Redding and Smith, the California fishery commissioners. In their presence I deposited the fish in the Sacramento River the same night at 10 p. m.; there were about ten thousand in good order. On the sixth and seventh days out they began to be very busy looking for food. Whenever I changed the water they would clean up all the food there was in it in five minutes. They did not suffer for food as long as the sack lasted on their bellies; that is about five days; then they needed sustenance. If I could get a change of water often enough from running streams I could carry them a long way, as nearly all streams are filled with small insects. With this view I examined the water of the Sacramento where I put them, and found plenty of food for the young fry. I then went down to the Pacific Ocean and found that there were plenty of sand-fleas, which are the principal food of the old shad in the Atlantic. And now I can only say that if they do not have shad in the Pacific Ocean there will be but one cause, the roily water, caused by washing the mountains down for gold. However, I think the fish will get through all right.

The shad did, and in 1873, Livingston Stone of the U. S. Fish Commission was dispatched east for a multitude of more shad and other species. In June, 1873, Stone set out for California by special railroad aquarium car with 20,000 shad eggs and young from the Hudson, 40,000 "freshwater" eels from the river, 1,500 "saltwater" eels from Martha's Vineyard (actually, the freshwater and saltwater eels were the same species, but no one knew this at the time), 60 black bass and 150 yellow perch from the vicinity of Lake Champlain, 1,000 brook trout from New Hampshire, and 162 lobsters and a barrel of oysters from Wood's Hole and Massachusetts Bay. But after passing Omaha, the train crashed into the Elk Horn River, and the whole carload was lost. Undaunted,

Stone returned to the Hudson where, following telegraphed orders, he took on 40,000 young shad and headed west. The shad survived this trip. He put 5,000 in the Jordan River, a tributary of Great Salt Lake, where they never were seen again, and the remaining 35,000 were "deposited safely and in good order in the Sacramento River." Mission accomplished, Stone and his assistants "turned away from the river, feeling as if a load of incalculable weight had been lifted from us."

Shad apparently do not have the strong "home stream" instinct that salmon do, and by 1876 the Hudson transplants ranged from the Golden Gate north to Vancouver Island, British Columbia. In 1880, mature shad were taken from the Columbia River. In 1885, shad fry from the Chesapeake Bay also were stocked in the Columbia River drainage system, and in recent years shad have come to outnumber the runs of native chinook and sockeye salmon in the Columbia. But the story of shad in the Columbia River does not end there. Present-day Pennsylvania fishermen, long irked by the loss of the shad run on the Susquehanna River because of the construction of unpassable power dams, prevailed upon authorities to stock shad anew. In 1967, to the blare of publicity, fertilized eggs stripped from shad in the Columbia River were flown east from Portland, Oregon, and planted in the Susquehanna less than a day later. Almost a hundred years had passed since Green and Stone went west with young shad, but descendants of their Hudson River fish have come home, almost.

With shad at a low point in the Hudson, Everett Nack of Claverack, a commercial fisherman, has expanded his operations by specializing in still another species that was introduced to the Hudson. This species is the goldfish (*Carassius auratus*). A domesticated cousin of the carp, goldfish originally came from China and Japan, and they possibly got into the Hudson when garden pools overflowed or, when aquarium owners tossed them into the river or flushed them down toilets. Whatever their precise point of origin, goldfish have thrived in the river, although after two or three generations in the wild, they apparently hybridize with carp and lose their coloring. Instead of being bright red, gold, or orange, the offspring become a sere yellow. Even so there are enough goldfish being flushed down toilets or holding their own genetically so that Nack is able to seine them for sale to wholesale aquarium fish dealers. There are thousands upon thousands, if not millions, of goldfish in the Hudson, some of them the size of a catcher's mitt, and they are in demand, especially for new garden pools in burgeoning suburbia. After several years of hauling a seine for goldfish, Nack has been able to hike his price up to seventy-five cents apiece from aquarium dealers, but, he says, "I know damn well some of those dealers get as much as ten dollars a pair." On the average, Everett nets three to four thousand goldfish a year. He could obtain more; he knows where there is a great concentration in the Hudson near Castleton, but he cannot get at the goldfish by hauling a seine out into the river because wastes from the Fort Orange Paper Company are piled to such a depth that dangerous holes in the natural river bottom are covered over. He tried seining there once, but in doing so he stepped into a deceptively shallow pile of pulp wastes and almost drowned when the sludge gave way.

Nack is a true river rat, one of a handful I know. A carpenter by trade, and tall and lean, almost Lincolnesque in appearance, he spends every minute he can on the Hudson or its feeder streams. He knows where the trout are near "Fatso's Bridge" on Claverack Creek (or at least where they were until a textile mill started pouring detergent into the "crick"), and he knows a sewage-polluted marsh where "the stink in August will knock your hat off." Despite the depredations committed allegedly in the cause of "progress," Everett continues to follow the river, and if there were to be a depression tomorrow, he would make out. He nets catfish, deemed unpalatable by others, and puts them in clear water tanks in his cellar, where the fish purge themselves and become a savory dish for the table. He seines the rivers for shiners and killifish ("minnies," in his lingo), which he sells as live bait. With his four sons—fourteen, thirteen, eleven, and seven—panting after him, he digs in the marshes for snapping turtles (*Chelydra serpentina*), vicious monsters which reach up to forty and fifty pounds; these are taken home, beheaded, scrubbed, cleaned, and chopped up before being dumped into the pot. Snapping turtles have very durable nerve endings, and individual pieces of meat will squirm and jump on the kitchen counter. "Man," Everett says, "there's nothing like turtle lasagna."

For several years, Everett used to sell the smaller snapping turtles to Donald Bartholomew in Hudson for a dollar apiece. Bartholomew, a tool and die maker by profession and a student of the Iroquois by avocation, used to take the shells to a reservation near Syracuse, where the Iroquois, the majority of them Onondagas with a scattering of Mohawks, Oneidas, and Tuscaroras, would hollow them out, place cherry pits inside, and use them as ceremonial rattles. "I started doing this when they had a shortage of the right size of turtles," Bartholomew says, "and I told them that on the Hudson we had trappers, such as Everett Nack, who caught the big turtles for food, but had no use for the small ones. I obtained them, and the Indians made the rattles. Some of those Hudson River turtles have ended up in museums all over the world." A couple of years ago, Bartholomew had a mold made, and he began making snapping turtle shells of fiberglass. "It's the exact duplicate of the original," he says. "I took some out to the reservation, and the Onondagas couldn't tell the difference." The Iroquois prefer the fiberglass shells because they hold up better, and the surplus is sold at roadside stands all across the country at so-called Indian trading posts.

In the winter, Nack traps. The river marshes are alive with muskrat (*Ondatra zibethicus*) and mink (*Mustela vison*). The muskrats, "rats" in the local vernacular, are in their prime form mid-January to the beginning of April. In the early spring, it is difficult to get good skins because the rats are in a mating mood, and a male rat caught in a trap is usually set upon and bitten by his anxious fellow rats. Hudson River rats have thick pelts and heavy fur, and there are trappers who say they are the best in the country. A dealer in Poughkeepsie pays anywhere from one dollar to three dollars for a skin; the price depends on the Russian catch. Muskrats are native to North America, but at the turn of the century, several were released near Prague by one Prince Collerdo-Mannsfeld, and their descendants have since spread over most of Europe. In most European countries, muskrats are regarded as pests because they undermine dikes and railroad embankments, but the Russians trap them and often sell considerable numbers of skins to American furriers.

Whether going after muskrats or turtles, Everett has to contend with a relatively new menace to the marshes, the tangles of water chestnut plants (*Trapa natans*) that enmesh the coves and shallow waters of the mid-Hudson. Once the plant gets a start, it grows so luxuriantly that it can soon take over a bay, enclosing the water surface in a tight lattice of green and smothering more desirable plants such as wild rice. It is impossible to row a boat through the dense growth. Everett has grown so distraught at the sight of this blight that he has tried to yank the water chestnut out by hand, but this is like pulling on the end of a line extending to infinity. The only known control, and it is not satisfactory, is spraying with a herbicide, 2,4-D. If applied in the spring, the herbicide will kill off the water chestnut for that year, but other plants do not have time to germinate and grow. Besides, the nuts or seeds of the water chestnut can remain viable for ten years. The hard seed itself is a menace; it is armed with four prongs, each as sharp and as barbed as a fishhook. The seeds have rich food value, but only muskrats eat them; the hard shell and the prongs are too much for birds.* The seeds drift about the river and pile up on shore. Bathers who step on them receive a nasty wound. The barbs can penetrate the bottom of a rubber boot. "If you get stabbed with one of those chestnuts, you get an awful infection," a river man once warned me. "The prong breaks off and stays inside, and it's covered with all the germs in the river."

Like the carp, the water chestnut is an import. In all likelihood, it was planted in 1884 by a clergyman, the Reverend John Herman Wibbe, in Collins Lake near Schenectady. He apparently thought it would make an interesting addition to local flora. A mile-long outlet connects the lake with the Mohawk River and the barge canal, but for years the water chestnut stayed in the lake. In the 1920s, possibly as the result of flooding, it spread into the Mohawk, and it was so prolific that it prompted an investigation by Professor W. C. Muenscher of Cornell, an authority on aquatic plants. In a paper published in the 1934 *Biological Survey of the Mohawk-Hudson Watershed*, Professor Muenscher reported that the water chestnut occupied one thousand to twelve hundred acres in the Mohawk above Lock 6. There were no water chestnut plants in the Hudson, but there were reports of seeds found as far south as Catskill, and Professor

* According to Stanley Smith at the state museum, the introduced Chinese mystery snail has been found feeding on the water chestnut plants in the river.

Muenscher urged that measures be taken to stop the plant from spreading. Nothing was done, and the plant is now found up in Lake Champlain as well as in the mid-Hudson down to the mouth of Wappinger's Creek and in the marshes at Constitution Island across from West Point. I myself have picked up seed husks on the shore at Croton.

During the spring and fall, the Hudson Valley is a place of passage for birds. Most migratory species utilize the low-lying parts of the valley, for birds, like people, have no wish to expend energy going over mountains. An exception to this are the hawks— red-tailed (*Buteo jamaicensis*), red shouldered (*B. lineatus*), and broad-winged (*B. platypterus*) for the most part—which migrate along the Shawangunk Mountains, a ridge of sandstone and quartz conglomerate that starts just south of the Catskills. The hawks soar easily in the rising air currents above the ridge, which curves southwestward away from the Hudson to the Delaware Water Gap and thence into Pennsylvania. From there the hawks have clear flying down the main spine of the Appalachians into Alabama. There is a small airport at Wurtsboro, New York, hard by the Shawangunk ridge, and it attracts a considerable number of sailplane enthusiasts who also like to soar above the ridge. The hawks are not as frightened by a noiseless sailplane as they would be by a conventional plane, and so on a fall day it is sometimes possible for a sailplane pilot to fly among them.

Along the Hudson itself, the American golden plover (*Pluvialis dominica*), which migrates from the Arctic to the pampas of Uruguay and Argentina, is a regular fall visitor. The plover stops in marshes or along the shore to feed on small clams, shrimp, and crickets. Another long-distance traveler is the white-rumped sandpiper (*Eriola fuscicollis*), which flies from Baffin Island to as far south as the Strait of Magellan. The snow goose (*Chen hyperborea*) is a high-altitude flier above the Hudson on its trip from the Arctic to the southeastern Atlantic coast. Occasionally, one sets down on the river.

The Canada goose (*Branta canadensis*), which used to be an abundant breeder in the Hudson Valley, is making a comeback, thanks in good part to the fact that it can grow used to man and become semi-domesticated. Indeed, it is one of the easiest birds for aviculturists to keep in captivity, and escapes and releases from waterfowl collections may have added to the local population. For the past several years, Canada geese have nested in the Bronx and Pocantico rivers in Westchester County, and as the population expanded, young geese, seeking territories of their own, have gradually spread up the Hudson Valley.

One of the most beautiful waterfowl, the wood duck (*Aix sponsa*), has also made a comeback. Its very beauty and trusting nature made it almost literally a sitting duck for gunners, and by World War I, hunters had almost shot it out of existence in the United States. Its resurgence now is due largely to the work of sportsmen and aviculturists, such as the late Alain White of Litchfield, Connecticut. Wood ducks are native to North America, but when White began his work in the 1920s, they were so rare that he had to buy breeding pairs from waterfowl collections in Europe. He hired a gamekeeper from England and began raising them, and in a few years, he started releasing banded wood ducks into the wild. By 1939, more than nine thousand had been freed and they had spread to forty-four states and several Canadian provinces. Wood duck are now re-established in such numbers in New York that they may be legally hunted.

Duck hunting along the Hudson is excellent. I know of hunters who do quite well off Ossining and Croton Point; the alert railroad commuter can see the blinds offshore. The best duck hunting on the river, however, is to be had in the mid-Hudson, and the most renowned hunter of all is a friend of Everett Nack, Crissy Wilson of Stottville, who is nicknamed Mr. Duck. Now in his late sixties and retired from the insurance business, Crissy has hunted ducks and geese on the river for more than forty years. He was named Crissy because he was born on Christmas Day. Short, stocky, and red-faced, he could be one of Henry Hudson's crew.

In the fall, Crissy is on or about the Hudson every day, often in the Tivoli marshes on either side of Cruger Island. The first birds to arrive are blue-wing teal (*Anas discors*). They stay until the first heavy frost and then depart for the West Indies and Latin America. Blacks (*A. rubripes*) and mallards (*A. platyrhynchos*) take their place. There are also widgeon (*Mareca americana*) and a smattering of shovelers (*Spatula clypeata*), and later in the season greater and lesser scaup (*Aythya marila* and *A. af-*

finis), a few redheads (*A. americana*), and "a pretty good flight" of canvasbacks (*A. valisineria*). But most of all, there are great flocks of Canada geese stringing the autumn sky in waving V's. "The geese are more in abundance on the Hudson than they've ever been since I started hunting," Crissy says. In recent years, for reasons not yet understood, migrating Canadas have taken to flying down the Hudson instead of along the coast, their customary route. There are also brant (*Branta bernicla*), but they rarely land on the river. "The brant we see go straight on to Long Island," Crissy says. "If they do stop, we butcher them. They're dumber than dumb. When they take off, they bunch instead of scattering. Dumber 'n dumb."

When the river is calm, Crissy likes to hunt by "creeping," an art unique to the Hudson and practiced on the river only between Albany and Kingston. To creep, a hunter uses a creeping boat, which looks like a wide canoe from the bottom and a two-man kayak from the top. Wire mats are set in holes in the foredeck, and rushes are attached upright to the mats as camouflage. The gunner sits up front peering through the rushes, while the creeper kneels in back with a creeping paddle, which has a foot-long handle and a three-foot blade. The paddle never leaves the water; the blade is slowly turned to the side and brought forward after each stroke. "I've seen some people scull," Crissy says, "but that's not near as effective as creeping. Usually I put decoys out five or six hundred feet from shore, and then, when the ducks come in, I creep out to them. The slower you go, the better creeper you are. It's always advisable to creep against the wind. You go too fast otherwise, and besides, the ducks always face to the wind. If you creep against the wind their backs are to you. When you're out creeping, you can get up so close to the ducks you can't hardly scare 'em out! Sometimes you have to stand up and wave your arms or hit the water with the paddle to get them to fly.

"Why, the very last day of hunting last year, my son and I were creeping, and we saw these two geese. I was shooting, and my son was creeping. He's a better creeper than I am. My knees ain't for kneeling any more. Anyway, we saw these two geese, and we started to creep. We got so close, I says, 'No point in getting any closer.' We raised up, and the geese jumped, one Canadian, other a snow. You can't shoot the snow. I waited until they separated, and I killed the Canadian."

Most of the ducks Crissy gets are blacks, while wood ducks are second in his bag. To foster wood duck breeding, he has put up nesting boxes on poles in the marshes and in old trees in the woods along the river. "The migration of ducks and geese is as great as it was twenty-five or thirty years ago along the Hudson," Crissy says, "but the ducks don't stay as long. You get 'em for one or two days, but then they're gone. My contention is that the biggest factor is the water chestnut. The wild rice, the wild celery, the wild oats, the duck potatoes, they're going or they're gone with the spread of the water chestnut."

All Crissy asks is a day on the river; he need not get his limit. Once we were sitting and talking, and Crissy hunched forward in his chair and said, "One year I went down to lower Tivoli Bay, where I had a blind. I was in the blind, just sitting and waiting, and there came fourteen geese. Oh, oh, I said to myself, we're going to be doing some business. So these came down and circled and lit right in front of my decoys. Only they weren't geese—they were whistling swans. They sat for an hour, and I didn't do a thing to move them. I just sat there still and watched. They just played around, stretched their necks around. Oh, my God! If they'd stayed there all day, I wouldn't have cared!"

7

THE HIGHLANDS

South of Newburgh, the river narrows, and the Hudson Highlands rear up against the sky. For a distance of fifteen miles, mountains line both banks of the river. Mountains may seem a strong word, but the hills of the Highlands, rising straight up from riverside, are truly majestic. Here the land immediately along the river is at its highest. Storm King, at the northern entrance, has an elevation of thirteen hundred feet, and there are peaks that go higher. Here, also, the Hudson is at its deepest. At World's End, the often turbulent bend in the river between West Point and Constitution Island, the mud bottom is 216 feet down. Engineers who worked on the Catskill Aqueduct did not encounter solid rock until a depth of almost eight hundred feet. The intermediate depths are composed of silt, sand, clay, and glacial rubble deposited in ages past.

Geologically, the Highlands vie with the Adirondacks in age. The rock formations include ancient Grenville sediments, which are also found in the Adirondacks and date back a billion years, and what is known as Storm King granite, which is six hundred million years old. Ordinarily, granite bespeaks solidity, but this is not the case with the granite in the vicinity of Storm King. Engineers who drilled the shaft and the tunnel 1,114 feet below the surface of the Hudson for the Catskill Aqueduct in 1914 ran into "popping rock" in the granite. The excavating placed a strain on the rock, and granite slabs broke off the walls with a distinct popping sound. The flying rock injured a number of workmen, and timber props had to be used. After the timber proved unsatisfactory a permanent steel support was installed. Still this did not solve the full problem. When water was run into the aqueduct, rock gave way again, this time in the downward shaft. Leaks sprang up, and to correct this, engineers had to drill a new shaft.

Without question, the Highlands comprise the most beautiful stretch of the Hudson. The mountain ramparts on both shores are heavily forested and, for the most part, protected against abuse. The Palisades Interstate Park system and the U. S. Military Reservation at West Point are on the west shore, as is Black Rock Forest, a thirty-six-hundred-acre experimental station in silviculture given to Harvard University in 1950 by the late Dr. Ernest Stillman of Cornwall. The Appalachian Trail, which runs from Maine to Georgia, passes through the Highlands, linked by the Bear Mountain Bridge the lowest point on the trail. On the east shore are the picturesque settlements of Cold Spring and Garrison, surrounded by large estates. There are even several castles: Bannerman's on Pollopel Island, and the Osborn and Dix castles near Garrison.

Ecologically, the Highlands can be likened to the heart of the Hudson Valley, serving as the major divide between northern and southern plants and animals. Among the northern plants are glacial relics: tundra bog moss (*Sphagnum squarrosum*), and subarctic black spruce (*Picea mariana*). The striped maple(*Acer pennsylvanicum*), not common further south, grows in the Highlands, while below Iona Island are southern arrowwood (*Viburnum dentatum*) and oblong fruited pinweed (*Lechea racemulosa*). Even though the forests of the Highlands were cut repeatedly in earlier days, studies at Black Rock show that the native forest composition, dominated by oak and hickory, has remained stable and resistant to invasion by foreign species. This is particularly true on the ridges, where the native trees are not only able to grow in the thin soil, but can withstand the ravages of periodic drought, such as those which occurred in the late 1940s and early 1960s. So far, exotic plants have not been able to adjust to the prevailing conditions, and as a result the higher elevations of the Highlands, at least in the Black Rock Forest, probably come as close as any area in the Hudson Valley today toward duplicating the woodlands the Dutch originally saw.

The higher elevations also offer habitats suitable for northern birds, such as the Blackburnian warbler (*Dendroica fusca*) and the brown creeper (*Certhia familiaris*), that are rare elsewhere along the lower Hudson. Conversely, the Highlands sometimes act as the northern boundary for southern birds, such as the fish crow (*Corvus ossifragus*). In recent years, there has been a most marked and interesting extension of range by southern birds. Besides the fish crow, the list includes the cardinal (*Richmondena cardinalis*), the mockingbird (*Mimus polyglottos*), the blue-gray gnatcatcher (*Polioptila caerulea*), and the tufted titmouse (*Parus bicolor*). All have established themselves the year round, and several have now gotten past or through the Highlands. The titmouse, for instance, has reached Newburgh, while further upriver the blue-gray gnatcatcher nests on Cruger Island. Another bird working its way north up the Hudson is the turkey vulture (*Cathartes aura*). Until the mid-1930s, it was a rare stray from the south; now it is common in the Highlands in back of Bear Mountain. A gradual warming trend in recent years probably has prompted the northward movement of southern birds, but in the case of the turkey vulture it also has been suggested that a couple of other factors have played a part: the resurgence of the deer population, which has periodically, resulted in overpopulation and consequent death by disease and starvation, and the presence of so many small animal carcasses on new highways. At any rate, during the summer, thirty to forty turkey vultures roost near West Mountain, doubtless keeping keen, beady eyes out for carrion on the Palisades Interstate Parkway below. Certainly, high-speed auto traffic on the Parkway and the Thruway, which parallels the Hudson from Nyack to Albany, supplies an abundance of dead creatures. The case might well be made that super-highways now rival the Hudson as an avenue of travel for birds and mammals seeking new territory. Ed Reilly has observed racoons (*Procyon lotor lotor*) and red and gray foxes (*Vulpes fulva fulva* and *Urocyon cinereoargenteus cinereoargenteus*) moving along parkways in southern Westchester, some apparently heading toward New York City. He was once intrigued to see a muskrat on Pinehurst Avenue, south of the Cloisters in northern Manhattan, emerge from one street drain and vanish into another. A couple of years ago, there was a hullabaloo when a black bear was seen foraging at the Rockland County dump south of the Highlands on the west shore of the Hudson. If reports by motorists are to be believed, the bear probably came down from the Catskills via the Thruway. The construction of the Thruway has prompted an inland invasion of salt-marsh plants. For instance, alkali grass (*Puccinilla distans*) and sand spurry (*Spergularia media*) are now found as far west as Buffalo. The salt put on the icy road in winter washes off into drainage ditches, providing the soil conditions these plants require.

A couple of birds appear to have outflanked the Highlands. The evening grosbeak (*Hesperiphona vespertina*) has come in from northwestern North America. Before 1890, it was unknown in New York. One was seen in 1911, and until the late 1940s there were only scattered sightings in the winter. Then the species suddenly increased, and by the early 1960s the evening grosbeak began breeding in the Hudson Valley. Several authorities have suggested that the bird was lured east by the planting of box elder trees in the Middle West and New England. The evening grosbeak has a marked fondness for the seeds of this tree, and almost continuous plantings of box elders across country set up a feeding route. In the Hudson Valley, the evening grosbeak is attracted to backyard bird feeders. "It is the world's best sunflower seed opener," says Ed Reilly. "I know of a woman who used up five hundred pounds of sunflower seeds feeding evening grosbeaks one winter."

The cerulean warbler (*Dendroica cerulea*) is another southern bird found along the Hudson. In *Birds of the New York Area*, John Bull of the American Museum of Natural History writes that "the most active observer is fortunate if he sees one or two in ten years" away from its breeding ground. In 1922, an isolated population of cerulean warblers was discovered breeding in Dutchess

County, "chiefly along wooded streams flowing into the Hudson River." At present, the warblers nest on Cruger Island. According to Bull, the warblers came not from the south up through the Highlands but from the west, "perhaps by way of the Delaware and Susquehanna valleys."

The gradual warming trend probably has caused a couple of amphibians, Fowler's toad (*Bufo terrestris americanus*) and the northern cricket frog (*Acris gryllus crepitans*), to invade the Hudson Valley. The northern cricket frog was unknown on the east bank of the Hudson until 1962, when it was discovered in Croton-on-Hudson. One southern mammal that has established itself in the river valley is the opposum (*Didelphis marsupialis virginiana*), which moved into the Highlands at least one hundred years ago.

Over the years, the Highlands have been a prime collecting ground for naturalists. The late Raymond Ditmars used to gather snakes in the region. Copperheads (*Ancistrodon contortrix mokeson*) still are common; they can be found in the Fahnestock State Park in Putnam County. The timber rattlesnake (*Crotalus horridus horridus*), which used to be abundant in the Peekskill area in the nineteenth century, is rare, though one was seen several years ago in Shrub Oak in northern Westchester, and they are sometimes seen back of Bear Mountain. As a boy, Theodore Roosevelt stayed with the Osborns in Garrison and collected amphibians. On one occasion, his pockets bulging with specimens, he tipped his hat to Secretary of State and Mrs. Hamilton Fish, whereupon a frog leaped off the top of his head.

One of the finest natural history surveys ever made of a region in the United States was that done of the Highlands by Dr. Edgar A. Mearns, a Highland Falls physician who became an Army surgeon. Dr. Mearns' report on the birds of the Highlands appeared in seven parts in the *Bulletin of the Essex Institute* from 1878 to 1881, and his report on other vertebrates, with observations on the mollusca, crustacea, lepidoptera, and flora, was published in the *Bulletin, American Museum of Natural History*, in 1898. Except for some confusion about the sturgeon, his notes on the fishes of the Hudson are remarkably well done. I have used them to track down certain species which I originally had no idea were in the river. With one or two minor exceptions, all the spe-

Lake Tear and the peak of Mount Marcy

The upper Hudson in the wild Adirondacks

The old queen of the river, the Mary Powell

Logs at the Big Boom at Glens Falls, 1900

ELGIN CIAMPI

Pattern of detergent pollution, Claverack Creek

The Penn Central oil pipe at Croton-on-Hudson

ROBERT HOEBERMANN

Con Edison's nuclear power nest at Indian Point

Typical despoliation of lush river marshland

Dead stripers at the Con Ed dump

Crissy Wilson and son "creeping" for ducks and geese

Everett Nack of Claverack with some of the goldfish he seines from the Hudson

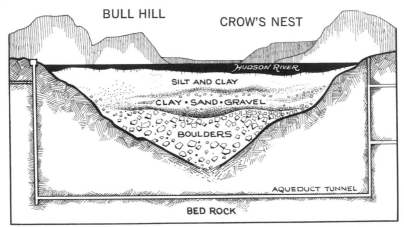

BREAKNECK MT.
STORM KING MT.
BULL HILL
CROW'S NEST

HUDSON RIVER

SILT AND CLAY
CLAY · SAND · GRAVEL
BOULDERS

AQUEDUCT TUNNEL

BED ROCK

Cross-section of the Hudson, looking south from the Highlands

Aerial view of the Highlands, looking north from West Point

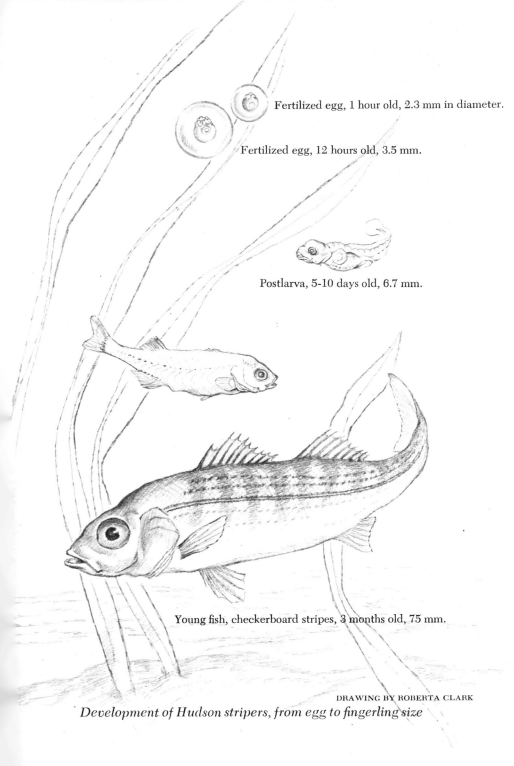

Fertilized egg, 1 hour old, 2.3 mm in diameter.

Fertilized egg, 12 hours old, 3.5 mm.

Postlarva, 5-10 days old, 6.7 mm.

Young fish, checkerboard stripes, 3 months old, 75 mm.

DRAWING BY ROBERTA CLARK

Development of Hudson stripers, from egg to fingerling size

Thirty-pound female striper netted during spawning run

*Ace Lent of Verplanck
with a female Atlantic
sea sturgeon that had
been struck by a ship*

Future caviar, eggs inside a shortnosed sturgeon

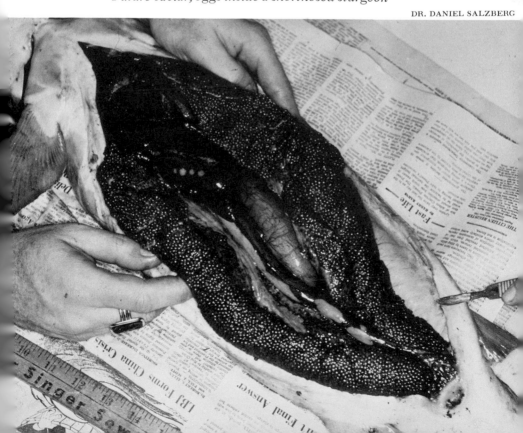

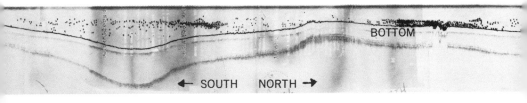

SURFACE

BOTTOM

← SOUTH   NORTH →

HOLE AT STONY POINT   CROSS SECTION OF HUDSON

ROBERT HOEBERMANN

Ace Lent, Charlie White, and Spitz Lent with roe shad taken near Verplanck

MAIN CHANNEL, VICINITY OF INDIAN POINT

JONES POINT, END OF VOYAGE NORTH ON FLOOD TIDE

Sonar readings of dense schools of striped bass and sturgeon wintering on the bottom near Stony Point

ELGIN CIAMPI

Mothballed ships off Dunderberg Mountain

The tributary Croton during low water in the fall

The Hudson meeting the Atlantic at New York Harbor

Finn Magnus with lancetfish he took during one of his offshore trips to the Hudson Canyon

cies Mearns found in the Hudson in the late nineteenth century are there now. The only quarrel I have with the doctor is over some of his collecting techniques. For instance, of the blue-black herring, he wrote: "When dozens of them are leaping out of the water it is not difficult to kill them with a shotgun."

Curiously enough, some of the mammals seem to have experienced violent ups and downs. This is the case with the white-tailed deer (*Odocoileus virginianus*) not only in the Highlands but along the length of the Hudson Valley to the Adirondacks. Until about the middle of the nineteenth century, deer were common in the valley. In fact, until the 1840s, deer were so numerous in the western Highlands that they were shot for the New York market. Then the deer population began to decline as the result of heavy hunting pressure. Moreover, survivors were unable to find browse or places to hide because forests were clear-cut as land was intensively developed for farming.

In 1861, the last deer in Ossining was shot. They were not long in leaving the Highlands and the rest of the river valley. In 1898, Dr. Mearns wrote: "The 'Middletown Journal,' issue of January 13, 1878, contains the notice of the capture of a deer, near Middletown, in Orange County, New York. This record brings the species within limits of the Hudson Highlands, and is the only authentic one that I know of; but I am informed that deer are still occasionally found in the extreme northwest corner of Orange County."

In 1880, farm acreage in New York State reached its point of greatest expansion, and in succeeding years land began to revert to second growth. With browse and cover now available, deer slowly began to return. On the east bank of the Hudson, the deer apparently came down from the Berkshires in New England. According to a study by C. W. Severinghaus and C. P. Brown, game research investigators with the state conservation department, a small deer population survived in the Berkshires during the 1870s, and as conditions improved, they multiplied and spread. At the turn of the century, a few deer appeared in the Hudson Valley, and the hunting season was gradually closed to protect them. This happened first in Putnam County, in the Highlands, in 1902; in Rensselaer County in 1903; in Dutchess and Columbia in 1904; and in Westchester in 1905. On the western shore of the river, the deer came from small herds that had persisted near the Pennsylvania state line and in the Catskills. Today, deer are common throughout most of the Hudson Valley. They are again in the Ossining area, and on the other side of the river, in Orange and Rockland counties, they have become abundant at times. Doubtless there has been some exchange between the deer populations on both shores. In September of 1965, my wife and I were out in our boat when we saw in the distance what looked like two seagulls sitting on a log. We went to see what it was, and it turned out to be a six-point buck swimming across the widest part of Haverstraw Bay, from Oscawana to Haverstraw, nearly four miles away. I thought this was unusual, but when I started to tell a commercial fisherman about it, he cut me short, saying that he often saw deer swimming the river, especially during the hunting season.

The gray squirrel (*Scirius carolinensis*) frequently swims across the Hudson. In the fall of 1968, there was a noticeable movement of squirrels across the river in both directions, and many were drowned. The previous year had been very productive for acorns and had prompted a bumper crop of baby squirrels. But acorns were in short supply in 1968, and a good many squirrels were forced to find new feeding grounds.

The Hudson itself as it flows through the Highlands is of great interest. The Highlands stretch of the river is fresh or brackish, depending upon the volume of downstream flow. In the spring, it is fresh, and at that time of year, it serves as a spawning ground for striped bass. Of all the fishes along the Atlantic Coast, none excites more passion on the part of anglers than the often-elusive, always unpredictable striped bass. In fact, the striper is the number one gamefish, the glamor fish of the East Coast. There are anglers who will sacrifice their jobs, their marriage, and even their sacred honor to fish for stripers. The intensity of interest is such that sport fishing for stripers amounts to a major industry on the Atlantic Coast. In 1960, the United States Bureau of Sport Fisheries and Wildlife, working in conjunction with the Bureau of the Census, estimated that anglers seeking stripers spent forty-five million dollars a year on the northeast coast alone. Numerous coastal communities derive considerable income during the summer from visiting striper fishermen, and in Maine the digging and shipping of bloodworms and sandworms, favorite baits for bass, has become a large marine industry in the state, with an annual revenue to worm diggers of more than one million dollars. There are more than four hundred charter boats in Connecticut, New York, and New Jersey waters, and they carry an estimated eighty thousand passengers a year, most of them striped bass fanatics. There are several hundred thousand surf casters on the coast, who will spend hour after hour, day after day, month after month, and (I suspect) year after year flailing away with plugs and spoons in the hopes of taking a bass. But for all this expenditure of time, effort, and money by a great many people, only a relative handful of anglers, perhaps fifty at best, regularly take advantage of the striper fishing that is to be had in the Hudson. For eight or nine months of the year, the tidal Hudson has an abundance of bass that is all but untouched. Of the estimated seventeen million stripers in the river, perhaps five million are sexually mature bass that migrate to the coast during the summer and the remaining twelve million juveniles that usually spend their first two years of life in the Hudson. In sum, there are so many stripers in the river that some commercial fishermen after other quarry refer to the bass in genuine exasperation as "trash fish."

The striper is intriguing to biologists as well as sportsmen. In terms of evolutionary development, the striped bass seems to be a fresh water species on its way to becoming a salt water fish. Twenty thousand years ago, when the last glacier still covered the Hudson Valley, striped bass probably were confined to rivers in the southeastern U. S. and the Gulf of Mexico, and the stripers found in the Hudson now may be descendants of some bass that moved up the coast after finding salt water to their liking. On the Gulf Coast, the stripers live in rivers in Louisiana, Alabama, and western Florida. On the Atlantic Coast, the striped bass is also a river fish in northern Florida, Georgia, and South Carolina. In the last state, there is a celebrated landlocked population in the Santee-Cooper Reservoir. In North Carolina, stripers from the Roanoke River appear to migrate to brackish Albemarle Sound but rarely to sea, and then not very far north. The urge to migrate to salt water in substantial numbers starts with striped bass originating in the Chesapeake Bay system. After spawning in fresh water, these fish move out along the coast, and the same holds true for stripers from the Delaware and Hudson rivers. So far as is known, striped bass do not spawn regularly in any New England rivers. This sometimes comes as a surprise to New Englanders, who often seem to take as much pride in their bass fishing as they do in being called Yankees, but the fish which they have in the summer are migrants from Chesapeake Bay and the Delaware and Hudson rivers. Historically, the striped bass has played an important role in the economy of New England. Indeed, the first public school in the New World was financed, at least in part, from the sale of stripers; in 1670, the Plymouth Colony decreed that the profits of the bass, mackerel, and herring fisheries at Cape Cod were to be used to found a free school. Curiously, there apparently are isolated spawning populations of striped bass in rivers in eastern Canada, notably in the St. John in New Brunswick. The striped bass on the Pacific Coast are transplants from the East Coast, and in all likelihood, the fish now so abundant in California and Oregon waters are, as in the case of the shad, descendants of Hudson River stock. In 1879 and 1882, 435 small stripers were taken from the Shrewsbury and Navesink rivers in northern New Jersey and planted in San Francisco Bay, where they grew and multiplied exceedingly well. Inasmuch as the Hudson is by far the nearest spawning river to the Shewsbury and Navesink, which in reality are tidal inlets rather than rivers, the fish taken there were probably youngsters that had come down from the Hudson. In California, as in the East, the striped bass is the number one saltwater gamefish, and the fanaticism is such that one enthusiast, Leon D. Adams, author of *Striped Bass Fishing in California and Oregon*, once ran thousands of punch cards, noting tides, weather conditions, localities, and other factors, through an IBM machine in an effort to pin down the best fishing.

To icthyologists, the striper is something of a puzzle. For years the fish bore the scientific name of *Roccus lineatus*. *Roccus* is Latin doggerel for "rocks," while *lineatus* refers to the characteristic stripes. Then, in the 1930s, the name was changed to *Roccus saxatilis* because *Roccus lineatus* was the name for a different fish in the Mediterranean. *Saxatilis* means "found among rocks." In 1967, after exhaustive research conducted by P. J. P. Whitehead and A. C. Wheeler at the British Museum, the striped bass and kindred fish, such as the white perch, were taken out of the genus *Roccus* and placed in the genus *Morone*, which, it develops, was the name originally used before *Roccus* and therefore has priority under the rules of nomenclature. So the striped bass is now known scientifically as *Morone saxatilis*, even though no one knows what *Morone* means. The change has been approved by the Committee on the Names of Fishes, composed of members of the American Fisheries Society and the American Society of Icthyologists and Herpetologists, and any striper nut who feels aggrieved at losing the good solid name of *Roccus* and wishes it retained in preference to the undistinguished, mushy, even moronic *Morone* must write an elaborate brief for presentation to the International Commission on Zoological Nomenclature. In this age of digit dialing and zip codes, I briefly felt moved to do so, but I was advised by Dr. C. Lavett Smith of the American Museum of Natural History that I did not have a prayer. Nonetheless, I am pleased to see that a number of biologists have felt outraged by the dropping of *Roccus* for *Morone*, and one of them, Miss Susan Smith (no kin to C. Lavett Smith) of the U.S. Bureau of Sport Fisheries and Wildlife Laboratory at Sandy Hook, New Jersey, wrote a poem "Taxonomic Tragedy," which goes:

> Oh, *Roccus saxatilis* is a name we'll surely miss.
> The culprit is, I'm sad to say, a taxonomic twist.
> You see the striped bass used to be
> *Morone saxatilis,*
> And now they've changed it back again—
> At least that's what they tell us.
>
> Yes, *Morone's* now the genus name
> I never figured why,
> But when that old name *Roccus* goes
> I'm sure I'm going to cry.
> Why, *Roccus* cracks right off the tongue!—
> Like speed and strength and size!
> While *Morone* kind of rolls around
> Then gives a sigh and dies.

For sure a proud and fighting fish,
I think it's quite a shame
That now he'll have to swim through life
With such a silly name.

Fiddling around with the reclassification of the striped bass has not been confined to the name of the genus. According to C. Lavett Smith, or Smitty as he is known, Dr. William A. Gosline of the University of Hawaii has been busy on the family level. For years, the striped bass and other members of the *Morone* and/or *Roccus* genus had been placed in the sea bass family, the Serranidae. Now, however, Gosline, with Smitty's support, has removed the striper and the rest of the *Morone* genus from the family Serranidae and placed them in the Percichthyidae, a hitherto obscure family that had contained only one genus, *Percichthys*, a Southern American fresh-water fish. Smitty reasons that the striper and other *Morone* fish were misplaced in the Serranidae because (1) they are not hermaphroditic, as sea basses are, and (2), they have only two spurs, not three, on the opercular bone near the gill. "Normally we would laugh at such things," Smitty says, "but the change makes sense."

Fishery biologists generally agree that the Chesapeake system is the leading supplier of stripers to the Atlantic coastal run during the warmer months, but the Hudson appears to play an important role, contributing perhaps from 10 to 20 per cent of the run. For years biologists were aware that striped bass spawned in the Hudson—after all, large numbers of baby stripers were present in the river—but until the 1950s no one knew where the spawning took place. Historically, New York State had (and has) done little in the way of studies on the resources of the Hudson, and, besides, collecting striper eggs presented certain difficulties. From what is known of striper spawning elsewhere, the eggs are broadcast into the water by a female and fertilized by anywhere from a dozen to fifty thrashing males. The fertilized eggs then drift with the tides and current. An eighth of an inch in diameter, the eggs are semi-bouyant, and moving water is necessary for their survival. The eggs whirl up and down in the river, like snowflakes in a blizzard, and they can be found just below the surface, at mid-depth or toward the bottom. Should they sink to the bottom and stay there, however, they will die; they must be free-floating. Incubation takes about two days in water with a temperature of 65° F. and three days at 58° F. The parent fish have no interest whatsoever in the eggs, which are literally at the mercy of the river. Perhaps because of this lack of parental concern, a female striped bass produces an enormous number of eggs. A ten-pounder carries about a million eggs, a fifty-pounder almost five million, and estimates are that a seventy-five-pounder would produce ten million in a single spawning season. The larger fish—from thirty pounds upwards—that anglers catch are dubbed bulls; in actuality the big fish are mostly cows. The females live longer and grow to a much greater size than the males.

After the eggs hatch, the young enter the larval stage. Like the eggs, larvae are about an eighth of an inch long; they are all but helpless as they are shifted about by tides and currents. They nourish themselves through a yolk sac. By the time the young bass are three to four weeks old, they are shaped like the adult fish and are silver in color. When two or three inches long, they have checkerboard sides; when they reach a length of four or five inches they assume the characteristic horizontal stripes of the adult.

Young striped bass range over most of the tidal Hudson, but many apparently come downriver to Haverstraw Bay and the Tappan Zee. They are omnivorous feeders; their principal foods are small crustaceans, such as *Latona, Cyclops,* and *Eurytemora;* small shrimp (*Gammarus* and *Palaemonetes*); insect larvae, especially those of midges; smaller fishes; and mud crabs. I have seen crabs lined up like a roll of Lifesavers in the stomachs of young bass. Most stripers probably stay in the river until they are two years old and ten inches long. Then they may begin to school and migrate to the coast in the summer.

I know of no fish with the charm of baby striped bass, and every July I go down to Senasqua Park in Croton to seine a dozen or so from the May-June spawning for my aquarium. Sometimes I catch them on tiny barbless flies, red and white-feathered streamers. One day at Senasqua, I helped two Maine biologists start to collect five thousand baby stripers in the river. As I have noted above, there is no known striper spawning in New England rivers, and Maine, which has suffered almost absolute loss of its Atlantic salmon runs from pollution and dams, would dearly love to establish striped bass. The Maine biologists needed the stripers for laboratory tests—maybe, for example, it is too cold for juvenile stripers to feed in Down East rivers—and after I showed them where the baby stripers were at Senasqua, I left them counting, "384, 385, 386 . . ." These bass were about an inch long. In my aquarium tank youngsters of this size are a constant delight. They are fast, alert, and exceedingly greedy. In personality, they are somewhat like Labrador pups, gamboling all over the tank to investigate whatever arouses their curiosity. When I drop in an earthworm that is too large for them to eat, they race over, pull up short, and then turn and flee. In a moment they are back again, and this time one may grab an end of the worm and swim off with his enormous prize as the others excitedly follow, nipping at the other end. Given a worm small enough to eat, a striper will pounce upon it at once and draw it inside its mouth much in the manner of a six-year-old boy sucking in a strand of spaghetti. It is all swiftly and deftly done, with none of the smash-and-grab tactics of the brutish largemouth bass.

In the course of this century, the numbers of striped bass have fluctuated widely. The number of fish may decrease over a period of years and then suddenly boom upward. In some years, stripers will inexplicably spawn an enormous brood, producing what biologists call a "dominant year-class." For instance, stripers were in low numbers in the Chesapeake Bay system in the early 1930s, but then there were very successful hatches in 1934, 1940, and 1942. In 1968, there apparently was a very successful hatch of stripers in the Hudson. I have never seen so many baby striped bass in my life as I did in September and October of that year. Small stripers were almost everywhere. On several days, I counted at least three thousand of them ranged in rows on the submerged concrete boat launch at Senasqua.

So far, no one has been able to pinpoint the exact reasons why a dominant-year class occurs. The biological, chemical, and physical conditions involved are very complex. In 1961, the late Dr. Romeo J. Mansueti of the Chesapeake Biological Laboratory published a most interesting paper, "Effects of Civilization on Striped Bass and other Estuarine Biota in Chesapeake Bay and Tributaries," in which he offered the hypothesis that "civilization and striped bass are compatible." He suggested that the man-made loads of silt, wastes, and fertilizers which empty into estuaries may be beneficial to the spawning of striped bass. Estuarine waters laden with excessive sedimentation, high turbidity, low light penetration, and the like may cause poor spawning for species which lay eggs on the bottom, but these conditions might be very favorable for stripers which produce eggs and larvae which float at or near the surface. In brief, Mansueti wrote, "increasing fertilization from artificial and natural sources brought down to the estuary by run-off and freshets may be directly responsible for the dominant year-classes." However, he was careful to warn, "It must be emphasized that at this time fertilization is uncontrolled and unpredictable, and that it can have deleterious as well as beneficial effects on striped bass."

In the early 1950s, the Atlantic States Marine Fisheries Commission, a gathering of state conservation commissions, sponsored a study of striped bass along the East Coast. The study was directed by Dr. Edward C. Raney of Cornell University, an outstanding expert on the striper. As part of the study the New York State Conservation Department assigned two young biologists, Warren F. Rathjen and Lewis C. Miller, to find the striper spawning grounds in the Hudson. Rathjen and Miller spent the summer and early fall of 1954 exploring the river for juvenile stripers and the spring of 1955 collecting eggs and larvae. In 1955, they worked ninety miles of the Hudson from Yonkers to Coxsackie, and they discovered that the stripers spawned in the river from mid-May to mid-June. All told, Rathjen and Miller collected a total of 71 eggs, with the great majority of them, 88.8 per cent, concentrated in a seven and a half mile stretch between Highland Falls in the Highlands and Denning Point just to the north. Rathjen and Miller had more luck collecting larval and young stripers, gathering a total of 583, a significant number of them in the Highlands portion of the river. After studying all data collected, the two biologists concluded,

> Collections made during 1955 reveal the spawning area of the striped bass to include a section of the Hudson River from Bear Mountain upstream to a point near Kingston. On the basis of these collections, the principal spawning area

was found to be centered in the vicinity of the United States
Military Academy at West Point. . . . a large percentage
of the total spawning occurred within a relatively short seg-
ment of the river. This location is characterized by strong
current, deep water, and rocky banks. Surface salinity here
was in all cases one part per thousand or less. By contrast the
river below Bear Mountain . . . becomes much wider and is
subjected to higher salinity.

The findings concerning the relationship of brackish water
to striped bass spawning are in close agreement with those of
studies made in Virginia . . . and . . . for rivers tributary
to Chesapeake Bay.

Rathjen and Miller published their findings in the January,
1957, issue of the *New York Fish and Game Journal,* and there it
lay in obscurity until the fight began to stop the Consolidated
Edison Company from building a mammoth power plant at
Storm King, just above West Point, a subject I will deal with
presently.

After spawning in the river, most of the sexually spent striped
bass move down the Hudson and disperse along the coast. Back
in the 1950s, Dr. Raney studied returns of bass tagged in Long
Island Sound, and found that most of the "school" stripers
(fish weighing from three to ten pounds) that were caught in
the western quarter of the Sound came from the Hudson. Raney
also did another interesting study. He and a colleague, Donald
P. de Sylva, published a paper on racial investigations of striped
bass, and in it they concluded that stripers from the Hudson
were racially distinct from those in the Chesapeake and Delaware systems. In other words, the Hudson stripers were of a
separate "race." Raney and de Sylva noted that when they added
up the total number of soft rays in the dorsal, the anal, and both
pectoral fins, stripers from the Hudson generally had fewer
than those from the Chesapeake or Delaware. Specifically, stripers from the Hudson were found to have a total of less than fifty-
five soft fin rays, while the Chesapeake and Delaware fish had
fifty-six or more. There are some icthyologists who do not hold
with all this, on the grounds that water temperature at the time
of larval development and not genetics may account for differ-

ences. In the late 1950s, Walter S. Murawski, a student of Dr. Raney, made a comparative study of different striped bass populations along the Atlantic and Gulf Coast. He counted the number of scales on the lateral line that runs from the gill to the tail on each fish. He examined hundreds of specimens and concluded that the Hudson River stripers were distinct from other populations. In general, they had fewer scales on the lateral line than stripers from more southerly systems. Murawski, who is now a biologist for the New Jersey Division of Fish and Game, concedes that environmental factors may play a role in determining the number of body parts, but he believes the differences between stripers from the Hudson and other areas are genetically fixed. Interestingly, Murawski examined some California striped bass and found no difference in lateral line scale counts between them and Hudson River fish.

John R. Clark, assistant director of the Bureau of Sport Fisheries lab at Sandy Hook has developed the most recent information of significance on Hudson River stripers. In a paper in the October, 1968, issue of the *Transactions of the American Fisheries Society,* he analyzed returns from a tagging program conducted from 1959 to 1963 by Don Manns of Flushing, New York, and fellow members of the Long Island League of Salt Water Sportsmen. During those years, League members, fishing from Maryland to Canada, caught, tagged, and released 6,679 stripers. Some members did yeoman work. Jim Maffucci of Ozone Park, New York, released more than two hundred bass in 1960 alone, including a thirty-two-pound fish. Out of all the tagged fish, a total of 498 were later recaptured, many in the Hudson, and according to Clark's analysis of the recaptures, the Hudson serves the spawning river for at least three different striper populations, or "contingents," as he calls them.

First of all, there is what Clark calls the Hudson-West Sound contingent, obviously the stripers identified earlier by Raney. From what I have learned from Clark's paper and other sources, these stripers pass the summer months in the western half of Long Island Sound, rarely traveling east of the Connecticut River. In September, they begin to leave the Sound and enter the East River, and early in October they swim up the Harlem River past Spuyten Duyvil to the Hudson. From what I have been able to gather from personal experience, these fish spend most of October in the lower Hudson, probably between Riverdale and Tarrytown. They do not go north of Croton Point in this period. Then sometime in the first week of November they move up past Croton Point into Haverstraw Bay. If one keeps a careful watch on the Hudson, it is almost possible to set a watch by them in the fall. That is a dangerously flat statement for me to make, given the unpredictability of stripers, but I think this is true as a general rule in the Hudson. For instance, every fall Henry Gourdine, a commercial fisherman in Ossining, sets his nets in Haverstraw Bay. On November 7, 1967, he caught a twenty-one-inch "school" striper that bore American Littoral Society tag Number 06739. Gourdine gave me the tag, and I mailed it to the ALS in Highlands, New Jersey. Graham Macmillan, who is in charge of the tagging program, wrote back that the striper had been caught, tagged, and released by one R. Berger at Stratford, Connecticut, on June 9, 1967, when it was fifteen inches long. This fish was in Gourdine's first sizeable catch of the fall. "I usually don't start getting stripers until the first week in November," Gourdine said. "The year before, 1966, they arrived on November 9." In 1968, the striped bass entered Haverstraw Bay on November 11. One of the fish caught in a net, a six-pounder, had a large yellow plug in its mouth.

The Long Island Sound fish winter in the Hudson, and after spawning in the spring they go down the Hudson, out the Harlem and East rivers, and into the Sound.

A second population of striped bass discerned by Clark, the Hudson Estuary contingent, adheres to approximately the same timetable. These stripers pass the summer on the south shore of Long Island, moving, by my records, possibly as far east as Westhampton Beach, and on the Jersey shore down to Barnegat Bay. Sometime in September or October, they move up through the Narrows into New York harbor to spend the winter in the Hudson. For instance, on December 6, 1967, I was out on Haverstraw Bay in my boat when I saw a commercial fisherman, Ace Lent, hauling. He had caught a number of "trash fish" while netting for sturgeon, and as he was tossing the stripers back into the river, he shouted, "Here's one of those goddamn fish with a tag in it!" He passed me a twenty-inch striper, I looked at the tag, a piece

of yellow plastic tubing, and read the message printed on it:
RETURN LITTORAL SOCIETY, HIGHLANDS N.J. 07951. The fish was in
good condition, so I put it back in the river with the tag in place.
Back home, I wrote to Macmillan, and this time he answered that
striper 07951 had been caught, tagged, and released by Dick
Koyama on October 20, 1967, at Coney Island.

After wintering in the Hudson, the Hudson Estuary fish spawn
in the river and then move down through the harbor for yet another summer off the south shore of Long Island and north Jersey. So far as can be determined from tagging, the Hudson Estuary and Long Island Sound fish never mix on their summer runs.
They may mingle when wintering in the river, but when summer
comes the stripers from each contingent go their separate ways.

According to Ace Lent and Henry Gourdine, there are great
concentrations of striped bass during the winter on the flats on
the east shore of Haverstraw Bay. The depth here is only ten to
twelve feet. It is illegal in New York to net striped bass from December into March, but when netting was legal in the 1940s,
Gourdine used to lower nets through fissures sawn in the ice
about a half mile off Croton, in a direct line with the red-tiled
roof of a house on the Albany Post Road, the old Starbuck place.

These contingents of striped bass apparently have good reason
to winter in the Hudson. If they stayed on the coast, they might
die. Coastal water is highly saline, and it does not freeze until the
temperature is 28°F. But striped bass will die at 30.5° because ice
crystals form in their blood. In order to escape death in Sandy
Hook Bay or Jamaica Bay or other shallow inlets, they must move
up into the lower Hudson, where the brackish water freezes at
31°. Here the bass are safe, even though they may be only half a
degree away from death under the winter ice cover on the river.

On March 6 and 7, 1968, just after the winter ice had broken
up, John Clark brought the Sandy Hook lab research vessel *Dolphin* up the Hudson for an exploratory cruise of Haverstraw Bay.
Clark hoped to find wintering populations of striped bass in this
stretch of the river, and inasmuch as the 107-foot-long *Dolphin*, a
converted seagoing tug, drew too much water to go over the east
shore flats, the vessel had to work the forty-foot ship channel on
the west side of the river. I was aboard both days, and I found
the cruise a thrilling experience. Never before had such a well-

equipped scientific vessel come up the Hudson, and then the striped bass were so numerous they could seemingly rival for sheer tonnage the vast herds of buffalo that Lewis and Clark saw on the western prairies.

On the afternoon of the first day, the *Dolphin* began a twelve-minute trawl of the bottom off the village of Haverstraw. When the forty-foot net was winched aboard, the bag of the net bulged with so many fish that the biologists and crew gasped. Roughly 70 per cent of the catch were stripers and the rest were mainly sea sturgeon. The fish were crushing one another, and Clark ordered future trawls restricted to five minutes. Clark and Dave Deuel of the lab managed to measure, tag, and release nineteen stripers that were not injured in the first trawl.

On the next set of the trawl, the net was torn on the propeller, and the crew had to spend the night docked at Hastings repairing the damage. The next morning, the *Dolphin* set out again off Haverstraw, and the trawls were incredibly productive. All told, Clark and Deuel examined, tagged, and released about three-hundred striped bass on the second day, the largest of which weighed approximately thirteen pounds. They could have tagged one thousand fish, peak work for a balmy summer day, but the weather conditions were very adverse. The morning air temperature was 18° F., the water temperature was 33° F., and the wind was out of the northwest at twenty-five miles per hour and gusting higher. I tagged and released five sturgeon for the heck of it, and even though I was wearing heavy gloves I thought my fingers were going to fall off. Clark and Deuel also dissected quantities of bass injured in the trawling. The fish were plump and in otherwise excellent condition. However, they were in a sluggish state, as though they had been asleep on the bottom of the river, and only one had remnants of food, a small fish, in its stomach. I spent part of the afternoon in the pilot house watching the electronic fathometer graph, on which a stylus drew a top-to-bottom profile of the river and any fish or obstructions beneath us. As we passed over the edge of the ninety-nine-foot hole off Stony Point, the fathometer graph revealed fish concentrated in cloud-like fashion at mid-depth. We made a midwater trawl with a smaller net and gathered in several hundred tomcod. They were of no interest to Clark, and as herring gulls squawked excitedly overhead the crew shoveled the writhing tommies off the deck and back into the river. From the northward edge of the Stony Point hole on up Tomkins Cove, we passed over enormous concentrations of fishes on the bottom. I thought the Japanese fleet was sunk down there. One continuous school was twenty feet thick in places and about a mile long and probably was composed of striped bass and sturgeon. Possibly they were in this part of the river in order to get in the hot water coming from the outlet pipes of the Con Edison nuclear plant at Indian Point and the Orange-Rockland powerhouse at Tomkins Cove. The Norwegian skipper of the *Dolphin*, Bob Landsvik, a veteran of trawling in the Atlantic on Nantucket Shoals and Georges Bank, was overwhelmed. He had never seen anything like the fishes in the Hudson, and one of the crew members, Lenny Castle, a retired Navy chief and a real striper fanatic—he had two rods hidden aboard—told me: "When I get back to Jersey and tell the guys what I saw, their eyeballs are going to flip around like the revolving cherries in a slot machine."

After the *Dolphin* returned to Sandy Hook, one of the tagged striped bass was soon recaptured. In the last week of March, Lee Sellazzo, a commercial fisherman who stakes his nets about a mile south of Sing Sing Prison, took eight thousand pounds of stripers in one haul, and a bass that Clark had tagged was among them. By late spring, the fish had started to move out of the Hudson to the coast, and Clark began getting tag returns from anglers. During the course of the summer and early fall, a dozen of the tagged fish were caught. In Long Island Sound, tagged stripers were caught at Norwalk, Connecticut; Bayville, Long Island; and Larchmont, in Westchester County. On the south shore of Long Island, three tagged stripers were taken at Fire Island Inlet, one at Rockaway Inlet, and another in Jamaica Bay immediately adjacent to John F. Kennedy International Airport. On the Jersey coast, one was taken at Sandy Hook and another at Sea Girt, twenty-five miles south. One tag was from the Fulton Fish Market.

There is a third contingent of striped bass that enters the Hudson, and this contingent is rather mysterious in its movement. Clark calls this group the Hudson-Atlantic contingent. These striped bass appear to spend the winter a mile or so off the coast from Delaware Bay south to the entrance of the Chesapeake. In the spring, they move up the coast and into the Hudson. They enter the river only to spawn. Having spawned, they immediately depart, this time apparently heading east and north, summering at Montauk Point, Naragansett Bay, and maybe Cape Cod.

The Hudson-Atlantic Contingent seems to be composed mostly of fairly large fish, from ten to fifty pounds or more. In late May and early June, these big bass start arriving off Sandy Hook, and charter boats from Sheepshead Bay and the Jersey shore do a banner business. In the Hudson, fish from this run, known locally as "June bass," have been caught by rod and reel off the reef at the south tip of Croton Point and near the Newburgh-Beacon Bridge. The largest so far has weighed thirty-seven pounds, but netters take bigger stripers. Several years ago, I heard of a netter taking a seventy-one pound bass near Storm King, and I would not be too surprised if the world record of seventy-three pounds on rod and reel, set in Vineyard Sound, Massachusetts, in 1913 by Charles B. Church, were to be broken in the Hudson some day when the June run is on.

It is quite likely that the Hudson has a fourth contingent of striped bass, not discovered by Clark because the stripers stay in the river. I will tentatively dub them the Hudson-Hudson contingent. These are mature bass which apparently do not leave the river at all during the summer. I have caught mature fish in the summer weighing up to six pounds, and once in late August I saw several big striped bass in the twenty-five- to thirty-pound class leap into the air off Croton Point. These fish were perhaps a hundred yards away, but the characteristic stripes on their flanks stood out like those on a convict uniform. Moreover, reliable acquaintances have informed me that they have either caught or observed mature stripers in the Hudson during the summer.

For the past half dozen years, I have devoted much of my spare time to seeking the best fishing grounds for stripers in the Hudson. I have done this by fishing, (pleasant task), by talking to veteran anglers and commercial fishermen, and by chasing down periodicals and books, however obscure, which might offer clues. Several books, a couple more than one hundred years old, have been most helpful; specific locations cited in them are still frequented by bass.

In fishing for stripers, the angler must bear in mind that the fish show a distinct preference for moving water, the faster the better, and a hard bottom. The specific epithet *saxatilis*, "found among rocks," is pertinent. Where there are rocks in the Hudson, there are almost sure to be striped bass. Tide is important; in the Hudson, stripers, and other species of fishes too, bite best on an ebbing tide. They will do almost nothing on the flood. They behave as though they were waiting for the ebb to wash minnows, small crabs, and other tidbits down river or from marshes, creeks, and tidal inlets. The tides make a difference. I would go so far as to say that the Hudson River has a split personality, that it is two completely different rivers, depending on the tide. Fish the flood, and you would swear there isn't a striper in the Hudson. Fish the ebb, and there will be times when you can't believe there are that many fish.

Here are my notes on the best locations on the Hudson, starting upriver and moving down:

Diamond Reef, New Hamburg. This reef is marked on the Coast and Geodetic survey charts, and it has been a well-known fishing spot for years. One of my best reference books is *The Angler's and Tourist's Gazetteer,* compiled by William C. Harris, editor of the *American Angler,* and published in New York in 1885. It offers an alphabetical, state-by-state, town-by-town rundown of the fishing that then existed in the United States, and it has an entry on Diamond Reef. One September when I was coming down river with Ronald Dagon, an ecologist, I recalled the entry and we anchored in a driving rainstorm off the reef. In half an hour, we caught and released forty small striped bass. We took them on light tackle and silver black bass spoons, and they were so numerous and eager that Dagon caught three in a row simply by dipping his spoon in the water next to the side of the boat. Diamond Reef is also mentioned in *The Isle of Long Ago,* the charming memoirs of Edwin C. Kent, a Hudson River sportsman and the great-grandnephew of Washington Irving. In the 1870s and 1880s, Kent fly-fished for snapper bluefish, herring, and shad at the reef. (One of the criticisms anglers have of the Hudson is that the shad cannot be caught on rod and reel because they do not pool up as they do in the Connecticut River below the Enfield Dam. The shad Kent caught were spent fish moving downriver, but I think there is a good chance shad could be taken at the reef in the spring.)

Denning Point south to Bannerman's Island on the east shore of Newburgh Bay. I have not fished here myself, but I have had excellent reports. In the late spring of 1968, a novice angler who had fished less than three weeks in his life caught a 34½-pound striper at the nearby Newburgh-Beacon Bridge. Kent wrote of this stretch:

> The striped bass came up in great numbers at the same time in May. They seemingly kept on the flats for I never heard of the drifters [for shad] taking them. Wherever there was a strip of beach where a seine could be hauled, the seiners shot their nets, taking the bass, a scattering of shad which had come on the flats looking for a spawning bed, and innumerable herring. In the early days herring were a drug on the market. I have often seen a seine drawn, the bag bulging with herring. The men would pick out the bass and shad, and then would stand on the cork line and let the herring go. The bass were all large, twenty-thirty-pounders were plenty, and I do not remember to have seen any under ten pounds weight. No one ever fished for the bass with rod or hand lines. When I, who was much excited by the size and number of the bass, asked about the possibility of taking them, I was told that they never bit. I did make some feeble efforts to still-fish for them, using shad spawn for bait, but it was a failure because I could not find where they were. I now believe that had I trolled on the flats with a squid I might have had great sport. In June the bass disappeared, but they appeared in the river again in September. I have seen the rocky flat between Polopels (now Bannerman's) Island and the shore covered with them. One afternoon I was going down to the little marsh at the mouth of Melzingah brook looking for rail and saw those flats seemingly covered with bass. My [boat] pusher, Jim Mosher, was a net fisherman, and proposed that we should go back for a dozen fykes he owned, anticipating a magnificent haul. We set the fykes and next morning early went there with high hopes. It was a pitiful failure. The net thread was altogether too frail and the bass

had wrecked the nets. We recovered only the hoops held together by strips of twine; even the wings were full of holes.

In the spring, the tidal outlets at the railroad trestle along the Constitution Island marsh attract striped bass. The same holds true of the mouth of Popolopen Creek near Bear Mountain and the outlet of Manitou Marsh directly across the river.

The railroad embankment at Roa Hook north of Peekskill is a favorite ground for local anglers who can stand the smell of the Cortlandt town dump, and so is Fish Island off Manitou Mountain. Once in a great while here an angler will catch one of the rarer denizens of the Hudson, a foot-long salamander, the mud puppy (*Necturus maculosus maculosus*). Local newspapers invariably term this salamander "a strange animal unknown to science."

One of the best striped bass grounds can be found on the old oyster beds covering the east-shore flats in Haverstraw Bay from Montrose Point south past Georges Island, a Westchester County park with a boat-launching ramp.

In the spring and fall, anglers often fish from the rocks all the way from Oscawana Island down to Croton. The fishing here is often excellent, with some anglers even insisting that the flood tide is good. A Croton acquaintance of mine, Jim Kleinert, caught a fifteen-pounder here on the flood in June, 1967.

Croton Point is an excellent place to fish from a boat. The 1885 *Angler's Guide* recommended both the north and south tips. The south tip, called Teller's Point locally, is especially good for trolling. A sand and rock reef, it is exposed at dead low tide for several hundred yards. When the tide is moving, the water is very turbulent, and doubtless all sorts of succulents are swirled toward the bass. Stripers up to thirty-seven pounds have been taken here. Trolled plugs and yellow bucktails with a worm trailer are usually successful. If I were to try to catch a really large striped bass, I would seine some herring in the late spring and then fish them live at once between Teller's Point and Buoy 10. When I'm at the reef I like to cast bucktails. Indeed, the first striped bass I ever caught in the river was taken here on a white bucktail. Howard Powley, the watch repairman in Croton and a longstanding striped bass fanatic, suggested I go there one day in May, 1962. "It's just the right time," he said, his jeweler's eyepiece screwed in his right eye, a cigarette with an inch-long ash teetering in the corner of his mouth. "The dogwoods are in bloom, and when the dogwoods are in bloom, it's time to cast bucktails at the point." I had less than an hour to spare, but I drove and slid down the muddy cliff to the reef. I put on a white bucktail, cast out, and retrieved it. A striper followed it right up between the two rocks I was straddling. I cast again, and this time I had a strike. I brought the fish in through the rocks and landed a three-pounder. How long had this been going on? I cast and had another fish. Then I had to leave.

In the spring, Henry Gourdine stakes his nets to the east of the reef in Croton Bay. He takes stripers there for the Fulton market, and it is a poor day when he doesn't take eight hundred to one thousand pounds of bass. Until after World War II, commercial fishermen were allowed to haul a seine in the Hudson for stripers. Seining is now illegal, but when Gourdine did seine, he worked Croton Bay in the spring with a two-thousand-foot net brought in by a winch set up on shore. He and other fishermen cleared the bay of logs and debris so the seine would not hang fast on obstructions, and with one sweep it was nothing for them to take considerable numbers of fish. Once they hauled in 13,000 pounds, with 2,000 pounds of the catch striped bass.

Further south, there is excellent fishing in the spring from just above Crawbuckie Beach in Ossining down to Bishop's Rocks near the Scarborough railroad station. As a matter of fact, I knew of a Sing Sing guard who was so carried away that he cast for stripers from his waterfront watchtower. Trollers like to work Patterson's Hole (named after the late Captain Joseph Patterson, founder and publisher of the New York *Daily News*, whose estate was nearby) near the mouth of the Croton River, while shore-based anglers do well at Crawbuckie Beach, which Ossining plans to fill in for "recreation." One of the great anglers of the river is Brother Andrew of Maryknoll, who fishes in the Ossining area. Using only a black rubber worm, Brother Andrew has landed in one afternoon as many as twenty stripers, ranging from five to seventeen pounds.

There are anglers who fish at Spuyten Duyvil and Riverdale in the fall, when bass are coming into the Hudson from Long Island Sound. The height of the migration is around Columbus Day, and anglers take fish with plugs, bucktails, and pieces of soft-shell crab secured to the hook with elastic sewing thread. The leading fishermen are Jimmy Pagano, a heating plant repair specialist; Artie Williams, who sells auto accessories; Barney Laughlin, a Wall Street insurance broker; George Lefferts, who works in Barney's office; and Louie Skapinac, who is with the New York City Department of Parks. These anglers call themselves the Rats and Art Glowka has written about them in *Outdoor Life*. The Rats have learned through long experience that at Spuyten Duyvil the stripers hit at slack water, while less than a third of a mile north at Riverdale, the fish prefer the flood tide. The Rats usually fish at night, and they designate their favorite spots by the numbers on the electric poles along the Central tracks. "Pole 172 is good," says Artie Williams. "So is 190. Mount Saint Vincent's station is a good spot. You have to move around. You've got to have a moving tide."

Given the abundance of striped bass to be found in the Hudson, one might expect that the river would be jammed with fishermen especially during the spring and fall months. But this is not the case. Except for a relative handful of anglers, the Hudson is empty and the fish ignored by sportsmen.

The reasons for this are twofold:

1) The stripers in the river have the reputation of tasting of oil. In 1962, my wife cooked a striped bass that was absolutely inedible. It so reeked of oil or gasoline that it tasted like a refinery. I have not had a bad fish since, and I have given away dozens of stripers to friends and acquaintances. I told some that the bass came from the river, and I purposely did not tell others, so that they would not approach the table with bias. I have had two complaints of oily fish. Believe me, when a striper is oily, it's bad. There is no mistaking that taste. I have had mixed reports from other fishermen. Interestingly, I have never had an oily white perch from the Hudson. (The white perch is closely related to the striper, but unlike the striper, it does not migrate to sea but stays in the river.) I suspect that some striped bass pick

up the oil flavor by lingering for a while in New York harbor, probably in the vicinity of Bayonne. Definite reports of oily fish appear to center on Bayonne. But then again there is the Penn Central oil discharge into the Hudson at Harmon. The obvious solution to the oil taste is strict and prompt enforcement of the laws. Fine the violators and put them in jail.

As early as 1887, a government report, *The Fisheries and Fishery Industries of the United States*, noted of Newark Bay:

> The fisheries in this bay are said to have been greatly injured by coal oil. Newark Bay shad sold at high prices in the neighboring towns, but as they often taste of oil they have lost their reputation. At times even the oysters in the bay are tainted with coal oil, and the fishermen complain loudly against the emptying of such substances into the rivers, as well as against the practice of carrying oil across them in submerged pipes.

In *From Sandy Hook to 62°*, published in 1929, Charles Edward Russell recalled:

> After the rapid development of the petroleum industry in the early eighties, when large refineries were established at Bayonne and elsewhere around the front yard of New York, much complaint used to be made that the waters of the bay were being polluted by the deposits of the oil offal, particularly of a fluid called "sludge acid" that was supposed to be most obnoxious. I think it must have been to fish, certainly, for I can remember when there used to be oyster beds in the East River, and the sludge acid did for them. The outcries of the populace finally found their way to the legislature, as such complaints do at times, and an investigation was instituted by many experts. Harvard graduates, chemists, scientists, and other Wise Men of the Earth were good enough to testify. These succeeded in establishing that:
> 1. There was much sludge acid in waters of the bay.
> 2. There was no sludge acid in the waters of the bay.
> 3. Sludge acid was an injurious and undesirable substance.

4. Sludge acid was an innocent substance that hurt nobody.

2) New York State authorities have neglected the river. Here I
do not have in mind pollution abatement authorities—although
they certainly must take their share of blame—but conservation
department officials. Years ago, for reasons I have not been able
to ascertain, the tidal Hudson River from New York harbor to the
Troy Dam was put under the jurisdiction of freshwater biologists
in the conservation department. However, the important and desirable fishes and shellfish that frequent the tidal Hudson, no matter whether the water is brackish or fresh, traditionally fall within
the professional competence of the saltwater or marine biologist.
Marine biologists are most familiar with striped bass, bluefish, sea
sturgeon, menhaden, shad, herring, blue crabs, grass shrimp, and
so on, while freshwater biologists are not. Moreover, the freshwater biologists in charge of the tidal Hudson simply do not have
the time or equipment to deal with the river.

This ridiculous situation could be corrected at once, with no
cost to the taxpayer, by a stroke of the pen up in Albany. The
conservation department should place the tidal Hudson up to
Troy Dam under the department's own Bureau of Marine Fisheries. The marine biologists in this bureau have the time, knowledge, vessels and equipment to explore and publicize the bounty
of the river. Indeed it is essential that this change be made, if
only because the Hudson supplies the coastal waters of the state
with striped bass and other fishes. A number of persons and organizations have been calling for this change for some time, and
in the summer of 1968 the conservation department responded by
giving its marine biologists jurisdiction over the Hudson to the
Tappan Zee Bridge. This makes no ecological or economic sense
whatever, unless Albany is planning to charge the stripers a toll.
Ecologically, the tidal Hudson is of the greatest importance to the
south shore of Long Island and the Sound.

I have no doubt that if the tidal Hudson were managed by the
Bureau of Marine Fisheries, the benefits would be many. The
sport fishery for striped bass alone could bring millions of dollars
into the Hudson Valley, for the fish are packed into the river

when they are not along the coast during the summer. Tarrytown, Nyack, Ossining, Croton, Haverstraw, Peekskill, and Cold Spring, to name some villages, could vie with Montauk for the title of "Striped Bass Capitol of the World." And with no harm to Montauk, since the bass are in the Hudson when they are not in the Atlantic.

8

POWER, POWER
EVERYWHERE

New York State's neglect of the Hudson River has been costly in many ways. A pattern of abuse has been established, and the river is prey to all sorts of damaging schemes. There are plans to fill in productive flats and marshes for roads, airports, or what are benignly described as "industrial parks" and "tank farms." Periodically there is a proposal to dam the wild and beautiful upper river at Blue Ledge for "multiple use," or a suggestion to dam the tidal Hudson, say at Yonkers or Bear Mountain, to "stop the pollution" from moving either up or down or to "stop the salt water" from mixing with the fresh.

One of the worst schemes has been the attempt, still unresolved at this point, by the Consolidated Edison Company, which supplies New York City and Westchester County with electricity, to build a pumped storage hydroelectric plant at Storm King Mountain near Cornwall. Certainly the battle to stop the Storm King plant has been one of the most fierce and publicized in the history of American conservation, and an account of the case may be instructive.

In late 1963, Consolidated Edison applied to the Federal Power Commission for a license to construct the Storm King plant. Located at the base of the mountain, the plant would be able to suck up to six billion gallons of river water during a single daily operating cycle. This water would be pumped from the river through a two-mile-long tunnel, forty feet in diameter, to a storage reservoir. When Con Ed wanted to generate electricity, the plug on the reservoir would be pulled, so to speak, and the water would then surge down the tunnel to turn turbines before flowing back into the Hudson. The plant would be able to generate two million kilowatts of electricity, and it would be the largest of its kind in the world.

To Con Ed, the Storm King plant seemed like an ingenious engineering feat, but some persons felt that the plant would be an intrusion in the Highlands and serve as the precedent for further despoliation. Prominent among them were Carl Carmer, the author, and the late Leo Rothschild, a Manhattan attorney and conservation chairman of the New York-New Jersey Trail Conference, an association of outing clubs whose members often hike through the Highlands. It so happened that shortly before Con Ed made its plans public, Rothschild was looking into the possibilities of state acquisition of the Beacon Mountain-Breakneck Ridge area, directly across the river from Storm King. It never occurred to Rothschild that Storm King would soon be under attack, because that landmark was considered "safe." In 1909, the state legislature had passed a law setting aside Storm King and nearby lands as a private forest preserve. According to the 1910 Annual Report of the State Forest, Fish and Game Commission, predecessor of the conservation department, the law was passed "at the request of residents who were desirous of seeing the beauty of the region preserved." In requesting passage of the law, the Forest, Fish and Game Commissioner himself wrote of the region:

It is an historical section of our state. It is the region commonly known as the Highlands of the Hudson. Except for the villages and settlements named, it presents substantially the same appearance today, except for a lesser tree growth, than it did when first discovered by Henry Hudson.

For many years foreign and American travelers have visited two great national attractions in the country, Niagara and the Hudson River, because they have been told . . . that these were of exceptional interest and beauty. Today, it is true, our great West has opened regions of dramatic interest and beauty; yet wonderful as the latter are, the Hudson River holds its high place in American scenery.

In 1910, the legislature repealed the 1909 law because it conflicted with an earlier law establishing the Palisades Park. However, the legislature directed park authorities to protect the Highlands region. In time, the Palisades Park Commission did acquire part of Storm King—in 1924, Dr. Ernest Stillman gave eight hundred acres to the park—and even though the mountain was not fully owned by the commission it was considered inviolate in the popular mind. Storm King was there, it would always be there, its integrity preserved from despoliation.

Con Ed obviously thought otherwise. To quote from one company brochure, "At Cornwall, 50 miles from the heart of Manhattan, nature has provided the physical requirements of a pumped storage hydroelectric station: a large source of water and a reservoir basin high above but near enough to store the water for generating power." As Con Ed went ahead with plans to present its application for a license to the FPC, Rothschild, Carmer, and several other conservationists formed the Scenic Hudson Preservation Conference to oppose the plant. Their objections were several: the plant would deface Storm King; it would open the Highlands to similar projects (it later developed that four or five more pumped storage plants were being considered for the Highlands and the Palisades); and high tension towers would scar the hills of Putnam and Westchester Counties. Rothschild and Carmer soon won support from a number of residents of the Highlands on both sides of the river: Mr. and Mrs. Stephen Duggan, Mr. and Mrs. Pierre Ledoux, and Dr. and Mrs. Albert Lamb of Cornwall, and Mr. and Mrs. Alexander Saunders and Mr. and Mrs. Benjamin Frazier of Garrison. Mrs. Duggan was particularly irate. Her mother had given the village of Cornwall a pond which was a part of the local reservoir system; Con Ed planned to convert it to the storage bowl for water pumped up from the Hudson at Storm King. Of course, this would render the pond useless for drinking water, and so Cornwall planned to tap the Catskill Aqueduct carrying water to New York City, which was then racked by drought. Cornwall officials were strong supporters of Con Ed, boasting of the tax benefits that would accrue from the Storm King plant.

All the early members of Scenic Hudson contributed to the cause in their own way, by raising hell or money (as of now, Scenic Hudson has spent more than $500,000 battling Con Ed), or by spreading news of the proposed plunder to other conservation organizations. Mrs. Saunders, for example, was of great assistance in the latter activity; she had been conservation chairman of the Garden Club of America. Ben Frazier had helped rescue Boscobel mansion from the wrecker's ball, and he was in touch with various historical societies and civic organizations. Stephen Duggan came up with the idea of hiring the Manhattan public relations firm of Selvage & Lee to carry the battle to Con Ed. James Cope, the chairman of the firm, and three of his aides, Lou Frankel, Mike Kitzmiller and the later Ray Baker, then went to work with a zest on behalf of Storm King, and Con Ed, not accustomed to taking it, found itself on the receiving end of a blizzard of press conferences and releases. If anything distinguished the early members of Scenic Hudson, it was their determination not to give in to the utility, no matter how much it goaded, bullied, or twisted the facts. Con Ed got better than it gave. When Con Ed distributed a circular denouncing opponents as "misinformed bird watchers, nature fakers, land grabbers, and militant adversaries of progress," Pierre Ledoux arose at a public meeting to announce, "Yes, I am a birdwatcher, and I have been watching buzzards and vultures." This remark, tendered in Ledoux's archest patrician tones, turned the meeting to him. The people present, from day laborers to estate owners, took delight in hearing the company scored upon. For years, Con Ed has been a notorious dispenser of high-priced electricity (the highest of any major utility in the nation), erroneous bills, and bad service, and outraged consumers were happy to have someone at last speak up to the monopoly. This was important, for public sympathy and support were vital. Support was forthcoming. I recall one dark night when most of the residents of the village of Croton-on-Hudson turned out their lights at ten o'clock in protest against the Storm King plant. This did Con Ed no harm economically. It was simply a gesture, but it was a gesture of protest that gave many persons who would otherwise not have been concerned a personal stake, a sense of direct involvement, in the outcome of the case. On another occasion, a number of boat owners staged a sail-in on the Hudson at Storm King. Bumper stickers appeared with the motto, "Dig They Won't—Save Storm King," in response to the company's slogan, "Dig We Must." Another motto, "Better Dead than Con Ed," spread by word of mouth, along with other quips.

The Storm King case was far from a laughing matter at the start. Rothschild, Carmer, and company had barely time to get organized for the hearing which the Federal Power Commission scheduled in Washington in February of 1964. Con Ed was all set; the utility presented a battery of company and hired "experts" who testified voluminously and seemingly knowingly about such subjects as kilowatt hours, "peaking" power, and fish life in the Hudson. An additional hearing was held in May. Thanks to the efforts of Dr. Walter Boardman, president of the Nature Conservancy, Scenic Hudson retained as attorney Dale Doty, a former member of the FPC, and Doty was able to get Scenic Hudson the legal status of "intervenor" in the case. Familiar with the ways of bureaucracy, Doty cut through the red tape which would befuddle the ordinary citizen seeking to have his say before a federal agency, and as a result Scenic Hudson had the right to present and cross-examine witnesses. Outmanned but not outgunned by a dense array of Con Ed lawyers, Doty conducted a clever Fabian campaign in which he drew attention to omissions and deficiencies in the hearing records. This was important, because if the FPC went ahead and licensed the plant, the fight might be carried to a federal court of appeals (a decision of the FPC is equivalent to a federal circuit court decision), and the judges on the court probably would be most interested.

At the hearings, Con Ed played, in Ben Frazier's words, "the role of lord of the manor." This perhaps was to be expected before the FPC, or the Atomic Energy Commission, for that matter.

Instead of acting as cops on the beat, as intended by Congress, these agencies actually embrace the industries they are supposed to police in the public interest. The reasons for this are subtle. For one, the same utilities and spokesmen invariably appear before them. A certain friendship springs up over the course of time. By contrast, the opponents are strangers. One week they may be farmers, the next week a group of fishermen, and after that ladies in silly hats. No matter what public interest they represent, they are strangers. Then, there has been a cozy flow of officials from government to industry. Wherever they work, their views are narrow—more power, more dams, more nuclear reactors. They may disagree on occasion on whether the power should be public or private, but they are for more power. One hand washes the other, but the dirty linen never gets aired. It's "Hiya, Bill," "Hello Charlie, howza family?" between government and industry. Today's ravisher of a river may be tomorrow's employer.

When Scenic Hudson presented its witnesses, Rothschild, Carmer, and Frazier were regarded as so many interlopers. After all, Con Ed had all the "experts." On July 31, 1964, Edward B. Marsh, the hearing examiner, recommended to the commissioners of the FPC that the plant be licensed.

Meanwhile, opposition was growing. The blizzard of testimony presented by Con Ed's witnesses and accepted as gospel by the FPC was being questioned by persons who knew better. It was one thing for Carmer or Frazier to testify about the aesthetic and historic riches of the Highlands, but it was another thing when persons who had expertise in certain technical matters began reading over the testimony given by the Con Ed experts. Controversy arose over the testimony given by Dr. Alfred Perlmutter of New York University on the effect the Storm King plant would have on fish life in the Hudson. Dr. Perlmutter, a former employee of the New York State Conservation Department, was hired as a Con Ed consultant; he was, most importantly, the only witness on either side who had testified on fish life. A number of persons interested in the fishes of the Hudson, such as Art Glowka, Dom Pirone, consulting biologist of the Long Island League of Salt Water Sportsmen, and myself, became involved in the Storm King case after reading Dr. Perlmutter's testimony. Dr. Perlmut-

ter stated that he could "almost guarantee" that the proposed
Storm King plant would have "little effect" on fish eggs. The
"best" spawning grounds for striped bass, he said, were "much
farther upriver" from Storm King. He also testified: "The last
study on the Hudson River was made in 1938 [sic] and it hasn't
been done since." Dr. Perlmutter made no mention whatsoever of
the Rathjen-Miller study published in 1957. They had reported
that striped bass spawned in the Hudson from Bear Mountain
upriver to Cruger Island, with the principal spawning area occur-
ring in the vicinity of West Point, only two miles south of Storm
King. In point of fact, Rathjen and Miller collected 88.8 per cent
of the total number of eggs between Highland Falls and Denning
Point, and Storm King sits squarely in the middle of this seven
and a half mile stretch.

Fishermen aware of the Rathjen-Miller study took issue with
Dr. Perlmutter's testimony. They feared that eggs, larvae, and
small stripers and other fishes would be killed by the plant. If
striper eggs and larvae were not shattered in the original trip up
the tunnel, they would be hard put to survive in the storage reservoir, because they need a current to keep them bouyant. If they
happened to survive that, they would then be subjected to whirl-
ing turbine blades on the trip back down the tunnel which Con
Ed has exultantly described as "a 'fall' six times higher than
Niagara."

Fishermen had an additional reason to be concerned. Word
was spreading that Con Ed already had a monstrous record of
killing fish in the Hudson, not tiny eggs and larvae but mature
fish, including striped bass weighing up to thirty-five pounds or
more. This slaughter occurred at Con Ed's nuclear power plant at
Indian Point, fifteen miles south of Storm King. Starting early in
1963, this new plant began killing fish by the ton day after day.
The exact number of fish killed probably never will be known,
because the state conservation department did its best to mini-
mize the mess, but the toll must have run into the millions. In a
statement in July, 1965, before the U.S. House Committee on Interior and Insular Affairs, Don Manns of the Long Island League
of Salt Water Sportsmen estimated the kill at seven million fish.
The exact cause of the kill has never been made precisely clear—
it is not a matter on which either the Consolidated Edison Com-

pany or the conservation department like to dwell—but apparently the fish were attracted by hot water discharged from the plant after it had been used to cool the condenser. Swimming in to investigate the hot water—many fishes have a knack for discovering such currents, especially in cold weather—they were then trapped underneath a pier which had sheathing partly down the sides to keep debris from the nearby intake pipe. As they jammed into the space under the pier, they could not find their way out. Some swam inside the bowels of the plant to meet their death; others milled around hopelessly, crowding all the closer as new recruits swam in under the boarding. Many apparently became enervated and diseased. This went on for at least six months, and Con Ed operated a huge wire basket elevator to remove the dead and dying.

Fishermen learned of the kill when great numbers of crows began concentrating at the plant dump to feast on the vast piles of rotting fish. On June 12, 1963, Dom Pirone, Harvey Hauptner, then the League's conservation chairman, Fred Luks, an outdoor columnist, and Art Glowka visited the Indian Point plant. Of that visit Pirone said: "We saw ten thousand dead and dying fish under the dock. We learned that Con Ed had two trucks hauling dead fish to the dump when the plant was in operation."

Several fishermen and at least one member of the New York State Conservation Department took pictures of the piles of the dead fish rotting at the dump, and those who saw them were horrified. Con Ed erected a fence at the dump and posted guards to keep away the curious, and the conservation department quietly began calling in every picture it could get of the slaughter.

Before the pictures disappeared into state files, Pirone saw some. A number of them were in color, and one Pirone distinctly remembers showed dead striped bass stacked a dozen feet high. In the December, 1963, issue of the *Southern New York Sportsman,* Ted Keatley, the editor, wrote: "I have a print of a picture taken at the dump. This was forwarded to me with the following commentary: 'Enclosed is a photo taken one evening in early March and showing just one section of the dump. The fish seen here were supposed to be about 1 or 2 days' accumulation. They were piled to a depth of several feet. They covered an area encompassing more than a city lot.'" In a previous issue of the magazine, Keatley had estimated the Con Ed kill at one million striped bass alone, but Assistant Commissioner W. Mason Lawrence of the conservation department in a letter to Keatley, tut-tutted that figure as unrealistic, and instead pegged the peak kill at only eight hundred stripers a day, "mostly of rather small fish." One wonders what the assistant commissioner would have done to a private citizen who was taking only eight hundred small stripers a day; the usual fine is $27.50 per fish. When Pirone and Glowka later visited the Poughkeepsie regional office of the conservation department to inquire about the kill at Indian Point, officials there acted dumb and denied ever having seen any pictures. The officials offered to open up their files on Indian Point, but when Pirone sought to examine them, he was informed by letter from one of the officials in Poughkeepsie that "we cannot release departmental reports to the public concerning matters still under investigation."

By the late summer of 1964 the aroma of the Indian Point kill was slowly leaking out for all to smell, and the testimony offered by Con Ed for permission to blast into Storm King was being scrutinized and questioned. Nineteen sixty-four was also a drought year, and the public was becoming interested in the Hudson as a possible water source. There was increasing interest in the river. A young Democrat, Richard Ottinger, was running for Congress in Westchester and Putnam Counties. He made pollution of the Hudson, the Indian Point kill, and the proposed Storm King plant prime issues. The district he sought to represent was overwhelmingly Republican, but he won on election day against the incumbent. As Congressman Ottinger said later, "I swam to office on the waters of the Hudson River." In the fall of 1964, State Assemblyman R. Watson Pomeroy, a Dutchess County Republican and chairman of the Joint Legislative Committee on Natural Resources, held hearings on the proposed Storm King plant at the Bear Mountain Inn. The hearing room was packed, and opponents outnumbered proponents by 10 to 1. Con Ed made the mistake of taking the opposition lightly, as if it were beneath contempt. Company followers swaggered about wearing buttons proclaiming, "Dig We Must!" Scenic Hudson and its allies kicked the stuffing out of Con Ed, the FPC, and compliant state officials. Ben Frazier overheard one official on the phone to

Albany. "What's happening?" he screamed. "They're murdering us!"

One of the most effective witnesses for Scenic Hudson was Alexander Lurkis, former chief engineer for the New York City Bureau of Gas and Electricity and senior engineer for the New York City Transit Authority, where he supervised the design and construction of power plants. Con Ed was not fond of Lurkis because he had blamed the Manhattan blackouts of 1959 and 1961 on breakdowns in the Con Ed distribution system and not on a lack of power, the company's favorite excuse for building another plant and then laying a new rate increase on the customers while the state Public Service Commission bows obediently. If Con Ed did need peaking power to meet sudden loads on the system, Lurkis told the Pomeroy committee, the company should abandon Storm King and use gas turbines in the city instead. Gas turbines would meet any alleged peaking need and would result in great savings to Con Ed. Gas turbines, furthermore, were desirable because they would eliminate the hazard of weather damage to transmission lines from Storm King. Moreover, Lurkis said, gas turbines were to be preferred to the Storm King plant because they would not contribute to air pollution. To pump water up Storm King, Con Ed would have to use power from coal-burning plants in the city. Interestingly, Con Ed would expend three kilowatts of power in city plants pumping water up for every two kilowatts it would get back when the plug was pulled in the reservoir. When this was learned the suspicion arose that the company really wanted the plant not for its own consumers but to market power elsewhere in the East.

After Lurkis finished I spoke about the fish life in the river, beginning with the slaughter at Indian Point and the supression of photographs, and ending with the Rathjen-Miller study. I might have been dismissed as a crank except that I was immediately followed by John Clark of the Sandy Hook lab, who spoke on the importance of Hudson River spawning grounds to striped bass fishing in Connecticut, New York, and New Jersey waters.

Upon completion of the hearing, the Pomeroy committee voted 5 to 0 to block the Storm King plant. However, the matter was out of the committee's hands. Thanks to Governor Nelson A. Rockefeller, New York State had given its blessing to the project, and the decision was up to the Federal Power Commission. The governor was solidly behind Con Ed; at one point he sarcastically suggested that the people who wanted to save Storm King should go buy the mountain. I once asked a prominent Republican why Rockefeller was so committed to Con Ed. "The people who own Con Ed are his people," was the reply. "They're in the same club." Whatever the reason for Governor Rockefeller's embrace of Con Ed, many persons were shocked by it. The Rockefellers, especially Laurance, the Governor's brother and chairman of the State Council of Parks, have reputations as conservationists. In truth, the Rockefellers are cosmetic conservationists at best. They do not seem able to envision the significance of an estuarine ecosystem, such as the lower Hudson, with its moving and myraid forms of life. They simply are not interested in such things.* Rockefeller projects, however estimable, such as Williamsburg or the Sleepy Hollow Restorations, are all run like Radio City Music Hall. The public stands in line to see a colonial candlestick maker, Washington Irving's desk, or Doris Day's newest movie. People are led through corridors of velvet ropes, admonished not to touch but only look, and then sent home while the staff gets ready for the next show. By contrast, it is not possible to put a glass bell over the Hudson Highlands and post a notice saying: STRIPED BASS SPAWNING AT TWO O'CLOCK. RESERVATIONS NECESSARY. Later on in 1965, as the Storm King battle waxed hotter, Governor Rockefeller got the legislature to create the state Hudson River Valley Commission. A powerless body, it was conjured into existence to appease public outcry and to give the illusion that the state could and would look after the Hudson. Previously, Representative Ottinger had introduced a bill into Congress calling for a three party Hudson River Valley Commission involving the federal government, New York, and New Jersey, and giving the Sec-

---

* According to the *Wall Street Journal*, April 14, 1969, David Rockefeller is the leading principal in a development group, Westbay Community Associates, which plans to fill in forty-eight hundred acres of San Francisco Bay as soon as possible. After that, the Rockefeller group plans to fill in another fifty-three hundred acres over a twenty- to thirty-year-period. Westbay also owns six-hundred acres of San Bruno mountain and for a time considered slicing up the mountain for bay fill. A Westbay spokesman, Warren T. Lindquist, said the fill project has the spirit of "pro bono publico" that characterizes Rockefeller ventures. Lindquist noted that "a few rabid conservationists" were depicting David Rockefeller as a "villain."

retary of the Interior veto power over projects affecting the river. The governor and his associates deemed this a federal intrusion. The fact that the very worst sort of federal agencies—the FPC, the Atomic Energy Commission, and the Corps of Engineers— already had life-or-death powers over the Hudson, or that citizens might need a federal club to beat these agencies off was never mentioned by the suddenly ardent states' righters. Instead, Governor Rockefeller came up with his own state Hudson River Valley Commission and named his very own cousin and assistant, Alexander Aldrich, as executive director. As might be expected, the state Hudson River Valley Commission never has paid any attention to the health or vitality of the river itself. Instead a curio-cabinet mentality has prevailed. I once heard Aldrich tell an annual meeting of the Hudson River Conservation Society of a most pressing problem facing the river—the need for funds to pay a curator to look into Frederick Church's old checkbooks and papers upstairs at Olana Castle. With indignation, Aldrich urged all present to write their state assemblymen and senators protesting against this ghastly omission in appropriations.

After the Pomeroy committee hearings, a number of conservation, civic, and fishing organizations joined Scenic Hudson and went through the tortuous legalisms required to file what is known as a "petition to intervene" before the Federal Power Commission. A taxpayer and consumer group, the Hilltop Cooperative of Queens, sought in a petition to present Lurkis' points about gas turbines. The FPC rejected it as not "timely," even though the commission was still several months from reaching a decision.

Simultaneously, the Cortlandt Conservation Association in Westchester, the Nassau County Fish & Game Association, the Long Island (commercial) Fishermen's Association, the National Party Boat Owners Alliance, the Hempstead (Long Island) Town Lands Resources Council, the village of Freeport, Long Island, and the town of Hempstead all sought to intervene. They wanted to present witnesses who could testify about the dangers the Storm King plant would pose for striped bass eggs and larvae, young shad, and other species. In its petition to the FPC, the Cortlandt Conservation Association described Con Ed's dismal record at Indian Point, cited the Rathjen-Miller study, which the commission had yet to consider, and added: "The Cortlandt Conservation Association finds it most surprising that Dr. Perlmutter did not mention the Rathjen-Miller report before the Federal Power Commission. 'He [Dr. Perlmutter] knew of our work,' says Miller. 'He was in charge of the unit. In fact, he hired us.' To which Rathjen adds, 'That's right.'" For its part, Con Ed told the FPC that any rebuttal on Storm King was dilatory and that "allegations" about Indian Point were "irrelevant." The FPC agreed and denied all the petitions. Con Ed was then able to boast that Dr. Perlmutter's testimony was "unchallenged on the record."

Although things looked black, Ottinger's election to Congress and the Pomeroy hearings marked a turning point. Scenic Hudson formally organized itself and hired Rod Vandivert as executive director. An advertising man who had become personally committed to saving coastal wetlands from destruction, Vandivert brought a special conservation expertise into the battle against Con Ed. Let the company hold a press conference on the need for Storm King, and Vandivert was ready with a counter-release five minutes later. He was everywhere. At sportsmen's shows, he distributed maps of the Hudson showing Storm King's strategic location. A black cross marked Con Ed's fish graveyard at Indian Point. In an effort to appease fishermen, Con Ed announced it would spend $150,000 to sponsor a three-year study of fish life in the river by the conservation department and the U.S. Fish and Wildlife Service. The company, of course, did not make any offer to withdraw from Storm King or halt construction if the study revealed the area to be critical for fishes.

On March 9, 1965, the Federal Power Commission, in a 3 to 1 vote, granted Con Ed a license to build its plant at Storm King. In its decision, the FPC dismissed the Indian Point kill as "outside the jurisdiction of this Commission" and endorsed Dr. Perlmutter as "an outstanding icthyologist." The dissenting commissioner, Charles Ross, wrote: "The continued existence of this [Hudson fish] resource is one of the primary issues in this case, and I, for one, am not willing to base an ultimate conclusion upon testimony about which serious doubts have arisen." As a sop, the FPC called for a hearing in May to determine the route of the high tension lines and the kind of screen to be placed over the intake tubes to protect fish life. Inasmuch as no known screen could exclude tiny striper eggs and larvae, the hearing promised to be ludicrous, but attorney Doty used it as an opportunity to present witnesses to stress this point for the official record. "We're going to go to court on this," Rod Vandivert said, "and when we get there the judges are going to be horrified by the contradictions." One of the expert witnesses who appeared for Scenic Hudson at the May hearing was Dr. Edward Raney of Cornell, whose name is synonymous with striped bass research.

Throughout all this, Con Ed kept getting blasted. A story in the *New York Times* quoted an unnamed high administration official as calling the Storm King plant "the rape of the Hudson." To many persons, the utility's bright orange repair trucks took on all the popularity of Soviet tanks on the streets of Budapest or Prague. From his Dutchess County dairy farm, James Cagney, the actor, wired Senators Thomas Kuchel of California and the late Robert Kennedy of New York beseeching them to stop Con Ed from ravaging the fisheries of the Hudson. Scenic Hudson saw to it that copies of Cagney's telegrams went to the press. The tabloids hopped on the story, and instead of seeming to be indignant bird watchers, Scenic Hudson members were snarling gut fighters. Other celebrities, if that is the word, who aided the cause were Brooks Atkinson, Henry Morgan, and Cornelia Otis Skinner. All told, it might be fairly said that Scenic Hudson went after Con Ed with such gusto that the company found itself questioned every which way. *Life* published a strong editorial in defense of Storm King, and the *Nation* and the *New Republic* ran stories. *Fortune* did an article on Con Ed and pronounced the management archaic and arrogant; the article was entitled, "Con Edison: the Company You Love to Hate." George Heinold, saltwater columnist for *Outdoor Life*, conducted his own investigation of the Storm King controversy and reported in a lengthy article: "My own investigation into the matter has convinced me that the concern sportsmen and conservationists feel for the future of the Hudson River's striped bass fishery is entirely justified." Heinold also wrote that he was dismayed to learn that "the conservation department wasn't taking any steps to protect the Hudson's striper spawning grounds from the threat offered by the proposed plant." Vandivert and Pirone spoke before civic groups, and they were so effective that Con Ed withdrew spokesmen before a scheduled public debate. I wrote about the Storm King threat in *Sports Illustrated,* and I also wrote editorials for the *Croton-Cortlandt News,* the local weekly. A Con Ed official, not knowing that I had written them, complained angrily to the publisher, A. A. Granovsky, who stood his ground. Con Ed is a big advertiser. Why a utility monopoly is allowed to advertise without limit is beyond me. I would like to know who pays for all the ads, the consumers or the stockholders? A consumer cannot take a wire across the Hudson and plug it into the socket of another power company. But utility monopolies are allowed to advertise without restriction, even though they have captive consumers. Con Ed runs ads either to praise itself or to entice consumers into "living better electrically" with more appliances, electric heating, etc., all the while pleading a "shortage" of power to meet "demand" before the FPC and AEC.

In my spare time, I kept up the search for any pictures of the Indian Point slaughter that might have escaped the state's secret files. After six months, I finally found a few, and *Sports Illustrated* published an article, "A Stink of Dead Stripers," showing one of the photographs in the April 26, 1965, issue. The pictures were Polaroid triplicates that had been saved by a sportsman. "I kept them because I figured a reporter would come along in a couple of years," the sportsman said. "The conservation department took all my originals, then a month later they asked if I had duplicates. I had to give them those, but they didn't ask about triplicates." I had to keep this man's identity secret; he worked for a bank, and he feared that fighting Con Ed publicly could cost him his job. Meanwhile Representative Ottinger was able to get the U.S. House Subcommittee on Fisheries and Wildlife Conservation to schedule a hearing on the problems of the Hudson. The hearing was held on May 10 and 11, 1965, a few days after the FPC session on fish screens for Storm King. Vandivert testified, so did I, and so did Dom Pirone, who told the subcommittee that when he tried to get Con Ed to take steps to stop the Indian Point kill a company official "called me a liar, he called me a troublemaker, he threatened suit." Pirone told the congressmen about a local outdoor editor who, after estimating that one million fishes had been killed at Indian Point, "was called up to the Mount Vernon office of Con Edison" to appear before a vice president. The editor "took out a series of thirty to forty pictures [of the kill], which I saw one night last year, and he spread these before the vice president and the subject of discussion was promptly changed." Before the subcommittee, Con Ed did not dare try to pull any of the bluster which it is wont to pile on private citizens or editors, and there was satisfaction of a sort when an attorney for the company, admitted "Well, the Indian Point thing was bad, there is no question about it." Although Con Ed, of course, attempted to justify its proposed rape of Storm King, Representative John Dingell of Michigan, who chaired part of the hearing, remarked that there was to be no protection whatever for striper eggs or larvae.

As a result of the congressional hearing, Con Ed found itself even more on the defensive. One amusing byproduct was the reaction of the New York State Conservation Department. Instead of making a clean breast of the kill at Indian Point department officials scurried around behind the scenes, demanding, "Who squealed to Boyle? Who gave the pictures to *Sports Illustrated?*" They even checked home phone bills of department members to see if anyone had called me. Publicly, the department head, Dr. Harold Wilm, made the gaffe of telling the Associated Press that the Indian Point slaughter was "almost in the vein of an act of God." Vandivert seized upon this to write a publicized letter to Wilm protesting against invocation of the Deity, and in an article I was writing for *The Garden Journal* in its "Conversations on Ecology" series—my pen never tires in a just cause—I sanctimoniously noted that I found the commissioner's statement so outrageous that I was almost moved to leave the ecologists to join the theologists to ask, "Is God dead?"

Given the FPC approval of the license for the Storm King plant, Scenic Hudson now sought redress in court. Thanks to the late Mr. and Mrs. Stephen Currier—she was a member of the Mellon family—Scenic Hudson was able to retain the services of the distinguished law firm of Paul, Weiss, Rifkind, Wharton and Garrison, and Lloyd Garrison went before the Federal Circuit Court of Appeals in New York in August of 1965 to ask that the FPC license for Storm King be set aside. All the points that the FPC had neglected to hear or explore, such as the Rathjen-Miller study, were presented for the court's consideration. On December

29, 1965, the three judges on the court of appeals, Lumbard, Waterman, and Hays, set aside the license and ordered the FPC to start all over again. I was only one of many people who got riotously drunk.

The court decision was a conservation landmark. The judges noted:

> If the Commission is properly to discharge its duty . . . the record on which it bases its determination must be complete. The petitioners and the public at large have a right to demand this completeness. It is our view, and we find, that the Commission has failed to compile a record which is sufficient to support its decision. The Commission has ignored certain relevant factors and failed to make a thorough study of possible alternatives to the Storm King project.

Specifically, the court upheld Scenic Hudson's contention that the FPC had not evaluated the effect on the scenery. "The highlands and gorge of the Hudson offer one of the finest pieces of river scenery in the world," the court said. The FPC, moreover, had not given consideration to alternate methods of generating power, such as gas turbines. The FPC also had not considered underground transmission wires. Finally, the FPC's record on fish life showed many "deficiencies." In sum, said the court, "In this case, as in many others, the Commission has claimed to be the representative of the public interest. This role does not permit it to act as an umpire blandly calling balls and strikes for adversaries appearing before it; the right of the public must receive active and affirmative protection at the hands of the Commission."

Con Ed sought to win back its license at Storm King in an appeal to the Supreme Court. The court refused to hear the case.

As a result, brand new hearings before the Federal Power Commission began in November of 1966. Con Ed was now talking of putting most of the powerhouse underground, a feat that would involve blasting a huge cavern out of Storm King. The FPC staff beamed approval. When Dr. Perlmutter reappeared, he suggested that if there were losses of striped bass after the plant went into operation, a hatchery could replace them. (To a striped bass enthusiast, this was news of revolutionary moment. Jack D. Bayless, head of the South Carolina Wildlife Resources Department Striped Bass Hatchery at Moncks Corner, where the most advanced research has been done, says it "would be very difficult to successfully procure and hatch striped bass eggs from the Hudson River." According to Bayless, "South Carolina has stocked an estimated hundred million larvae in a fourteen-thousand-acre reservoir and no significant survival has been detected to date. North Carolina has been stocking coastal rivers for at least ten years and, as far as I know, no fingerling or adult fish have been found which could be attributed to these stockings.")

Fortunately, Vandivert and Scenic Hudson were well prepared for the new round of hearings. Among the organizations which opposed Con Ed at Storm King were:

Cornwall Taxpayers Water Protection Association
Town of Cortlandt
Town of Putnam Valley
Town of Yorktown
Sportsmen's Council, Marine District of New York State
The Hempstead Town Lands Resources Council
National Party Boat Owners Alliance, Inc.
Nassau County Fish and Game Association, Inc.
The Constitution Island Association, Inc.
National Parks Association
The Long Island League of Salt Water Sportsmen, Inc.
Cortlandt Conservation Association, Inc.
The Sierra Club
Atlantic Chapter of the Sierra Club
Town of Philipstown
The Nature Conservancy, Inc.
County of Putnam
Putnam County Historical Society
The Hudson River Conservation Society
Citizens Committee on Natural Resources
The Izaak Walton League of America
The National Trust for Historic Preservation in the United States
Village of Freeport, Long Island
Westport Striped Bass Club
The Hudson River Fishermen's Association, Inc.
Appalachian Mountain Club
Boscobel Restoration
Federation of New York State Bird Clubs, Inc.
County of Nassau.

Many of the intervenors presented expert witnesses on all sorts of pertinent subjects. Natural beauty occupied a prominent role. Here Con Ed was at a loss, even though the Court of Appeals had ordered consideration of this. One Con Ed witness, a landscape architect, was asked if the utility's storage reservoir would be more attractive than the pond there now, and he replied, "Any large lake is handsomer than a small lake." By contrast, witnesses presented by Scenic Hudson and the Sierra Club were most explicit. Charles Callison, now executive vice president of the National Audubon Society, called the Highlands "the most beautiful stretch of river scenery in the United States." The beauty of the Highlands, Callison said, was directly related "to the dominant geological feature of the eastern United States, the Appalachian Mountains." The Highlands stretch "is one of the very few places where the main chain of the Appalachians is broken by a river." Asked if there were other rivers breaking through the main chain of the Appalachians, Callison replied:

> Yes there are. For example the French Broad, at the base of the Great Smokies, cuts through the main chain. And the Susquehanna, starting in central New York's Otsego Lake, journeys southwest and then turns southeast to go through several of the Appalachian ridges of Pennsylvania. The Delaware, Connecticut, and James Rivers also cut through one or more of the main chains of the mountains, often with striking beauty. Yet nowhere, in my opinion, is the impact as great as it is through the Highlands. In the Smokies, of course, the French Broad cuts a deeper valley and is flanked by higher mountains. But there the river is shallow and narrow, a small stream practically hidden by the scale of the mountains. At the Delaware Water Gap there are also high hills. Yet in the Highlands—and only in the Highlands—the river cuts the Appalachian at sea level. And with a relative breadth it creates river scenery of an unequaled scale, bounded on both banks by the precipitous hills. Here we have not simply a river, but an estuary . . . with the tides of the Atlantic literally cutting through the mountains. Here alone we have ocean-going vessels passing through a great mountain chain and traveling ninety miles on to the heartland. And here, too, and again here alone—we have Storm King Mountain—a headland unique in its height and sheer rise from the river.

Richard Edes Harrison, the distinguished cartographer, exhibited three-dimensional shaded maps of the water gaps of the Appalachians, and after comparing them testified, "Storm King is uniquely dramatic and, in my opinion, the most scenic of the water gaps in the eastern United States." Professor Charles W. Eliot, II, of Harvard, landscape architect and planner, testified that the Highlands provide "a very special kind of natural beauty, rarely found anywhere and particularly valuable near the great metropolis of New York." Indeed, the beauty of the Highlands was such, in Eliot's opinion, that they fully qualified for National Park status. Perhaps the most lyric witness was Professor Vincent J. Scully, Jr., of Yale, an expert in art history. Of Storm King he said, as Con Ed's lawyers doubtless ransacked reference books:

It rises like a brown bear out of the river, a dome of living granite, swelling with animal power. It is not picturesque in the softer sense of the word but awesome, a primitive embodiment of the energies of the earth. It makes the character of wild nature physically visible in monumental form. As such it strongly reminds me of some of the natural formations which mark sacred sites in Greece and signal the presence of the Gods; it recalls Lerna in Argolis, for example, where Herakles fought the Hydra, and various sites of Artemis and Aphrodite where the mother of the beasts rises savagely out of the water. While Breakneck Ridge across the river resembles the winged hill of tilted strata that looms into the Gulf of Corinth near Calydon.

Hence Storm King and Breakneck Ridge form an ideal portal for the grand stretch of the Hudson below them. The dome of one is balanced by the horns of the other; but they are both crude shapes, and appropriately so, since the urbanistic point of the Hudson in that area lies in the fact that it preserves and embodies the most savage and untrammeled characteristics of the wild at the very threshold of New York. It can still make the city dweller emotionally aware of what he most needs to know: that nature still exists, with its own laws, rhythms, and powers, separate from human desires.

There were other surprises for Con Ed. After testifying for the Hudson River Fishermen's Association, ecologist Ronald Dagon went to Hartford to appear before a hearing conducted by a committee of the Connecticut legislature. As a result of work by H. Philip Arras of Naugatuck, Conn., who had formed the Connecticut Friends of the Hudson River Highlands, the legislature was considering a bill to have the state intervene before the FPC on the grounds that the Storm King plant could do harm to Connecticut's striped bass fishery. Dagon was a most persuasive witness, and the committee approved the bill. So did the legislature and Governor John Dempsey signed it.

The hearings before the FPC ground on into the spring of 1967. There then came a long silence as the hearing examiner, Ewing Simpson, went over the more than sixteen thousand pages of testimony. The cost of obtaining a full set of the hearings is staggering, but I must say that I do derive a certain sense of righteous bliss just gazing at selective chunks of testimony that lie heaped on my desk like the thigh bones of a mastodon. On August 6, 1968, the hearing examiner finally emerged with his recommendation: the FPC should license the Storm King plant. Simpson's decision appeared to dismiss whatever points Scenic Hudson and its allies had scored (e.g., "A number of these opponents would have a decision on the license application await the outcome of fishery studies and research now in progress along the River and at the site"), while he bestowed high marks to Con Ed's contentions.

But the Storm King case was far from concluded. New York City finally moved to intervene on the grounds that all the drilling and blasting in the "bad rock" of Storm King would imperil the Catskill Aqueduct, which supplies the city with 40 per cent of its water. After the city was granted the status of intervenor, the flexible FPC staff simply recommended that the plant be switched to a site a mile and half downriver. "They don't give up easily," Vandivert said with a smile. Inasmuch as this new site was within the boundaries of the Palisades Interstate Park System, the park commission got understandably edgy, and it became an intervenor in new hearings that began in March of 1969.

In all likelihood, the Storm King case will not be finally resolved until 1970 or later. I hope and pray that Con Ed will be beaten, and that the Highlands will be left undespoiled. Thus far, the case has had several beneficial results. Among them, it has focused attention on the Hudson and its problems and made many persons cognizant of them. The controversy also has made people aware that they "can do something" to meet those problems.

There is no need to fall back on the old defeatist slogan that "you can't beat City Hall" or Con Ed. The Federal Court of Appeals decision is proof of this, and that decision is far-reaching, having application not only to the Hudson but to rivers and natural resources elsewhere in the United States. The Storm King case also stirred Congress into action, with the passage of Ottinger's bill calling for a Hudson River compact between the federal government and New York and New Jersey.

Without question, Storm King has prompted a few superficial changes at Con Ed, the Tammany Hall of utilities. The company has hired new advertising and public relations firms to recast its "image." The irksome slogan, "Dig We Must," has been buried at last in favor of a new one that smacks of the company's asphalt prose style: "Clean Energy." (Clean Energy, Con Edison, get it?) The company's trucks also have been repainted. They are now a vivid blue instead of orange.

Meanwhile, Con Ed is still seeking to protect the fifteen million dollars it has sunk into Storm King. It is also busy pioneering a new threat to the well-being of the Hudson, thermal pollution from nuclear power plants.

All steam power plants, whether run by fossil fuels or a nuclear reactor, use water to cool their condensers, but nuclear plants, or "nukes," as they are coming to be called, require enormous amounts of water because of their large output. Because of this, nuclear plants are now planned for construction next to natural bodies of water, such as the Hudson, Lake Michigan, Barnegat Bay, Biscayne Bay, Long Island Sound, the Mississippi River, and the Columbia. A nuke sucks in the water, heats it anywhere from 11°F. to 25°F., and then spews it back into the river, bay, or lake. This is done around the clock. Heating water like this could be especially deadly for the estuarine Hudson during the warmer summer months, when the tidal river slides back and forth. Peak temperatures for the lower Hudson hover around 80°F., although the U.S. Geological Survey, which maintains a recording thermometer in the river across from Peekskill, has recorded sporadic highs of 85° for an hour or two. This is the borderline for most of the life in the river. Huge artificial hot water discharges pouring into the Hudson from nuclear plants could raise absolute havoc. For instance, a strong dose of hot water can decrease the dissolved oxygen content of the river water, increase the toxicity of pollutants, spur the growth of noxious blue-green algae that can stink so badly as to peel the paint of nearby houses and make people vomit, increase the metabolic rates of fishes and other aquatic organisms, alter the behavior of fishes or interfere with their reproductive cycles, foster fish diseases, or simply kill organisms outright. Increased temperatures in the Hudson could wipe out various species of plankton or unbalance their natural relative population numbers. In a recent paper, Dr. Gwyneth Parry Howells of New York University, co-director of an ecological survey of the river, writes:

> In the classic studies in the Potomac and Patuxent rivers it has been shown that as environmental water temperature change from < 90° to > 90°, the species making up the micro fauna and flora will change. There is a reduction in the variety of organisms as the less heat tolerant cannot survive in competition with the others. There is a loss of protozoa and an increase in microbial growth, perhaps because the reduced protozoan population no longer browses on them. . . .
>
> The planktonic copepod *Acartia* (present in the Hudson) shows a critical dependence on temperature in relation to egg hatching. A reduction in the abundance of larval nauplii would deplete the food supply for young fish, and it would also remove the population responsible for cropping algae and diatoms. Again, many invertebrates such as soft-shelled clams, oysters and crabs are directly or indirectly affected by temperature changes.

Every species has its own lethal temperature, and fishes, it should be noted, live within relatively narrow temperature spans as compared to man or other mammals. Aside from trout, whose thermal limits were mentioned previously in the chapter on the Adirondacks, here are the lethal temperatures for some fishes found in the Hudson:

> Striped bass, 77° to 80.6° for mature fish; temperature for larvae probably 74° to 80°.
> Common shiner, 86°.
> Bluegill sunfish, 87°.

Carp, 89° to 93°.
Largemouth bass, 91° to 97.5°.

Even if a creature is able to survive in water heated a few degrees below its lethal temperature, it might not be able to thrive because its metabolism is somehow impaired. There is the curious example of the shrimplike *Gammarus*, abundant in the Hudson and a most important organism in the food chain. At temperatures above 46°, *Gammarus* produces only female offspring.

There is no need for any power plant to cook the Hudson. A plant can use a closed circulating cooling system, similar in priciple to an automobile radiator. However, the Atomic Energy Commission, which licenses nuclear plants, has refused to take thermal pollution into consideration. The AEC takes the stand that it has authority from Congress to deal only with radiological hazards and thus has no jurisdiction over hot water pouring from a nuclear plant, no matter what damage it may inflict.

The damage done on the Hudson by Con Ed's first nuclear plant at Indian Point is minor compared with what could happen. As of now, Con Ed is building two more nuclear plants adjacent to Indian Point One, and together the three will take in and spew out 2.1 million gallons of river water a minute when in operation. That is Con Ed's figure; the company also admits that this water will be returned to the Hudson 16.4° hotter than the temperature of the river.

Con Ed also has plans for a fourth unit at Indian Point, and early in 1968, the company announced that it was going to put two more nukes at unspoiled Montrose Point, two miles south of Indian Point as the crow flies from the dump. This announcement came as a surprise to the Catholic Kolping Society, which owns a fifty-acre estate on Montrose Point. The society is composed in good part of old-country Germans, artisans and craftsmen, and Con Ed's plans to take their land got their Dutch up, especially when surveyors working for the company landed unannounced and uninvited one evening from a barge in the river. The Kolping Society has refused offers from Con Ed to sell out, and the utility responded with a blunt threat to institute condemnation proceedings. This really inflamed the members, and they began to fight back with so much vigor that they prompted the New York *Daily News* headline, "A-Plant Land Grab May Explode," over the sort of story that makes Con Ed P.R. men order a new color of paint for the company trucks.

Where Con Ed will eventually attempt to build more nukes is anyone's guess. There were reports Con Ed was casting covetous corporate eyes at Bowline Point across the river near Haverstraw, and there were strong rumors that the Orange-Rockland power company, which operates a monstrously ugly, smoke-belching coalfired plant at Tomkins Cove on the river opposite Con Ed's original industrial error at Indian Point, was planning a nuke of its own nearby. If I added up all the dreadful possibilities anywhere from six to nine nukes might be in operation on both sides of the Hudson in just the five-mile stretch from Haverstraw to Tomkins Cove. Upriver, other utilities were making ominous noises, and a spokesman for the state's Hudson River Valley Commission told me that a total of twenty-four sites were being surveyed along the Hudson for possible nuclear plants.

The fact that nuclear plants might proliferate all over the Hudson was not lost on the Hudson River Fishermen's Association, several of whose officers, notably Dom Pirone and Art Glowka, had been active in exposing the original Indian Point kill. In early May of 1968, Richie Garrett, the president of the HRFA, and five directors—Pirone, Glowka, Dr. James Alexander of the Biology Department at Fordham, Ric Riccardi, and myself—met with four Con Edison officials. The meeting was private, with no fanfare. The HRFA was already locked in battle with Con Ed over the proposed Storm King pumped storage plant, and the officers of the Association had no wish to get into another publicized, costly, and time-consuming dispute with the company. This meeting was to be held with white flags on both sides. When we met, we told Con Ed that the HRFA had no objection to nuclear plants on the river as long as they did not pollute or damage the Hudson. We told the company to cool the water with closed-circuit systems. If Con Ed agreed to do this, the HRFA was willing, perhaps naïvely, to join with the company to gain public acceptance of nuclear plants. If Con Ed balked, the HRFA was bound to fight. William Cahill, a newly promoted vice-president of Con Ed, who appeared to be the senior official present, judging from the deference shown to him by the other Con Ed representatives, disputed the cost of cooling devices. When I pointed out that New York State supposedly had thermal standards which required that tidal salt water, such as the lower Hudson, could not be heated more than 1.5° during the critical summer months and that therefore Con Ed would have to play ball, Arthur Pearson spoke up. Pearson, an engineer for Con Ed, is usually billed as the company's "expert" on ecology. None of us could quite believe our ears as Pearson waved my objections aside and smugly announced that Con Ed would not have to cool any water because the utility was going to get the state to reclassify the lower Hudson from tidal salt water to "freshwater stream."

After the meeting, Pirone, then the corresponding secretary of the HRFA, wrote to R. Stewart Kilborne, the state conservation commissioner, who has succeeded Dr. Wilm of "act of God" fame, to ask if the lower Hudson was indeed going to be changed from tidal salt water to "freshwater stream" by fiat. The reply came from A. G. Hall, director of the Division of Fish and Game. "It is impossible to classify the Hudson River to the Troy dam as anything but an estuary. However, as compared to estuaries in most of our country, the Hudson is a relatively cool water estuary. This provides justification for permitting a temperature rise greater than 1.5°F. which would be the limitation in a more southerly estuary where temperatures are close to upper thermal levels for many species." When another conservation department official was asked how come the Hudson had suddenly become "a relatively cool estuary," he said, perhaps with tongue in cheek, "Well, the Hudson is cooler than estuaries in Alabama, Louisiana, and Florida."

Additional nuclear plants are under construction or planned for Long Island Sound, the south shore of Long Island, and the Jersey coast. Here too the utilities involved have refused to recognize thermal discharges as a problem. As a result, a number of persons and organizations, such as the HRFA, who were originally willing to live with nuclear power as long as there was no thermal pollution, began to raise other questions. What about the risk of radiation exposure? The plant at Indian Point does in fact routinely discharge radionuclides into the Hudson and the atmosphere. Other plants will do the same. To be sure, the AEC has established regulations on the release of radionuclides, but as Dr. Malcolm L. Peterson of Washington University School of Medicine, wrote in the November, 1965, issue of *Scientist and Citizen:*

These regulations are derived from *estimates* of how the radioactive materials move through the biosphere and *man's body*, how much radiation an average individual would receive from radioactive materials if he consumes an average diet and how much radiation damage would be expected to cause detectable health damage.

It is apparent that these are difficult estimates to make because we are only learning just how the radionuclides are concentrated under the widely varied conditions of nature and how they behave in human tissues. Furthermore, there are wide differences in dietary habits which might cause some people to concentrate these substances more than others. Current knowledge does not permit us to say how much damage would be the result of exposure to small doses of radioactivity. Nevertheless, we are faced with the necessity of making *some* estimates. . . .

It is apparent that "permissible" levels of radioactivity in reactor effluents cannot be asserted to be absolutely "safe" levels.

There is the possible effect that radionuclides could have on the Hudson ecosystem. In a paper published in 1968 in an effort to stop the New York State Electric and Gas Corporation from fouling Cayuga Lake with a nuclear plant, a committee of Cornell scientists wrote:

Localized concentration of radionuclides by currents, eddies or wave action is a likely possibility. After a few years of plant operation and accumulation of radionuclides in the lake, these processes could result in local concentrations in excess of maximum permissible concentrations. There will be also be concentration of radionuclides in aquatic organisms. Many plants and animals concentrate specific radionuclides in certain organs or tissues. For example, iodine is concentrated in the thyroids of higher animals and strontium in bones, scales, and shells. Tritium behaves much like ordinary hydrogen in metabolic pathways. Zinc-65 (formed by activation of reactor components and released to condenser cooling water) may be transferred by many routes from water to various plants and animals (including man). The extent to which different radionuclides are concentrated under various conditions by different organisms varies widely. The scientific literature contains reports of concentration factors for strontium-90 by freshwater organisms up to 500,000 for filamentous green algae, 100,000 for insect larvae, and 20,000 to 30,000 for fishes. [The concentration factor is the number of times the radioactivity of an organism exceeds that of the water in which it lives.] Each element can be expected to behave differently in different organisms, and the effects of very few radionuclides have been determined for very few freshwater organisms. Though radionuclide levels in human diets may not be significantly increased or exceed "permissible" levels, no one can accurately predict the effects such accumulations might have on aquatic organisms. Additions of radionuclides and the resulting increase in radiation exposure may be particularly damaging to aquatic organisms, because they are normally subjected to relatively small amounts of ionizing radiation.

The Cornell scientists, some of whom took issue with thermal pollution in an earlier paper, have proposed a closed-circuit cooling system for the Cayuga Lake plant. This would greatly reduce the volume of cooling water returned to the lake and thus diminish the amount of radionuclides discharged as well.

In spite of the protests thus far, New York State and the utility companies are engaged in a headlong rush to build nukes. In May of 1968, Governor Rockefeller rammed a bill through the legislature giving enormous powers to the State Atomic and Space Development Authority. No public hearings were held on the bill. Even public debate was stifled before it could start, because it was just about impossible for an outsider to procure a copy. Indeed, some legislators have since privately admitted that they did not even bother to read the provisions of the bill. Specifically charged with "the maximum development and use of atomic energy," the atomic authority is to have enormous sums of money at its command to subsidize both public and private plants. It has sweeping powers to condemn lands in the state. Moreover, the authority is not subject to the state public service and conservation laws. In the language of the bill, such laws are "deemed to be superseded," and should any provision of these laws appear to be in conflict with the powers of the authority, these provisions shall be "deemed to be superseded, modified or repealed as the case may require."

9

ACE AND
VERPLANCK

The Hudson leaves the Highlands at Peekskill. The river widens at Peekskill Bay, then veers to the southwest and narrows between Stony Point, which Mad Anthony Wayne stormed during the Revolution, and Verplanck Point. After the surrender of Cornwallis, Verplanck became the scene of "the grandest international military review in the history of the nation," according to one local history. French troops marched north from Virginia and crossed to Verplanck, where eight thousand Continentals hailed them with cheers and cannon salutes. Tents were decked with laurel and evergreen, and on October 1, 1782, Washington reviewed the French. On the next day, French officers reviewed the Americans, who were wearing their first decent uniforms.

It would be understatement to term Verplanck picturesque. It is today a weird settlement, by turns beautiful and scarred, but almost always fascinating. It is a cross between Cannery Row and an undiscovered Williamsburg. It sits out in the river on a long peninsula, Verplanck Point. The main line of the Penn Central cuts inland, and the Point is one of the few places on the east shore not girded by railroad tracks. Most of the houses are of sturdy red brick, which came out of the local clay pits worked during the nineteenth century. Spacious boulevards out of a surrealist dream offer sweeping vistas of the Hudson and the mothball fleet off Dunderberg Mountain, and down by the river at Steamboat Dock are brick tenements out of an O'Casey play. Ace Lent, a commercial fisherman, lives in the first of these on the second floor rear. Next door is a bar and grill, and beyond that is a lovely old wooden building with fluted wooden columns on the porch. One of the columns has tumbled into the river, and the building itself, Federal in style, bears the faded lettering on its front: EXCELSIOR POOL HALL ROOM. The bottom parts of some of the letters are missing; they were cut out for windows by past tenants.

Verplanck is an old Dutch settlement. Politically, it is neither village nor town. It is just there. It has always been there. Ace Lent's ancestors go so far back he does not know when they first arrived; possibly it was shortly after Peter Stuyvesant. There are Lents all over the Point; the name is as common as Johnson in Minneapolis. There is a Lent Street, and there is a Lents Cove, with no apostrophe, around the north bend at Indian Point, where Con Ed is busy adding to Hiroshima-on-Hudson. Before Con Ed got wired into the landscape, Indian Point was a park for excursionists on the Hudson River Day Line.

Besides the Dutch, there are Irish and Italians. The Irish, who came to work in the brickyards way back, are old-timers compared to the Italians, and they are in the social ascendancy. The "mayor" of Verplanck is Punchy Keefe, who wears a top hat in parades and is given to writing long odes about life along the river. Irish names are everywhere. There are McGuire's Brook, Murphy's ice cream store, and Mitchell's bar on King's Ferry Road, named after the ferry that ran to Stony Point in colonial times. Except for a couple of small neon signs, Mitchell's bar could pass for just another house. The proprietor, Sonny Mitchell, sees no reason to advertise. Like all Pointers, Sonny sticks to his own crowd, "the regulars"; Sonny and the regulars dote on the river, and during the spring and fall striper runs, many of them repair to the bar at night to compare catches. In season, Sonny keeps a platter of fried sturgeon on hand, and behind the bar is a twenty-gallon aquarium filled with river water and seething with life—small eels, killifish, and the resident boss, a six-inch striper.

Sometimes when I feel the world is too much with me, I like to go over to Verplanck. On occasion, I drop into Mitchell's for a beer, but most of the time I go over to Ace's. We look at the catch of fish in the shack out back, and then we go inside and talk while a pot of sturgeon chowder simmers on the stove. Ace's grandfather and father fished the river. In his father's day, fishing was a way of life at the Point. In the spring, Pointers netted shad and sturgeon, and the sturgeon were piled on barges and shipped upstate in such numbers that they were called Albany beef. In the summer, Pointers worked in the brickyards or the rock quarry, and in the fall and winter, they netted sturgeon and stripers or cut ice from Lake Meahagh, which was formed by a stream dammed off from the river. When the ice business and the brickyards collapsed, Pointers took year-round jobs in the factories of Peekskill and Buchanan, including the very industries that were among the worst polluters of the river; one is Standard Brands. The fishing was left to a handful who couldn't get the river out of their system, such as Jimmy Carey, Pete Smith, and Ace.

Ace has a regular job as a guard in the state armory in Peekskill, but the Hudson is his passion, his Moby Dick, his Holy Grail. Ace is a big man, six feet even and 250 pounds. Much of what I know about the river, I learned from him. Where he gets his unsparing nature I do not know. I never have asked him a personal question, and he says little about himself except as it relates to some fact about the river. I do not know whether Ace derives his inner spirit from some family tradition, or whether he has absorbed it from his life on the Hudson. So many of us are cut off from reality, from nature, by man's plunder and devastation, by prettily wrapped packages, supermarkets, and television that we do not know the world in its natural state. Ace does. I do not say this to make him any seer or a holier-than-thou person. He says "jeez" and "Jesus Christ," and "God damn," and "son of a bitch," and more, but he is unassuming in the truest sense. The first time

I ever saw him, he and some pals were down at the beach off the Steamboat Dock. The nets were drying on a pipe rack beneath a willow tree, bushel baskets of shad and sturgeon lay in the shade, and Ace was wearing a torn undershirt, the old fashioned kind with shoulder loops. All I could think of was a scene from the Bible.

As heavy as Ace is, he is fast on his feet and nimble with his hands. He builds his own boats and makes his own nets, usually from tug hawsers he has found along the river. He unwinds the hawsers and then weaves the strands into a net. He is not garrulous, but the river can get him talking, and when he starts talking I never know what I am going to learn. One day he got going about wrecks or "fasts" on the bottom of the river near Verplanck. "There's the Mary Warner sunk off Grassy Point in forty feet of water," he said. "You can hang up on that fast with a drift net, but I guess she's worn to the bottom by now. Not far away is the Midwater Fast. Who knows what the hell it is. Midwater Fast, that's all it is. There's the Cement Mixer off the quarry north of Stony Point. It's big, and I suppose it's a cement mixer. And off Jones Point are the Newsburgh Poles. I guess somebody was shipping poles to Newsburgh when they dropped off." When I said that he had never told me about these fasts, which do not show on the charts, Ace replied, "Jeez, you never asked me." I let it go at that.

The river is his life. "I love the Hudson," he says. "Even if I couldn't fish it, I'd just like to sit and look at it. My God, it's beautiful. But what I'd like to see is the bottom. Imagine if it was as clear as glass, and you could look down on all the fish—the stripers, the sturgeon, the herring, the perch, all of them. Jesus Christ, that would be something to see. I'd bet people would buy tickets to look at that. Jeez, what a river!" Ace has been away from the Point only once, and that was during World War II, when he was a radio operator on a B-26. On the way to England, the bomber passed over Verplanck, and Ace could see his mother's laundry hanging out to dry.

Ace's son, Billy, a quiet teenager now in the Army in Vietnam, has little interest in fishing with his father. Every once in a while, Ace teams up to fish with his cousin, Spitz. Spitz Lent is short, round, red-faced, and jolly, and at Christmas time he plays Santa

Claus at the Sears Roebuck store in Peekskill. His interest in fishing is sporadic. Spitz seems mainly interested in the eggs from the round-nosed sturgeon, which he likes to fry up in an omelette for breakfast. "You can tell when the eggs are done," Spitz says. "The stuff begins to pop all over the places like beebees going off." At present, Ace's fishing partner is Charlie White, who is also six foot and about 250 pounds. Charlie is a very pleasant fellow, but he is less talkative than Ace. When I drop into the house after a haul, the two of them are usually sitting exhausted at the kitchen table like two silent, giant Buddhas.

In late February or early March, when the ice starts to break up, Ace gets out his nets for shad. "Maybe they'll run good, like they used to," he says. "Jeez, you shoulda seen it in the old days. You'd look out on the river, and there'd be twenty-five boats off the Point, all of them catching shad."

Ace uses two nets, each two hundred feet long and twenty feet wide. He takes them out to the river and sets them near Stony Point. The bottom of each net is weighted with rocks. Long ropes extend from each end of the net, and old Clorox bottles and glass jugs are tied to them as floats marking the location. Of course, Ace does manage to catch some shad, but it is almost impossible for him to catch anything at all when the spring thaw comes in March. The melting snow from upstate surges down the Hudson, shoving trees, old timbers, logs, toilet seats, and plastic bags before it. "Those plastic bags kill me," Ace says. "That plastic never rots, and all those bags hit the net and hang there. Every fish in the river sees the net like a big bedsheet or a flag, and they all go around it. I can't catch a damn one. What the hell can be done? Damn, I wish the plastic stuff had never been invented."

Ten or fifteen years ago, Ace used to fish with a two-thousand-foot-long drift net for shad. "A net like that is no longer worth using," he says. "There aren't that many shad." On a good day Ace gets twenty or thirty shad, and half of these are bucks which have no roe. In good part, Ace blames the decline on overfishing. "I have to lift my nets out of the water Friday morning and keep them out until Sunday morning," he says. "All the nets are supposed to be out of the river for that time so the shad can swim up the Hudson to spawn. But it doesn't work out that way, at least not the way I figure it. The shad don't get up to the spawning grounds in enough numbers because they move with the tide. You see, the way I figure it, they come up on the flood tide and then drop back a bit on the ebb. All right, on Friday morning, we all stop fishing, and take our nets out. I get mine, the fellows in Ossining get theirs, and so do the fellows down near the Tappan Zee Bridge and the fellows fishing Jersey. The lift period lasts until Sunday morning. So what happens? The shad that have come up with the flood tide to the Jersey side of the river or up to the Tappan Zee bridge get past the fellows down there. But then when I put my nets in, I catch them. I know because I catch the shad on Mondays and Tuesdays. They don't have enough time to get past me. And if they do get past me, a fellow upriver at Peekskill is going to get them. I could see this when the Hudson was filled with shad, millions of them. That was when everybody was getting shad. After the lift, we'd put our nets back in, and we'd catch fish like crazy on Mondays, then a little less on Tuesdays. On Wednesday, the catch would drop way off, and on Thursday we wouldn't get a damn thing at all. This happened week after week, year after year. All the while we'd go on lifting the nets and all the time the shad were getting less and less. Now the fish are scarce, damn scarce. I figure there should be some way of staggering out the lift periods so what shad are down below can get up above to spawn without anyone catching them. These shad, or a certain amount of them, just have to get through, or otherwise we're not going to be able to catch shad anymore.

"Then there's the striped bass," Ace goes on. "That striper is getting to be nothing but a trash fish. Those striped bass are all over the river, and I think the shad are down because those stripers are everywhere. Now I can't *prove* that the striped bass are eating *all* the shad, but those stripers are sure as hell eating them. You've got that striper so protected now he has become a trash fish." Up until after World War II, commercial fishermen were allowed to haul seines in the river, and it was nothing to take great numbers of stripers in a sweep of certain grounds, such as the south side of Croton Point. Some sportsmen, including, ironically, a manufacturer who was a notorious polluter, raised a fuss and sent letters to Albany, protesting against the seining. A number of commercial fishermen (Ace was not among them) banded together and raised a thousand-dollar defense fund to stave off the sportsmen in Albany. The commercial fishermen lost, scining in the river was outlawed, and now striped bass may be taken only in gill nets from March 16 to November 30. Years ago, Ace's father used to take stripers in the winter off Georges Island by lowering a net through fissures chopped in the ice. Ace himself has no market for the stripers he catches in his nets. Local people can easily get what they need by fishing with rod and reel. The peculiar thing is that although Ace, as a commercial fisherman, has scant regard for stripers, he is fond of fishing for them himself with rod and reel. "Isn't that a beauty!" I've heard him exclaim, holding up a five-pounder. A couple of hours earlier, he might have been cursing out a thirty-pound bass that got into one of his nets.

With shad in short supply in the spring, Ace has taken to fishing for alewives, which jam into the Hudson in April from the sea and measure about a foot in length. Ace fishes for the alewives with a sixty-foot-long drift net he made from a spool of four-pound test nylon fishing line. ("I like to went blind putting that net together," he said.) In the morning before going to work at the armory, he takes his boat a quarter mile upriver to the quarry and puts the net overboard. As the net drifts downstream, on an ebb tide, the floats on top shake and dance whenever an alewife swims into it. "There's nothing like an early-morning drift on the river," Ace says. "Just me in the boat drifting with the net, the water glassy-smooth. No wind up as yet. A little bit of haze with the sun trying to come through. Everything is so quiet and peaceful and beautiful. Now tell me, could anyone ask for more?" In a twenty-minute drift to the Steamboat Dock, Ace may net as many as two hundred fat alewives bearing roe. He cleverly made the mesh of the net wide enough for the slimmer bucks to pass through. There is no market at all for buck alewives, and as yet Ace has little call for the roes, but he is trying to create a demand for them by giving the fish to friends. The roe of a female alewife is only a quarter as large as that of a shad, but it is finer-grained and has a more delicate and subtle taste. To me, the testes of the buck alewife are even tastier. On occasion, Ace will set a trot line, a long line with hooks, for catfish, and when he does, he uses a chunk of alewife as bait. "Those catfish go crazy over the herring," he says. "Why, by the time I'm halfway out still putting on bait, the line I've already put in the water is bouncing up and down loaded with catfish."

Ace occasionally gets a call for eels before Italian feast days, and eels have been dubbed, in Verplanck vernacular, "Eyetalian turkeys." Eels are a nuisance for Ace to catch. He has to make his own eelpots out of wire mesh, and state law requires that an irksome fifty-cent license fee be paid for each pot, which is like charging for swatting flies. Then again, teenagers out on the river in boats find it amusing to take an eelpot out of the water and remove the captives. "The hell with all that trouble," Ace says. He prefers to catch eels by bobbing for them. He sews a couple of hundred earthworms into a ball with a fine thread and lowers the gob to the bottom on the end of a line. When an eel strikes, the line is quickly retrieved, and the greedy eel does not let go of the ball of worms until he is in the boat. "That's a lot of fun," Ace says.

The only argument I ever had with Ace was about eels. He was telling me about the millions of inch-long "glass" eels that swarm in the river in the spring by the outlet from Lake Meahagh. "I wonder where they came from?" he asked. I told him that eels spawned in the Sargasso Sea and that the larvae were carried north by the Gulf Stream. When the larvae developed into the glass stage, they were able to fend for themselves, and they then headed inshore for coastal rivers. Ace refused to believe me, and he would not change his mind when I showed him a couple of books on the subject. He said, "I can't believe that that many little eels could come all the way up here from down there."

"It's true, Ace."

"I don't believe it, no siree. Can't be."

"But it is."

"It *can't* be," he said with finality. "I know there are a lot of strange things going on, but I can't believe this. I just don't think it's so. The whole thing sounds crazy."

I let the matter drop. Ace raised it once since at his house one morning when Spitz was there. "Hey, tell Spitz where all those millions of little eels come from," Ace said, with a smile. I didn't want to get involved for hours, so I pretended I hadn't heard and went on asking about sturgeon.

Sturgeon fascinate Ace. There are two species in the Hudson, the sea sturgeon (*Acipenser oxyrhynchus*) and the short-nosed or round-nosed sturgeon (*A. brevirostrum*). There are times when the Hudson off Verplanck seems alive with sturgeon. For unknown reasons, sturgeon will suddenly leap from the river, falling back with a loud splash. According to Washington Irving, a large sturgeon played a part in the naming of Anthony's Nose, the mountain just north of Peekskill. Irving wrote:

And now I am going to tell a fact, which I doubt me much my readers will hesitate to believe; but if they do, they are welcome not to believe a word in this whole history, for nothing which it contains is more true. It must be known then that the nose of Anthony the trumpeter was of a very lusty size, strutting boldly from his countenance like a mountain of Golconda; being sumptuously bedecked with rubies and other precious stones—the true regalia of a king of good fellows, which jolly Bacchus grants to all who bouse it heartily at the flaggon. Now thus it happened, that bright and early in the morning, the good Anthony having washed his burly visage, was leaning over the quarter-railing of the gallery, contemplating it in the glassy face below—Just at this moment the illustrious sun, breaking in all his splendour from behind one of the high bluffs of the Highlands, did dart one of his most potent beams full upon the refulgent nose of the sounder of brass—the reflection of which shot straightaway down, hissing hot, into the water, and killed a mighty sturgeon that was sporting beside the vessel! This huge monster being with infinite labour hoisted on board, furnished a luxurious repast to all the crew, being accounted of excellent flavor, excepting about the wound, where it smacked a little of brimstone—and this, on my veracity, was the first time that ever sturgeon was eaten in these parts, by Christian people.

When this astonishing miracle came to be made known to Peter Stuyvesant, and that he tasted of the unknown fish, he, as may well be supposed, marvelled exceedingly; and as a monument thereof, he gave the name of *Anthony's Nose* to

a stout promontory in the neighborhood—and it has continued to be called Anthony's nose ever since that time.

Ace has his best sturgeon fishing in the late fall and early winter, just before the ice comes. The fish are more active in colder
weather, and as Ace says, the rougher the weather the better, because "a good blow seems to put the fish on the move." I well remember the first time I went out with Ace and Spitz to haul a
sturgeon net. It was a cold and windy December day a week or
so before Christmas. I threw on an old overcoat and a pair of
snow boots and drove over to Verplanck. The net was set about a
mile away in the deep hole off Stony Point, where the bottom is
ninety-nine feet down.

A twenty-knot wind was blowing from the northwest as we
started off from the beach at Verplanck, and water soon slopped
over the ribs of the eighteen-foot boat. "A good day for sturgeon,"
Ace said, as I sat huddled with him on the rear seat by the out-
board. Up forward, Spitz crouched, searching for the floating bottles that marked the position of the net in the breaking white
caps. It is no use pretending that the Hudson River is the Grand
Banks in a nor'easter or a surging tropic sea stung by a typhoon,
but Haverstraw Bay can get nasty. I recall the comment of one of
the speedboat hotshots who entered the Albany-New York race a
couple of years ago. Everything had gone fine, he said, until he
hit the churning waters of Haverstraw Bay, where he felt as
though he were "roller skating over railroad tracks."

Water soaked my neck and trickled down my back. Pneumonia
seemed imminent. Even my hands, thrust deep into my overcoat
pockets, were soaked. The overcoat was wool, and I tried to tell
myself that wool warms and cotton chills, but this textbook
thought did little good. I was wet and cold. Ace and Spitz were
dry and comfortable in oilskin slickers.

The ebbing tide had not yet finished its run, and we circled
about the bobbing Clorox bottles for a half hour waiting for slack
water. The tug of the tide is so strong in either direction that
hauls have to be made on the slack. At last the ebb ceased, and
Ace moved up forward with Spitz to grab a line and pull the net
from below. "We've got sturgeon, a lot of them!" Ace yelled. He

could tell because there were bubbles on the water between the whitecaps; sturgeon are the only fish that emit bubbles as they come up in the net.

Most of the fishes in the net were sea sturgeon between twenty and fifty inches long. The legal size is thirty inches. Writhing in the net, they were especially primitive in appearance. Indeed, they might be called living fossils, for they are among the oldest fish species on the earth. They have long, leathery snouts on the front of the head, while the bottom part is soft and white, with a vacuum-cleaner type mouth that can hang down like the sleeve on an old coat. The eyes are small and glistening, like threatening peas, and the hard body is almost crocodilian, armed with five longitudinal rows of sharp shields, or scutes. Ace and Spitz had a time of it extricating the fish from the net because the scutes caught and fouled in the mesh. Pulling a sturgeon through the mesh was like attempting to push a needle with a broken eyelet through fine silk. Mixed in with the sea sturgeon were short-nosed or round-nosed sturgeon, legal keepers at twenty inches.

Ace and Spitz threw the shorts of both species back into the Hudson, but legal-sized sea sturgeon began piling up in the boat in such numbers that I started stacking them around me like cordwood to ward off the wind. By the time Ace and Spitz had finished, I was literally up to my neck in sturgeon. At last we chugged back to shore. Ace and Spitz carried bushel baskets of the fish to the shack in back, where a noose was affixed to a stout pole. Spitz handed Ace a sturgeon, and he hung it from the noose by the tail. He stuck a knife behind the dorsal row of scutes near the tail and sliced downward. Instantly the first row of scutes was cut off. Deftly turning the fish from side to side, Ace skinned it completely in no more than a minute. He gutted the carcass and chopped off the head. The final touch was to remove the gelatinous cord inside the spine. If left in the fish when cooked, the cord imparts too strong a flavor. Ace gently notched the skin around the tail, being careful not to cut through the spine. He then gave the tail a few twists to the right, tugged, and then pulled the tail and the attached cord from the fish. The only innards that he kept were the black egg sacs from ripe round-nosed females. These Spitz took. In Russia, the cords are washed, pressed, dried, and put up for sale as *vyaziga,* an ingredient of fish pie. The Russians also use the inner lining of the swim bladder to make glue or gelatine; in the nineteenth century, the lining was also used in Russia and the United States for isinglass. In Russia, *golovizna*, the head of the sturgeon, rich in gelatinous substances, is sold as food. I never had the courage or desire to try either *golovizna* or *vyaziga*, but I once had the dandy idea of making boot laces from the spinal cords. I squeezed out the gelatinous substance from the cords, carefully scissored them into long strips, and hung them up to dry. Two days later, I took them down, and humming merrily to myself, began lacing a pair of boots. Unfortunately, the cord strips snapped every time they were turned through an eyelet. When I told Ace about my experiment, he just stared at me.

After my first trip out with Ace and Spitz, I became very much interested in the two species of sturgeon in the Hudson. The more common of the two is the sea sturgeon, which originally ranged from Florida north to Canada. In early 1967, after the passage of the "Endangered Species Act" by Congress, the Interior Department classified the sea sturgeon as rare in the United States. "Rare" is officially defined as meaning that the species "is in such small numbers throughout its range that it may be endangered if its environment worsens. Close watch on its status is necessary." The sea sturgeon may be rare elsewhere on the Coast, but in the lower Hudson it is abundant, and New York State has no closed season or catch limit on the fish. Little is known about certain aspects of its life history. From what I have been able to gather, sea sturgeon hatched in the Hudson remain in the river until they are about eight or nine years old and have grown to a length of from three to four feet. These are the bulk of the fish that Ace catches. To Ace and other river fishermen, these juvenile sturgeon are known as "pelicans" or "peelicans." The pelicans apparently feed on small catfish and killies; on bottom invertebrates such as shrimps, sludgeworms, chironomid, and dragonfly larvae, *Asellus communis*, the aquatic cousin of the sowbug that is found on land under logs, and on small clams, *Pisidium*. The Hudson is rich in such provender.

At present, there is no sport fishing for sturgeon in the Hudson, but Ace has caught them on a trot line, the hooks of which he baited with live killies. In view of the great number of sturgeon in the Hudson, particularly in the ship channel in Haverstraw Bay, an excellent sport fishery potential exists. Sport fisheries for sturgeon have been started on the West Coast and in Florida, among other places, and there is no reason why the Hudson could not boast one of its own.

After reaching eight or nine years of age, the sea sturgeon move out to the Atlantic, probably venturing to the edge of the Continental Shelf. They have been taken off the Long Island and Jersey coasts, on Nantucket Shoals and Georges Bank, and in the Gulf of Maine. In the Atlantic, sea sturgeon grow at a rapid rate, and after maturing, they return to coastal rivers to spawn. One unspent male, taken in the Hudson in 1936, measured seven feet four inches long, weighed 176 pounds, and was twelve years old. Sea sturgeon are supposed to live to a fairly advanced age, but exactly how advanced no one knows because little research has been done. Moreover, determining the age of a sturgeon is rather involved. Many species, such as largemouth bass or striped bass can be aged by their scales, which show annual growth marks much like the rings in a tree trunk. But the scutes of the sturgeon do not show growth marks. Instead, biologists must dissect the ear stones or otoliths from the sacculus of the internal ear, and then only after much delicate sawing and grinding can they then determine the age through microscope examination of a cross section.

Mature sea sturgeon enter the Hudson to spawn probably in late April, certainly in May and June, and possibly in July. Precisely where they spawn is unknown. My own guess is that they spawn from Peekskill north to Coxsackie or Castleton. In 1875, Seth Green, the fish culturist who first carried shad from the Hudson to California, artificially propagated sturgeon with eggs and milt taken from fish captured near the mouth of Wappinger Creek. I have no doubt that in the late spring and early summer mature sea sturgeon are in the Hudson in considerable numbers. The evidence for this is obvious. First of all, there are the countless juveniles in the river, and you get small sturgeon only from big sturgeon. Secondly, it is not unusual to see the big fish leaping from the water. In June, 1968, while flying by helicopter from Croton to New York City, Ronald Dagon saw sturgeon schooling heavily near the mouth of the Croton River. Dagon said the sturgeon were in the thousands, "some up to six feet long." On occasion the big sturgeon hit a shad net. The strands of a shad net are not strong enough to contain these powerful fish, and they punch through like a torpedo smashing into a ship.

Ace has had several run-ins with large sturgeon. One incident occurred on May 2, 1966, when he went out to lift his shad net off Stony Point. As he pulled and grunted, the net slowly came to the surface, and there was a monstrous sturgeon. Ace took a good long look at it. The fish had rolled itself into the net, and, Ace told me later, "it was three-quarters the length of the boat," which meant that the fish was twelve feet long and probably weighed in the neighborhood of five or six hundred pounds. Ace sat down on the middle seat and pondered what to do next. The sturgeon was quiet; perhaps it had exhausted itself battling the net. Reaching overboard, Ace decided to boat the fish by grabbing it above the tail. He had no sooner put both hands on the sturgeon than it immediately came to life and thrashed wildly. Ace hung on, but then the fish decided to dive, and as it did it lifted Ace, no lightweight, straight up from his seat and into the air. Ace let go, and with a resounding splat, the sturgeon broke free of the net and escaped. All atremble, Ace came back to shore, where his father told him, "You were damn lucky you didn't get him into the boat. He'd have sunk it and drowned you."

Almost a year to the day later, on May 4, 1967, Ace saw another big sturgeon in the river. This one was floating on the surface, and it was dead. Part of the back and tail had been sheared off, most likely by a ship's propeller. Ace slipped a hawser around the fish, towed it into the beach and phoned me. I went over to the Point to see it. Before running into the ship, the sturgeon must have been seven feet long. A plump female, it weighed, by my rough estimate, between 175 and 225 pounds and contained from fifty to one hundred pounds of golden-brown eggs. After I photographed the fish, Ace towed the sturgeon back out into the river, where, no doubt, eels and catfish polished off the remains.

Even less is known about the life history of the round-nosed sturgeon. The Interior Department has classified this species as endangered, the same status given to the whooping crane. An endangered species is "one whose prospects of survival and reproduction are in immediate jeopardy. Its peril may result from one or many causes—loss of habitat or change in habitat, over-exploitation, predation, competition, disease. An endangered species must have help, or extinction probably will follow." Originally, the round-nosed sturgeon ranged in rivers from Florida to New Brunswick. It was found nowhere else in the world. According to the Interior Department all recent catches, except for one Florida specimen, have been from the Hudson River. "The species is gone in most of the rivers of its former range," states an Interior report, *Rare and Endangered Wildlife of the United States;* "[It] is probably not yet extinct."

Ace laughed when he heard this. He is not one to mock an endangered species, but the round-nosed sturgeon is far from an unusual fish in the Hudson. The state allows round-nosed to be taken from July 2 to April 29, supposedly the beginning of the spawning season. Although the round-nosed has been caught at sea, the fish apparently spends all its life in the river and ordinarily does not go into the Atlantic. The smallest of all the species of sturgeons in the world, round-nosed males mature when only nineteen or twenty inches long and females at about twenty-four inches.

Considering that the Interior Department has deemed the round-nosed endangered, Ace has taken some highly unusual specimens. For instance, he caught a hermaphroditic round-nosed in 1965. He gave me the sex organs, which I passed along to John Clark at Sandy Hook. Clark, in turn, passed the organs along to Dr. James Atz at the American Museum of Natural History. Atz, who had recently finished a paper on hermaphroditic fishes, said this was the first case he had ever encountered among the sturgeons. In 1969, Ace caught another hermaphroditic round-nosed, which he passed on to an astonished Atz.

According to Bigelow and Schroeder's authoritative *Fishes of the Gulf of Maine,* the heaviest round-nosed on record weighed seven pounds four ounces. In a more recent study, Vadim D. Vladykov and John R. Greeley give the maximum weight as "about nine pounds." However, Ace and Charlie White have taken fish weighing up to twenty-five or thirty pounds. Unfortunately, Pointers put such a high gourmet value on the large round-nosed that I have had difficulty procuring a record fish, which I want to give to the American Museum. Once Ace promised me a twenty-pounder, but when I went over to get it, he said: "So and so ate it. He came in, saw the fish, and bought it. How the hell could I have turned him down?" The same thing happened with a fifteen-pounder. The Pointers go on eating supposedly endangered fish of world record size. When I finally stressed the importance of a record round-nosed to Ace, he promised me he would save the next one for me. When he called, I drove over immediately and procured an eleven-pound four-ounce specimen for the museum. It was a female and contained forty-four ounces of eggs. I gave the fish to Ron Dagon, who has a large freezer, for safekeeping. Alas, Dagon lost the key to the freezer, and the museum has yet to get its record fish.

During the colder months, the female round-nosed sturgeon contain eggs which can be made into caviar. Whenever Spitz isn't around, Ace has been kind enough to give them to me. At first, I was faced with the problem of preparing caviar properly, and a Croton acquaintance, Dr. Dan Salzberg, joined in the quest for informative how-to-do-it literature. Such literature proved to be lacking, aside from a nineteenth-century report that I discovered on taking a hundred pounds of eggs and letting them sit in brine of fine grained Luneberg salt from Germany. Salzberg found a book in the New York Public Library with the title *Caviar,* but it turned out to be a dreary novel about some high-living Mittel Europeans in the 1920s, and it had nothing whatsoever to do with caviar. As is his bent, Salzberg read it and insisted upon telling me the plot one evening. Finally we chanced upon the printed advice of General Malcolm Beyer, the president of Iron Gate Products Company in Manhattan, the gourmet foods subsidiary of 21. Beyer, a retired Marine brigadier general, is the largest single American purchaser of caviar from the Soviet Union, and his instructions for making caviar are to be found in that estimable work, *McClane's Standard Fishing Encyclopedia and International Angling Guide.* Following the general's instructions, Salzberg and I remove the eggs sacs from the fish and place them on very fine mesh from a minnow seine stretched across a bowl and held in place by a rubber band. We gently rub the sacs back and forth across the mesh. The tissues adhere to the mesh, while the eggs separate and fall into the bowl. The eggs are carefully stirred and rinsed in cold tap water four or five times. After the final rinsing and draining, we have a bowlful of glistening, pearly-black eggs. We place the eggs in a colander and allow them to drain for no longer than ten minutes. We slide the eggs back into the bowl, which has been wiped dry. We add 3 per cent salt by volume to the eggs, mixing in the salt gently with a cake spatula. We then ladle the eggs into small sterilized glass jars until the jars are filled to the brim. The jars are capped and placed in the refrigerator. A week later, the caviar is ready, and it can be kept for up to six months. On no account should caviar be placed in a freezer; freezing will cause the eggs to burst. The caviar from the round-nosed sturgeon is of excellent quality. I gave a jarful to General Beyer, and, to quote Hamlet, "'twas caviare to the general." He pronounced it equal to the best *Sevruga* caviar from the Soviet Union and he offered to buy any round-nosed caviar available at the wholesale price of ten dollars a pound.

Pointers themselves are very fond of cooking skinned sea sturgeon which has a strong taste uniquely its own. The round-nosed, a naturally oilier fish, is even stronger. Properly prepared, either kind of sturgeon can be excellent. In appearance and flavor both are more like turkey than fish. Because of the strong flavor, many Pointers parboil or marinate their fish, cut it into steaks, and sauté it. I once gave a sturgeon to Jerry Tax, an editor of *Sports Illustrated*, and he and his wife, who baked the fish, pronounced it superb. Here is Mrs. Tax's recipe:

First put up to boil three good-sized potatoes, sliced, in salted water, along with a few carrots and two large onions. Cover and boil steadily for about fifteen to twenty minutes. Half done, in other words.

Slice the sturgeon into 1½- to 2-inch steaks. Season well. Sturgeon absorbs all kinds of seasoning heavily. Dot with butter and arrange loosely, with plenty of space around each piece, into a shallow pan lined with foil. Arrange the parboiled vegetables all around the pan, and pour in the liquid —all of it, it's delicious. Bake in a medium oven for about twenty minutes, basting the fish occasionally. You can also add slices of tomatoes to the baking dish when putting in the fish.

Insert a piece of raw garlic into each piece of fish before putting it into the baking dish. The size depends on your taste. We use practically a whole clove in each piece.

As for other seasoning, we just use salt, pepper, and paprika. Do not cover the baking pan.

I have yet to try Mrs. Tax's recipe; frankly, I do not care for sturgeon, either round-nosed or pelican, as a dinner dish. However, I do like smoked sturgeon. I buy the fish from Ace and take them to Ralph Mann, a carpenter and jazz musician in Croton, who smokes them over applewood gathered from abandoned orchards.

Many persons, ichthyologists included, have been flabbergasted by the abundance of sturgeon in the Hudson. A couple of years ago, John Clark asked me to collect some live striped bass from the Hudson for the Sandy Hook lab. I did so with Seth Rosenbaum, a systems engineer from the city, about whom more will be said in the next chapter. Following Clark's arrangements, Seth took off for the New York Aquarium at Coney Island with three striped bass swimming around in a container on the front seat of his aging convertible. An air hose plugged into the cigarette lighter assured them of a supply of oxygen. As an added treat for Clark, we added a few small sea sturgeon to the container. The New York Aquarium was to hold the stripers for Clark in a temporary tank until he could get over from Sandy Hook to pick them up. When Seth roared up at the aquarium, he asked Charlie Young, the keeper, the whereabouts of the holding tank. In an off-hand fashion, Young pointed to the tank, and Seth dumped in the fishes. Young did a double take when he saw the sturgeon. "Where did you get those?" he asked. "Up the Hudson," Seth replied airily. A day later I had a call from Young, and not long afterwards he and Eddie Dols were up to see Ace at the Point. Every once in a while, Young and Dols explained, the Aquarium got the chance to pick up a six- or seven-foot-long sea sturgeon from the pound nets off Long Island and the Jersey coast. Although such fish were of interest to the Aquarium, they took up a lot of space in an exhibit tank. On the other hand, Young and Dols went on, small sea sturgeon were rarities. In fact, aquariums all over the world wanted them. The small sturgeon did not take up much space, and they were genuine show stoppers for the viewing public. Surplus juvenile sturgeon were also excellent for trading with other aquariums. In fact, an aquarium that had an assured supply, a lock on the market, if you will, was in the position of a major league baseball club that had an unlimited number of Willie Mayses down on the farm teams. Ace was happy to help. The New York Aquarium has a scientific license allowing it to collect fishes of less than legal size, and under this permit, Ace supplied Young and Dols with a dozen sea sturgeon, some as short as nine inches. Several of them are on exhibit at Coney Island while others have been air-expressed to the Shedd Aquarium in Chicago and the Steinhart Aquarium in San Francisco. At one time, I kept a fourteen-inch sea sturgeon in my living room aquarium. For the most part, the fish swam counter clockwise around the tank, sporadically sticking its snout out of the water. Afraid that the sturgeon would electrocute itself on the light wires above, I lowered the water level several inches. Unfortunately, I could not get the fish to feed, and after two months it expired. In public aquaria, sea sturgeon thrive in a tank of thirty thousand gallons or more on a diet of cut shrimp and bait fish. So far, I have not been able to get the brass of the New York Aquarium interested in keeping round-nosed sturgeon from the Hudson. None of this species has ever been kept in captivity anywhere, so far as I can determine, and their confinement would mark a first. Surely their presence in a tank of sufficient size would contribute considerable knowledge to their feeding habits and behavior. It might even be possible to induce the round-nosed to spawn in captivity, and considering the rarity of this species elsewhere along the coast, such an event might do much toward relieving its endangered status.

In view of the lack of knowledge about sturgeon, fishery biologists are very much interested in getting freshly preserved specimens for taxonomic study. Several years ago, while on a trip to Miami, I was asked for specimens by George Miller of the U.S. Bureau of Commercial Fisheries Tropical Atlantic Biological Laboratory. Miller said that Jim Atz at the American Museum of Natural History would arrange for shipment to Miami. After returning home, I collected fifteen small sea sturgeon and phoned Atz, whom I had yet to meet in person, and he said to come on down. I drove to the museum with the fish frozen in a large plastic bag. After wending my way through labyrinths of dinosaurs and Pleistocene elk, I found the Department of Ichthyology, where a secretary directed me to Atz's office. As I entered with the booty for Miller, Atz, garbed in a long white coat, was bent over a microscope examining some tiny cichlid from British Guiana. He waved me to a seat. Five minutes later, he arose and wandered over. "What have you got here?" he asked.

"Sea sturgeon from the Hudson for George Miller in Miami," I said. "He said you would ship them to him."

Atz looked at the bag of fish on the counter. His eyes seemed to pop. "Oh my God!" he exclaimed. Then he shouted. "Donn! Donn! Come here." Dr. Donn Rosen, the head of the department, hurried from his office across the hall. He and Atz stood in wonder at the fish in the melting bag. "Oh," said Atz, "They're beautiful. They're lovely." He sighed over them like a lifer let loose with Elizabeth Taylor. "They're just beautiful. Hmmm, look at those tails. How lovely!" Rosen sighed in agreement. After much oohing and aahing, Atz turned toward me. "You know, our sturgeon collection here is very meager," he said. I nodded stupidly. "We'd love to have these for the museum," he continued. "Of course, I'll send George some. Would you mind?" I said I would not, that I could get plenty more for George. After this, we all had a very long and pleasant conversation, which was joined by C. Lavett Smith, and the end result was that I agreed to collect sturgeon and other Hudson River species for the museum and its new Hall of Ocean Life.

Given the abundance of sturgeon in the Hudson, I began to wonder a few years ago if there might not be more of a commercial market for Ace. In my mind, I began to formulate fantasies of a corporation to be known as the Greater Verplanck Caviar Company. Ace and Charlie were to wax rich as joint managing directors and net haulers, while I would draw a modest fee as consultant. One day, I told them about my idea.

First off, Ace and Charlie would have to capture the big sea sturgeon entering the river to spawn in the late spring and early summer. To do this, they would need very strong netting. This would cost approximately a thousand dollars, a figure which caused Ace and Charlie to look askance. At the time, they were running a leaky boat with an elderly five horsepower engine held together with string—ha, they still are! I suggested a new boat and engine would be in order. "Why not go first class?" I said. They looked askance again. "He's dreaming Charlie," said Ace. But as I sketched out the possibilities, they hunched over the kitchen table in silence. There was no hard and fast figure on how many big fish they could harvest, I went on. More research was needed (and certainly the Greater Verplanck Caviar Company should back that research), but the chances were that maybe five thousand big fish, weighing one hundred pounds and upwards, could be taken each year without harm to the stock. "He's still dreaming, Charlie" said Ace. If research disclosed that only one thousand should be taken, then only one thousand would be taken. If seventy-five hundred could be taken, we could work toward that figure each year. Over all, five thousand was a nice, round working figure. According to the law of averages, and from what is known about sturgeon populations, about half of these five thousand fish would be females, and the typical female would contain, to set a low figure, about fifty pounds of eggs. Twenty-five hundred females each with fifty pounds of eggs added up to 125,000 pounds of caviar. At the very least, that caviar would fetch a minimum wholesale price of ten dollars a pound. There was the chance it would bring more, because the eggs of the sea sturgeon, unlike the eggs of the round-nosed, are not pearly-black but golden-brown. In Europe, the golden-brown eggs are the cream of the caviar trade to knowing gourmets. Known as *Osietr,* this golden-brown caviar fetches sixty dollars a pound retail. It ranks with *Beluga,* which is the caviar most American gourmets know, while *Sevruga* is next in esteem.

"Now, boys," I said to Ace and Charlie, "I'm not saying our sea sturgeon will have the *Osietr* caviar. But I think they will because European sea sturgeon, *Acipenser sturio,* is probably, possibly, the same fish as *Acipenser oxyrhynchus,* except that some taxonomists have noted slight differences. The eggs are quality stuff." For starters, we could still figure on the wholesale price of ten dollars a pound raw. But, I went on, even at the low price of ten dollars a pound, 125,000 pounds of eggs would be worth $1,250,-000. There were great laughs from across the table, as though we had just robbed a British mail train. Moreover, I continued, the flesh of both the female and male fish would be worth a minimum of fifty cents a pound, possibly far more if the Greater Verplanck Caviar Company went into smoking sturgeon. Figuring the average fish had one hundred pounds of meat, that meant the flesh would bring $250,000. In sum, the value of the total catch, eggs and meat, would amount to $1,500,000 for three months of work. Silence. An exchange of glances around the table.

Financing was in order. A few persons with whom I discussed the prospects of the Greater Verplanck Caviar Company were immediately enthusiastic, but they had even less business judgment than I. By chance, I happened to run into a Time Inc. colleague, Seymour Freedgood of *Fortune,* who had, at least for a journalist, some business sense. With great fervor, Sy at once began seeking to organize and finance the company. Ever the backer of improbable causes, he was so smitten with the prospects that he drove up to Verplanck with an immense seine that he had bought from a commercial fisherman on Long Island. The seine was worthless for what we had in mind, but Ace and Charlie expressed their thanks while Sy went back to sounding out moguls on Wall Street. Sy and I had lunch with General Beyer, who was very interested in buying what the company caught. For one thing, the general liked sturgeon I had brought him from Ace; as a matter of fact, he had even served one smoked to amazed friends at 21. Secondly, the general had liked the *Sevruga* caviar from the round-nosed sturgeon, and although this fish was not present in enough numbers in the Hudson to support a sustained commercial yield, the possibilities of *Osietr* caviar from the big sea sturgeon was most intriguing. Thirdly, the general had his difficulties in dealing with the Russians, and the Russians, moreover, were having difficulties of their own. The Caspian Sea, the major source of the Russian sturgeon fishery, is badly polluted, so badly polluted that in the 1930s Soviet biologists had to stock a marine worm, *Nereis diversicolor,* from the Black Sea, in order to provide food for the sturgeon in the Caspian. Furthermore—and this will strike an ironic response in the Hudson Valley— the Volga spawning grounds are threatened by hydroelectric projects, and marshlands on the Caspian are being "reclaimed" for agriculture.

Unfortunately for the Greater Verplanck Caviar Company and for all those who knew him, Sy Freedgood died. Plans for the company have been put aside for the nonce. Nonetheless, General Beyer is still very much interested in the Hudson sturgeon and their eggs, and Ace and Charlie are talking about weaving a net to hold the big ones. In fact, not long ago they went for a walk along the beach at the Point looking for an old black tug hawser. Ace found one, and he is now taking the hawser apart strand by strand to weave into a gigantic net. "I could finish it in a month," Ace says. "This black stuff is as strong as hell."

Whatever happens, Ace will go on fishing the river. Recently he realized one of his dreams. He hunted up the owner of the old Excelsior Pool Hall Room and bought it to use as a home. Now he is painting the place over and putting in new windowpanes. The old poolroom is right on the riverbank, and any debris that floats close to shore is swept into a little cove by the house where Ace keeps his boat. The pickings can be good, especially after abnormally high tides. Within the space of a week, Ace picked up an old rowboat, a ladder, a chair, and a twenty-by-ten-foot wooden pier that he plans to nail into place. In the years to come, he doubtless will be able to furnish the old place from the flotsam that floats by. The Hudson seems to have a way of taking care of her own.

10

HAVERSTRAW BAY
AND
SENASQUA BEACH

David Starr Jordan was a great American ichthyologist and the first president of Stanford University; in his two-volume autobiography, *The Days of a Man*, there is a chapter which has, for anyone who is interested in what lies below the surface of flowing water, the exciting opening sentence, "In the summer of 1876 I set out to explore the fish fauna of the streams of Georgia, a large region from which practically no records had been made." The Haverstraw Bay reach of the Hudson River is my equivalent of Jordan's streams of Georgia. Although the bay is only some thirty miles north of the Battery, it is largely unknown. If I have a personal wish about the Hudson, it is to know the bay in its entirety, to know every fish, every crab and shrimp, every bird and every plant, and to mark their shifts and movements with the ebb and flow of tide and change of season. The bay is an incredible place, and it is subject to so many variables, to so many unknowns and rhythms as yet unperceived that it exhausts the imagination. One would have to be God to see it all.

From Croton, where I live, over to Haverstraw, beneath High Tor, the bay is more than three miles across; this is the river at its widest. From Croton Point, composed of glacial moraine and alluvial outwash, north to the peninsulas of Stony Point and Verplanck, where the river narrows, the bay is about six miles long. In appearance, Haverstraw Bay looks more like a lake than a river, and it has been compared by some admirers to Lake Como for beauty. In this age of rapid despoliation, the comparison is perhaps optimistic.

The bay is a place of moods. There are the gloomy days of late December when dark billows of clouds scud low and a northwest wind lathers whitecaps on the rocks of the Penn Central tracks. The air temperature may fall below freezing, but the wind beats with such force that the river cannot ice over. Ice needs peace and quiet to form. But if there should be two or three still days, the ice suddenly appears, at first a thin glaze of white stretching from shore to shore. Cracks zigzag crazily across the expanse of glare as the tides change, but the ice holds and thickens to a depth of half a foot or more.

In a normal winter, Haverstraw Bay is frozen from January to early March, and Coast Guard icebreakers keep the ship channel open to Albany. In a rare winter, ice may not come at all. In another year, ice may come early in December, melt during a warm spell in January, then form a second time. When Haverstraw Bay is frozen over, ice boaters flock in from a hundred miles around on weekends. Ice boating got its start on the Hudson—the Roosevelt family, including FDR himself, were great enthusiasts—and it is much preferred to ice boating on lakes in the region. There is almost always a good wind on the bay, and there are great distances over which to skim at exhilarating speeds. To ice boaters, the bay has all the attributes that the Bonneville salt flats hold for automobile speed enthusiasts.

The first signs of spring are Canada geese on the move northward. For the most part, the geese, wily creatures that they are, eschew the shorelines of the Hudson, settling instead for refuge in the middle of the bay. The geese gather in large rafts, as many as five hundred or one thousand at one time, and when disturbed they take to the air with a great beating and rustling of wings, lining the sky with shifting V's. I have been about on local ponds in the spring, wading and watching for the early movements of pickerel, when suddenly I have been startled to see and hear geese land nearby. They come soaring in above my head. I stand stock still, and they fly lower and spread their giant wings. Air rushes through the stiffened feathers with the peculiar hissing sound of a jet coming in with flaps down. With a soft splash, they land on the pond. The geese espy me, and padding furiously toward me, they deliver angry, raucous honks that seem to say, "Get out, get out!" I do. I retreat from the pond and into the woods, exhilarated at having met my masters.

When the water temperature is 35° in Haverstraw Bay, I know that vast schools of striped bass are somnolent in the depths. Sturgeon are lively and stirring about, but the bass are almost comatose, shifting about the bottom of the bay with the change in tide. At 40°, smelt are on the move in the spring. Sharp-toothed, delicate, slender creatures, they flash along the bottom of the bay, doubtless tracking, through some keen inbred sense of chemistry, the mouths of freshwater brooks, up which they will swim and spawn. Between 42° to 45°, the striped bass sort of yawn, wake up, and begin to feed. By now alewives are starting to throng up the Hudson, seeking out nuptial streams or death in the Albany pool. Waking stripers, large enough to take alewives whole, do so with avidity and ease. Smaller stripers nose about the bottom, tails flicking upward, as they pick out tidbits. These bass appear to feed by opening their mouths and inhaling their prey; I have found bits of oyster shells and other detritus in their stomachs.

As Haverstraw Bay comes to life in the spring I try to envision the bay as a moving whole. In spring, summer, fall, or winter the mud bottom of the bay in the deeper water and ship channel is covered with a green, bristly sort of grass. Actually, this grass is an alga, of the genus *Cladophora*. Thick and bristly, the *Cladophora* harbors enormous amounts of rock crabs and shrimp upon which sturgeon, striped bass, and other fishes prey. If the waters of the bay were crystal-clear and it were possible to see to the *Cladophora* at the bottom, the river would appear carpeted with a pasture of green hair.

The water in the bay is usually murky, except in the early fall, when there is little rain or runoff. Visibility then is four or five feet, but most other times it is barely a foot and often only six to eight inches. In color, the water varies from gray to green to brown. Some of the turbidity is caused by sediments in suspension, and some by plankton, the free-floating populations of minute animals and plants. In the spring, the water may appear green because of the growth of algae, especially the diatoms, single-celled plants that flourish upon the nutrients in the water. These plants serve as the grass on which minute crustaceans and other animals can graze, and, in turn, these creatures serve as the food for larger invertebrates and fishes. The plankton is of the greatest importance to the river, but it has been largely ignored.

In 1936, when the state conservation department conducted its biological survey of the lower Hudson watershed, the entire report on plankton dealt with the plankton in lakes and ponds and not at all with that in the river. Only recently have scientists begun to appreciate the significance of microorganisms in rivers. Thus it is impossible to say how much pollution or other factors have altered the composition of plankton in the Hudson over the years. Even so, according to Dr. Gwyneth Parry Howells of New York University, the Hudson has a rich population of plankton. To be sure, there are a number of organisms usually associated with sewage pollution, for example, *Phormidium* and *Oscillatoria*, blue-green algae. Even so, compared to other polluted rivers in the East, such as the Raritan and the Delaware, the Hudson apparently has a richer fauna of plankton not associated with pollution. Twenty different species of rotifers and about thirty protozoans have been found in the lower Hudson, and a biologist friend says these numbers do not even begin to give a true picture of what the river holds.

One of the ecological strengths of Haverstraw Bay is that it offers diverse habitats. On the rocky west shore, the bottom slopes steeply to the ship channel, reaching an average depth of about forty feet. Proceeding eastward, the dark gray mud bottom begins to shoal, rising quickly within the space of a few yards to a depth of twelve feet. This eastern half of the bay is uniformly shallow, and it is covered, where not silted over with mucky clay, with millions of old, empty oyster shells. These oyster beds apparently flourished between four and six thousand years ago, when the bay was more saline.

I cannot get enough of the bay, and aside from Ace and Charlie and the other commercial fishermen at Verplanck, I am often the first out on the bay in the spring in my boat, a small Boston Whaler, and the last to leave in winter when the ice sets in for good. My trips or expeditions usually have some specific purpose behind them, and often I am accompanied by friends, acquaintances, or scientists interested in a particular aspect of the Hudson. These jaunts give me the greatest pleasure, not the least of which is simply dreaming about what to explore. The rocky beaches of the Palisades? The bottom off the north tip of Croton Point? The shallows, cluttered with old bricks, off Grassy Point? The marsh at the mouth of Furnace Brook? All these places, for all the horrors done to the Hudson, have their surprises.

There are glorious days when the wind is still and the bay is smooth as a mirror. Off we go at eight in the morning, the boat laden with a depth finder, a plankton net, a seine coiled in a plastic garbage pail, a cardboard box stuffed with mason jars full of formalin for specimens, waders or worn-out sneakers (broken glass and tin cans are all too common on the river bottom), a couple of sandwiches, and a thermos of milk. Time passes quickly, and suddenly it is nightfall, and we are back at the launch. The deck of the Whaler is gritty with mud and sand, the seine has been torn and requires mending, the sandwiches are half eaten, and the milk is warm. But the jars bulge with specimens, and there is another day to be remembered when ice grips the river.

Yet these expeditions have drawbacks. For one, I simply do not have the money to do all I would like to do. An Ekman dredge is expensive, and so is a shrimp trawl, ideal for collecting in the depths of the ship channel or obscure holes known only to the chartmakers. But what defeats me, what has made me at times despair, is that the bay is so vast and time so short. There simply is too much to be done, to be collected, studied, or pondered if I am ever to see in my mind's eye the entire workings of the bay.

Still, I try to build bit by bit. The commercial fishermen help out, and instead of throwing back strange fishes, they keep them for me. So far, Ace alone has come up with three species never before reported in the scientific literature as being in the Hudson. They are codfish (*Gadus morhua*), silver hake (*Merluccius bilinearis*), and the longhorn sculpin (*Myoxocephalus octodecemspinosus*), and all were caught in November and December, when he was fishing for sturgeon.

For my own part, I have not given up in my determination to know Haverstraw Bay firsthand, and thus what I have done is to retrench, to make what time I have more valuable by concentrating on the shoreline of the bay. I have set up certain collecting stations that are easily reached by car, and I visit them as often as possible the year round. One station has yielded some unusual specimens; this is Senasqua Beach at Croton. Perhaps it has yielded the most because I have studied it the most intensively; it is only five minutes away from my house.

A small bay one hundred yards long, it is flanked on the north by the barges serving as a breakwater for the Croton Yacht Club and on the south by a landfill, Senasqua Park. The beach runs parallel with the Central tracks, only fifty feet away. Behind me as I work, trains roar and rumble—the rusting ghost of the 20th Century Limited bound for Chicago, the Hendrick Hudson late as always from Albany, lengthy freights from the Middle West— Pacific Fruit, Rath Packing, the Route of the Phoebe Snow, Canadian Pacific, Union Pacific, Burlington, Milwaukee Road. The litany of cars clickety-clacks a metallic rhythm to the valley. A switch engine, shunting cars weighted with auto frames for the General Motors plant at Tarrytown, tootles by. The freights move, people move; from a train the river is an enticing blur. Next to the tracks is the unknown drama of the life in the river: great schools of stripers and sturgeon on the move, acres of killies and catfish and eels buried in the winter mud, the stray cod fumbling in the murk to find the sea. A train passes, the last echo dies in the distance, and a stillness descends upon the valley. The transients are gone, oblivious to what lies beneath the lapping waves. I remember the flickering passage of a dining car— mulatto waiters moved about, two pairs of white hands touched briefly over a vase of flowers, and then they were gone, and I turned back to the river.

Like Haverstraw Bay Senasqua Beach offers a diversity of habitats: from north to south, there is a foot-deep mucky bottom with heavy vegetation during the summer months; rock rubble and wooden pilings, the foundations of a nineteenth-century village pier; and a smooth sand bottom, bordered by boulders, that serves as a bathing beach for swimmers at Senasqua Park. Although the bay is polluted, the water hereabouts is usually clean enough for health authorities to certify the beach as safe for swimming.

I collect with a sixty-foot-long, six-foot-deep seine. Made to my special order, the seine is of quarter-inch mesh, and it has a collecting bag called the cod-end in the middle. I have seined alone, but wading out into the river and bringing back both ends of the net evenly is a tricky business, and my children or friends and acquaintances often lend a hand. There is Ed Hatzmann, a Croton neighbor; Murzban Jhabvala, a local high school boy of Parsee ancestry who hopes to become a marine biologist; Richie Garrett, an ardent river rat; Dom Pirone; and Seth Rosenbaum, whose dream is to own a marine collecting station in the West Indies and who has seined in Bermuda, in Puerto Rico, and along the East Coast. Seth is nuts about fish. He goes marlin fishing just to catch remoras for his aquarium. I always wear thick wool socks, trousers, and waders when I seine in cold weather, but Seth persists in showing up in only bathing trunks and sneakers, even when the water temperature is in the low forties. Seth and I have a mutual acquaintance, Joe Mintzer, and I only wish I could inveigle Joe to Croton more often, because he is a great fish collector, probably the greatest in northern waters. A native New Yorker with a noticeable local accent, Joe is in his mid-fifties, stubby, and of middling height. He has curly red hair, a preoccupied expression, and a predilection for cigars. He works nights as an electrician in Manhattan, and he spends his days off collecting at Rockaway Beach, Sheepshead Bay, and other points near the mouth of the harbor. "Fish are beautiful," Joe says. "They're like boids."

He travels to his collecting sites by subway, toting snorkle gear, buckets, and nets. He has disdain for a seine, and instead uses nets of his own design, employing mesh from nylon shopping bags. He has hand nets with square, round, elliptical, and triangular frames which are bent to shape for him by a lamp-shade maker. Each net serves a special purpose; the triangular net, for instance, is used to corner fish in crevices. Joe also has special nets which he wears like a bib. To collect fishes that hide in vegetation, he swims face down through the water, holding out the hem of a green apron net. To get fishes that like to hide in dark holes, Joe uses a black hand net. He goes underwater and waits for a fish to come by. Then he scares it with his bare left hand and the fish foolishly takes refuge in the black net held in Joe's right hand.

Joe lives on the top floor of a seven-story walk-up in the hippie district on the Lower East Side, and his apartment looks as though fishes rent it and he is just a boarder. Tanks are everywhere. Unfortunately, Joe's fishes are difficult to see in captivity because he overfeeds them and the water is heavily clouded with bacteria. Pointing to a tank, Joe will say, "There's a triggerfish in there, I think." He will then stand waiting patiently for fifteen or twenty minutes until suddenly a figure looms out of the murk next to the glass. "There he is! There he is!" Joe exclaims, as the fish disappears back into the aquatic smog.

Seth and I both keep fishes from the Hudson alive in aquaria, and we have had, thank God, more luck than Joe. My principal tank is six feet long, two feet deep, and almost two feet wide, and it holds 120 gallons. It is set close to the floor in my living room. Originally, I used the aquarium to duplicate a local largemouth bass and sunfish pond, even to the point of stocking dragonfly and mayfly nymphs, but for the past several years I have concentrated on re-creating the Hudson River at Senasqua, or at least a clear version of it. All the fishes in the tank have been taken at Senasqua sometime or other, and I have put rocks and old oyster shells on the bottom. At night, after a few beers, I like to get down on my back on the floor and look up at the stripers, small perch, and eels swimming around, and imagine that I have my own private view of Haverstraw Bay, unbeclouded by plankton or silt. Sometimes I think I ought to stock a broken Coke bottle or a couple of beer cans to add to the air of reality.

I release most of the fishes I seine at Senasqua, though I make it a point to take a number of specimens of everything from time to time for the American Museum of Natural History. Sometimes I collect specimens, either live or preserved, for other institutions, such as the New York Aquarium, the King's College in Briarcliff, Adelphi College, or the U.S. Marine Gamefish Laboratory at Sandy Hook. The Sandy Hook Lab has dibs on all bluefish I take; the lab is attempting to do a life history study of this important marine gamefish. Recently, I began collecting blood samples of fishes for a professor at the University of California who is attempting to reclassify fishes on the basis of blood chemistry. The classical taxonomists of the nineteenth century, who set down the orders, families, genera, and species we have today, did so largely on the basis of bone and fin structure. Maybe the professor in California will come up with something new to explain the development and relationship of fishes. As long as he sends me the necessary equipment (hypodermic needles, pipettes, fixative solution, bottles, and so on) and pays the postage, I am willing to help. I am also interested in any findings any specialist can report, however seemingly obscure, about life at Senasqua Beach, Haverstraw Bay, or the Hudson.

I have been seining Senasqua Beach for several years. Catches vary slightly from year to year, but I have ascertained fairly well the rhythm of seasonal cycles. Here, then, is what is likely to be found beneath the surface of the Hudson inshore at Croton from the late winter to the fall:

LATE WINTER AND EARLY SPRING

SMELT (*Osmerus mordax*). There is a tremendous run of smelt up the Hudson starting in March. They are related to salmon and trout, and they often occur inshore at Senasqua by the hundreds, perhaps thousands.

KILLIFISH, HARDHEAD, MUMMICHOG. There are two species of killifish at Senasqua, the common (*Fundulus heteroclitus*) and the eastern barred killifish (*F. diaphanus*). These fish throng the river by the millions, if not billions, feeding upon small crustaceans and mosquito larvae. They are often seined by anglers for bait. The true saltwater killie (*F. majalis*) is absent. The common killie has extraordinary endurance. It can be impaled on a hook through the lips and cast time after time as bait and still be lively. I have taken them alive and well out of the stomachs of largemouth bass. Their only drawback as bait is their drab green color. Inasmuch as killies can withstand almost anything, I have dyed them red with neutral red, a laboratory stain, to make them conspicuous underwater as bait. They can spend several hours out of the water and survive. I have seen killies in my aquarium stacked on top of one another out of the water, with the bottommost killies resting on the stems of water hyacinths. They do this to escape largemouth bass on the prowl below. In the laboratory, killies have lived in water with three times the salinity of sea water. In late May, I have seen them spawning in the ditches of Iona marsh. During spawning, the male common killie takes on a vivid blue and yellow coloration.

GOLDEN SHINER (*Notemigonus crysoleucas*). Sometimes called roach, they are almost a foot long at Senasqua. I once showed some giant specimens to Richie Ferris, a Croton bait dealer, and he said, "The Poles at the hat factory used to fish for them." The hat factory used to be at Peekskill, and both it and the Poles have departed, the latter, I hope, to better angling. In Britain, a slightly different species of roach is much sought after by anglers. Thus in the *Angler's Bedside Book*, edited by Maurice Wiggin, there is a picture of three dozen roach, all smaller than those I seine at Senasqua, with the caption, "This bag of beauties represents the most dreamed of the mostest." Maybe the Poles at the hat factory knew what they were doing. Roach are supposed to be good eating, but I have never tried them. In the Hudson Valley roach are a capital bait for largemouth bass in lakes and ponds, and they sell for one dollar a dozen. Those that come from the Hudson appear to be much hardier than those from ponds, and when I once remarked upon this to a biologist, he said that I was seeing natural selection at work—conditions in the river were causing a strain of tough shiners to develop.

SPOTTAIL SHINER. This is the *Notropis hudsonius* described by De Witt Clinton. It is abundant at Senasqua from the spring through the fall.

ALEWIFE OR HERRING. I have seined adults from ten to twelve inches long in the spring. In the summer and fall, baby herring are very common. Alewives are landlocked in the Kensico Reservoir in Westchester, where the larvae used to pass into the New

York City water supply distribution system and emerge from household taps.

BLUEBACK HERRING (*Alosa aestivalis*). Juveniles are common at Senasqua. They very much resemble alewives, except that they are more slender. According to Bigelow and Schroeder's *Fishes of the Gulf of Maine*, "The most dependable distinction between the two (though requiring the use of a knife) is that the lining of the belly cavity is sooty or blackish in the blueback, but pearl gray or pinkish gray in the alewife." Both the blueback and the alewife are delicate fishes, and juveniles usually die when netted unless the greatest care is taken.

COMMON SUCKER, WHITE SUCKER (*Catostomus commersoni*). I have taken perhaps a dozen over the course of three years, and these were all seined in the spring. Suckers are more common up-river, and it may be that they visit Haverstraw Bay mainly during the torrents of spring, when salinity is at its lowest.

JOHNNY DARTER (*Etheostoma nigrum*). I usually take from two to a dozen in a haul at Senasqua. The johnny darter is a very attractive aquarium fish. It walks about on the bottom using its pectoral fins as if they were legs. It does not swim so much as it darts and leaps. It is attracted by light, and it has very keen sight. It has the ability to roll its eyeballs and turn its neck, and it is interesting to watch them feed on small shrimp. As the shrimp shower down, the darters eagerly turn their heads back and forth in the manner of spectators at a tennis match. Small fish, rarely more than four inches long, they are members of the perch family. They are well distributed up and down the Hudson and in tributary streams.

YELLOW PERCH. Found at Senasqua from the late spring to late fall.

PUMPKINSEED SUNFISH (*Lepomis gibbosus*). Common at Senasqua from spring to fall.

RED-BREASTED SUNFISH (*Lepomis auritus*). Also common throughout most of the year. I have seen both species of sunnies guarding nests in the brackish waters of the lower Croton River.

CALICO BASS OR CRAPPIE (*Pomoxis nigromaculatus*). Not as common as the above. I may take a dozen in the course of a year.

LARGEMOUTH BASS. Sometimes taken in the spring, but more

common in the summer at Senasqua. Specimens ranged in size from one to ten inches. One eight-inch bass had a two-inch barred killie in its stomach. I have never known of an angler to take a largemouth from Haverstraw Bay with rod and reel. Ace Lent has caught them in his gill net on occasion, and they are sometimes taken in fyke nets set in the mouths of tributaries, such as the Croton River, Annsville Creek, and Popolopen Creek.

In both natural waters and the aquarium, largemouth bass are extremely aggressive. They have a strong sense of territory, with the toughest bass, usually the biggest, taking the most preferred area, such as the choicest feeding ground. I have put ten large-mouths into my aquarium at one time, and within a week, they all had their own territories, with the lion's share—half the tank—belonging to the dominant bass. Woe to any other largemouths that stray over the line. The boss bass immediately rams the intruder in the flank with his head and nips at the fins. If there is a marked discrepancy in size, the bigger largemouth will eat the smaller by swallowing him whole. One night, I tossed a field-mouse into the aquarium, and a two-and-a-half-pound largemouth seized him at once, turned him around head first, and swallowed him, with the tail of the mouse slowly receding from view. It is impossible to keep striped bass with largemouths because the largemouths have a marked liking for stripers. Once I put a two and a half inch largemouth in with twenty two- to four-inch stripers and perhaps twenty small killies. In six weeks the largemouth had grown to five inches. He had wiped out the killies and all but five or six of the larger stripers, and these stripers were having a hard time of it. The largemouth would try to swallow them and when unsuccessful would spit them out. The rough handling loosened the scales of the stripers and made them subject to fungus infections.

BROWN BULLHEAD OR CATFISH (*Ictalurus nebulosus*). Common at Senasqua from April to October. The species is found in brackish and fresh water. Bullheads are supposed to bury themselves in the mud upon the approach of cold weather. They feed by taste and smell; their sight is very poor. They are interesting aquarium fish. When pieces of cut herring or earthworms are dropped into the tank, bullheads go into a frenzy, dipping and sweeping the bottom sands with their taste-organ barbels or whiskers. A bullhead five inches long once attacked and demolished a two-inch crayfish in the tank. The fight raged in a dark cleft between some rocks, and it was waged with such primitive elan by both participants as to make *Frankenstein Meets the Wolfman* a lackluster affair.

WHITE CATFISH (*Ictalurus catus*). An occasional visitor at Senasqua. Black in color, it is called the white catfish because it has white barbels.

AMERICAN EEL (*Anguilla rostrata*). The eel is very common at Senasqua from the spring through the fall, and I have taken eels that were from an inch to two and a half feet long. They are usually found over the mud near the Croton Yacht Club barges, but I sometimes gather them from under the rocks at low tide. In the spring young "glass" eels are abundant.

My first experience with an eel in my aquarium was most enlightening. I got a twelve-inch eel from the river, and as my family gathered around, I dumped him into the aquarium, which then contained eight largemouth bass, the largest of which weighed three and a half pounds. I thought that the eel would be too fast for the bass, but this was not the case. Immediately after the eel entered the tank, the three and a half pound bass grabbed the eel, and swallowed him. Or at least we all thought the bass had swallowed the eel. But lo, the eel's tail started to poke through the gill flap of the bass. The startled bass relinquished his grip, and the eel shot free through the flap. In an instant another bass seized the eel, and the eel again wriggled free through the flap. The eel did this to every frenzied bass in the tank. Sometimes the eel poked his head through first, other times his tail. Whatever end he used, his unique method of escape worked on every bass. On several occasions, the eel would be working his way out of one bass when another would grab the free end. The eel would thread his way through both. Finally, the three and a half pounder hit the eel a second time, and this time the eel, undoubtedly battered and woozy from his Houdini-like escapes, had lost his zip, and our hero disappeared for good into the bass's stomach. In the wild, of course, the bass never would have had a second chance. The eel is literally a slippery customer.

Even herring gulls (*Larus argentatus*) which abound on the Hudson and are capable of bolting a small rat, seem to have difficulty with eels. An acquaintance of mine, Ted Marsi, once caught an eel while fishing for stripers on their fall run up the Harlem River to the Hudson. He unhooked the eel and threw it back. No sooner had he done this than a gull swooped down, grabbed the eel in its beak, and flew off, swallowing hard. Suddenly the gull started screaming and swooping. As Marsi watched, the eel emerged through the bird's anus and fell back into the water. The gull flew off, still screaming, and as Marsi said, "I've never seen such an angry bird."

In an aquarium, eels along with catfish serve a useful purpose as scavengers. Any stray bits of food that might fall to the bottom and eventually cloud the tank are swiftly consumed by them. Eels seem to have very poor eyesight, and ordinarily, they spend the daylight hours buried in the sand or even snuggled up inside the glass wool of the filters, but when something odorous enters the water, they are out at once tracking the quarry by smell.

WHITE PERCH (*Morone americanus*). I have taken perhaps as many as five hundred to one thousand white perch with one haul of the seine at Senasqua. Perch bite freely from mid-May to October, and it is no trick for an angler to catch a hundred in a few hours, with the average fish about eight inches long. The favorite bait is a small piece of bloodworm or a grass shrimp impaled on a small hook. The white perch is a superb fish to eat, especially when it is filleted and sauted. There are some persons who deem it the best eating fish of all, and there are times when I agree.

At the outlet to Lake Meahagh, I once seined a ten-inch perch with a large bulge in its stomach. I pressed gently, and a bullfrog tadpole, which probably had washed out of the lake, emerged. I put the perch and the amphibian Jonah back in the Hudson and both swam off their separate ways. The white perch, incidentally, does not do well in an aquarium. It is strangely delicate for a fish that thrives in the Hudson.

HOGCHOKER OR RIVER SOLE (*Trinectes maculatus*). This is the only flatfish found the year round in Haverstraw Bay—the summer flounder or fluke (*Paralichthys dentatus*) and winter flounder (*Pseudopleuronectes americanus*) have been taken on rare occasion in the lower Hudson—and the hogchoker generally frequents the bottom of the deeper parts of the bay. It is the closest relative in North America of the famed Dover sole, but it is too small—from two to six inches long—to eat. In the aquarium, hog-chokers usually stay on the bottom and cover themselves with sand, where they wait for some smaller creature to venture by. Sometimes they will stick against the glass sides.

TOMCOD (*Microgadus tomcod*). An anadromous member of the cod family. Adults from six to ten inches long are present in the fall. On May 4, 1965, while out fishing with Ace Lent at Georges Island, we scooped up several larval tomcod that were swimming on the surface. (The frozen larvae were later given to the Sandy Hook lab.) This was noteworthy, inasmuch as Bigelow and Schroeder report in *Fishes of the Gulf of Maine:* "Although great numbers of tomcod have been hatched artificially by the State of New York, its later larval stages have not been described, nor have we seen them ourselves." Bigelow and Schroeder state that tomcod spawn from November to February. In the Hudson, they probably spawn in April. In the fall and winter months, anglers along the shore catch tommies in numbers. They have the reputation of being a toothsome fish, although the saying goes that it takes twenty to make a dozen. I have found as many as four or five tommies in the stomachs of striped bass caught near Georges Island in November and early December.

The whereabouts of tommies during the winter has always been a subject of local speculation, but the *Dolphin* cruise on March 7, 1968, located them in great numbers in midwater over the hole off Stony Point.

LATE SPRING AND EARLY SUMMER

A number of invertebrates may be present the year round at Senasqua, but they are most evident starting in the late spring.

FRESHWATER SHRIMP OR SCUD (*Gammarus*). *Gammarus* is found in abundance at Senasqua. These are tiny creatures about 12 millimeters long, and at low tide they can be found clinging to the underside of wet rocks. They may also be entwined in vegetation or algal mats. These are doubtless one of the most important fish foods in the Hudson, especially for young fish. I once found a pair of *Gammarus* copulating inside a cleft in a wad of discarded gum.

GRASS OR GLASS SHRIMP (*Palaemonetes vulgaris*). Abundant in the submerged vegetation at Senasqua during the summer. They may also be found in coves and inlets along Haverstraw Bay. They grow to an inch in length. Like *Gammarus,* grass shrimp are very important fish food, and knowing anglers use them as a deadly bait for white perch, striped bass, snapper bluefish, black bass, and trout. On several occasions when I had the water drawn down in my big aquarium, I put in two or three dozen grass shrimp as food for stripers and largemouth bass. The basses went wild over them, and in an effort to escape the shrimp jumped and plastered themselves on the glass above the water line, where their transparency made them all but invisible.

PRAWN OR SAND SHRIMP (*Crago septemspinosus*). Common in the mud bottom near the barges at Senasqua. Sometimes reaches a length of almost two inches. Prawns are easily collected by pushing a window screen along the bottom.

MUD CRAB OR HARRIS CRAB (*Rhethroparopus harrissi*). A small, brown crab, it is found beneath the rock rubble at low tide. One of the favorite foods of small striped bass.

BLUE CRAB (*Callinectes sapidus*). One of the most exquisitely beautiful of living creatures. Found at Senasqua from late July into September. The crab population of the river has fluctuated wildly in recent years. In the early 1960s, it began to dip, and from all reports reached a low in 1965. In 1966, the crabs were back in fair number but they were scarce in 1967 and 1968. By scarce I mean I saw only two or three in the river over the course of both years. The reasons for the fluctuation in population is unknown. In 1968, there were noticeable declines elsewhere on the coast. In the Hudson, blue crabs range up to Poughkeepsie, and crabbing is a favorite summer diversion along the river. The crabs are superb eating.

BARNACLE (*Balanus improvisus*). Barnacles are on the rocks at Senasqua, and they are common in the river at least as far north as Peekskill.

HARDSHELL CLAM (*Venus mercenaria*). The year-round presence of this mollusk, never before reported from the bay, has yet to be documented for certain. The trouble is that no one has searched for them. In December, 1966, hardshell clams approximately two inches in width were scattered by the hundreds along the tide line at Senasqua after several days of strong northwest winds. The winds and wave action might have rooted them from the bottom and pushed them onshore, a common occurrence along the coast. Then again, the clams might have come into the bay that particular year because of increasing salinity caused by drought.

The mollusks of the river offer a rich field for study. In the 1950s, Morris K. Jacobson and William K. Emerson found a huge colony of brackish water mussels, *Congeria leucophaeata*, attached to submerged logs, floats, and buoys off Croton Point, and along both shores of the river from northern Manhattan to Bear Mountain. Previously this mussel was not thought to be north of Chesapeake Bay.

DAMSELFLIES AND DRAGONFLIES. The damselflies are *Lestes congener* and *L. disjunctus;* the nymphs may be found in the vegetation. The dragonflies are the little amberwing, *Perithemis tenera,* and *Celithemis elisa.* I have seen dragonfly adults laying eggs—ovipositing to use entomological jargon—but I have yet to discover any nymphs.

To return to fish. FOURSPINE STICKLEBACK (*Apeltes quadracus*). There are usually one or two of these little fish in a haul of the seine at Senasqua Beach during the summer. The stickleback is found when vegetation is present.

CARP. Specimens up to fifty or sixty pounds are common at Senasqua from June onward. I have seen monsters of this size swimming in the confines of the Croton Yacht Club. In the summer, it is nothing to take half a dozen at one sweep of the seine. One day Charlie Young and Eddie Dols of the New York Aquarium were up collecting, and one of the fish they wanted was a twenty-pound carp. As we brought the seine in, carp began leaping and smashing back into the water. It was as though small bombs were going off inside the net. We landed close to a dozen, the largest about forty pounds, and as the carp lay flopping on the beach, Eddie and Charlie were jumping up and down, exclaiming over the wonder of it all. A netful of big carp is a sight to draw people to the beach. On the dirt road between the beach and the railroad tracks, motorists screech to a halt and jump from their cars at the sight of the fish. Bathers on the beach below leave the water to run up. The most expressive face I ever saw belonged to the engineer of a Central switch engine. Dom Pirone and I had netted half a dozen big carp when I heard the engine coming up the tracks. I purposely timed bringing in the net with the arrival of the engineer, who was looking out toward the river. Just as he passed, the carp came thrashing ashore in the net, and the engineer almost fell out of the cab. He pointed wildly to the fish and then began tooting the whistle and waving like a madman as the engine moved away.

I used to have difficulty wrestling the carp into submission, until a commercial fisherman told me to put a finger in the carp's mouth. I do this now, and the carp immediately go limp, much in the manner of a squalling baby given a pacifier.

GOLDFISH. Found at Senasqua in the summer. Young and Dols have taken two-pounders here for exhibit at the aquarium. There's no business like show business.

SPEARING, SILVERSIDE. There are two species of spearing at Senasqua, the common (*Menidia menidia*), and the tidewater (*Menidia beryllina*). Both are slender fish and beautiful to behold. They are a translucent bottle-green with a glittering silver band along each side. The two species may be differentiated by examination of the anal fin; that of the tidewater is much shorter, with only fifteen or sixteen rays. The New York State Conservation Department nominated the tidewater spearing for inclusion on the rare and endangered list maintained by the Bureau of Sports Fisheries and Wildlife, and there it is listed as "status undetermined." I have found ripe females at Senasqua in late June. The common spearing is in great abundance in Haverstraw Bay from late July through November, and they are among the favorite prey of bluefish and striped bass. There must be millions of spearing in the river. It is no trick at all to take several hundred at Senasqua with a small umbrella net. The net, held outstretched by stiff metal ribbing, is dropped to the bottom in two or three feet of water with a cord attached. Bread or cracker crumbs are then cast upon the water as bait. In a few minutes, spearing move into feed, and the net is lifted from the water with the fish. Spearing are delicious to eat and simple to clean. I hold one in my right hand, and gut the innards with a forward motion of the thumbnail. I snap off the head with the left hand and rinse the fish under the tap. The spearing are fried in cooking oil. In restaurants they are sold under the name of whitebait.

Dead or alive, spearing are also a killing bait for black bass and big pickerel in local ponds and lakes.

STRIPED BASS. Curiously, I have not taken many striped bass at Senasqua in the early spring. I do get a few, but not as many as from July on into November. In early July, the vegetation at Senasqua is thick with thousands upon thousands of inch-long striped bass, the result of the spawning upriver in May and June. At times in the early fall, striped bass may be the the the most common species in the seine, after spearing.

SHAD. Young shad, three inches long, may be found at Senasqua in late August and September. Like the herrings, they are a delicate fish and almost invariably die upon contact with the net.

ATLANTIC MENHADEN OR MOSSBUNKER (*Brevoortia tyrannus*). Juvenile menhaden, two to three inches long, are found often in great numbers during August and September. I once took ten thousand in a single haul. They utilize the lower Hudson as a nursery ground. Once in a while adult fish, up to fifteen inches long, are to be found in Haverstraw Bay. Very delicate, the menhaden can easily die when seined. Menhaden belong to the same family of fish, the Clupeidae, as the alewife, blueback herring, and shad. Their excessive natural oiliness makes them unfit for human consumption, but they are the leading commercial fish taken along the Atlantic coast. They are used to make oil and fertilizer. They are very difficult to keep in an aquarium, because they bang their heads in the corner until they hemorrhage. However, as Joe Mintzer says, "If you can get one of them to live, you can't kill him." Joe uses small menhaden to clean up the water in his tanks.

PIPEFISH (*Syngnathus fuscus*). Reported as "rare" in the state biological survey of 1936, pipefish are very common in the late summer and early fall at Senasqua. They are to be found in the vegetation, where they probably feed on *Gammarus* and other small crustaceans. From three to five inches long, the pipefish have thin S-shaped bodies; when mating, they intertwine their bodies, looking, according to one observer, "very much like the U.S. Army Medical Corps insignia."

The male pipefish incubates the eggs in a brood pouch, and the hatched young stay there until eight or nine millimeters long. Pipefish supposedly protect themselves from predators by giving off a stink, but I have smelled nothing. I have never been able to keep one in an aquarium for more than a few days.

Pipefish are related to the American sea horse, which was first discovered in the Hudson in 1842 by James DeKay and named, appropriately, *Hippocampus hudsonius*. I have yet to find sea horses at Senasqua, but several years ago, Ed Brandon, an aquarium dealer in Bedford, discovered them clinging to the latticework of a sunken boat off Tarrytown.

ANCHOVY (*Anchoa mitchilli*). Common in the early fall.

ATLANTIC NEEDLEFISH, BILLFISH, SILVER GAR, OR "SWORDFISH" (*Strongylura marina*). The needlefish is one of several marine species which enter the Hudson in late summer and early fall. I have found baby needlefish, two to three inches in length, as early as mid-July, but schools of larger needlefish do not arrive until September at Senasqua. These fish range in length from nine to twenty-two inches, and I have taken as many as a hundred in one haul of the seine. The needlefish is shaped somewhat like a squarish garden hose and has a long, pointed beak with sharp teeth. The fish must be handled carefully because they will attempt to bite, even when held by the tail. Needlefish are surface feeders, and they sometimes leap from the water after their prey. In so doing, they have been known in southern waters to skewer people accidentally. (Needlefish belong to the same order, Beloniformes, as the flying fishes.)

Needlefish make a unique contribution to the aquarium. They stay on the top of the water and can dive only with the greatest difficulty. I feed them live spearing, which the needlefish instantly seize crosswise in their beaks and then turn lengthwise, swallowing them head first. On one occasion, when I neglected to feed two needlefish for several days, they staged a savage battle for the one spearing I had to offer. One needlefish took the spearing crosswise, and the other attempted to steal it. Their beaks clashed, and the duel was on between Douglas Fairbanks and Ramon Navarro. The fight ended when one needlefish used his beak to give the other a scissors grip across the midsection.

In the Hudson, needlefish range to Poughkeepsie, and some local people refer to them as swordfish. DeKay called them a dish for epicures, but warned that most persons were alarmed by the bones, which turn green when cooked. Needlefish are the tastiest fish I have ever eaten. They have a subtle, nutty flavor that make Florida pompano seem coarse.

BLUEFISH (*Pomatomus saltatrix*). Starting early in July, baby bluefish an inch and a half long may be found at Senasqua and other points in the Tappan Zee and Haverstraw Bay. I have seined only a handful, but Tony Morabito of Ossining and Jimmy Mowbray of Peekskill, both commercial bait seiners, have encountered large schools of baby bluefish on separate occasions. Morabito ran into several hundred at Kemey Cove north of the Scarborough railroad station, and Mowbray once netted several thousand in the cove at the mouth of Annsville Creek while trying to fill an order for live killies. In late August and September, so-called snapper bluefish from eight to twelve inches long are present at Senasqua, and I have taken them there in the seine with such freshwater fishes as sunnies and largemouth bass. In the Hudson, snapper blues travel as far as Diamond Reef, New Hamburg, sixty-seven miles north of the Battery.

There probably is no fish that can match the bluefish for rapacity. Back in the 1870s, Spencer Fullerton Baird, the first head of the old U.S. Fish Commission, described the bluefish as "an animated chopping machine."

"Going in large schools, in pursuit of fish not much inferior to themselves in size," Baird wrote, "they move along like a pack of hungry wolves, destroying everything before them. Their trail is marked by fragments of fish and by the stain of blood in the sea, as where the fish is too large to be swallowed entire, the hinder portion will be bitten off and the anterior part allowed to float away or sink."

Blues are the only fish that can excite the herring gulls at Croton Point. The Croton Point gulls, glutted with garbage being dumped at the marsh, are ordinarily a blasé lot, but when the blues start chasing bait fish to the surface of the river, the gulls suddenly become interested and involved. With much screaming and squawking and flapping of wings, the gulls dive bomb the water for the bait fish driven to the top by the marauding blues. I recall one September morning in 1965 when all was quiet off Croton Point, and about five hundred gulls were sitting on the water near the north tip off Potato Rock. They seemed to be out of their usual torpor, but nothing was happening. I was with Don Manns,

the guiding spirit of the Long Island League of Salt Water Sportsmen, and, anxious to show him some action, I continued on in the
boat to the reef at the south tip of the point, where one can
usually catch snappers casting blind. There we spent a fruitless
hour, and I headed back upriver. Just before we reached the
north tip, we saw a wild melee in the water. Perhaps five acres of
the river surface was boiling with twelve-inch snappers, frightened spearing, and bombing gulls. This mob came right at us,
and for twenty minutes the action was absolutely frantic, as we
tried to keep up with the school of blues and frantic gulls chasing
the spearing down river. I would gun the boat to the head of the
school, we would cast, catch fish, and then start the engine to get
in front again. The air was so thick with gulls that Manns inadvertently snared one in his line while bringing in a snapper. The
bird, which did not take kindly to handling, was freed, and we
kept on casting until the blues suddenly sounded after reaching
the reef. There were a few last jumps here and there, like stray
rifle shots at the end of battle, and then all was quiet, and the
gorged gulls lazily flapped back to their usual station at the
dump.

On occasion there are larger fish. On another September morning, also in 1965, Bill Gaddis, a Croton neighbor, and I went out
to fish for snappers. The water was glassy-slick and the sky gray
when we launched at high tide. We went up to Furnace Brook,
where the tide was just going down. The fishing then is usually
very good, as all sorts of titbits are washing out of the marsh behind the trestle. But no snappers showed, and we decided to drift
downriver with the tide. Off Oscawana Island, we came upon a
double-crested cormorant (*Phalacrocorax auritus*) and for several
minutes we started to count aloud the number of seconds the
cormorant stayed under every time he dived. Suddenly there was
a splash ten feet off the bow. A blue had come out of the water,
arching its back. I grabbed the light spinning rod we had in the
boat and cast a two-inch silver spoon, ordinarily used for black
bass, toward the widening ripples. Instantly the rod throbbed. A
hooked blue leapt from the water and dove deep, ripping four-
pound test line from the reel. After about five minutes, I brought
him alongside, where Gaddis netted him. The blue was almost
seventeen inches long and weighed about two pounds. Its size

made it not a snapper blue but what some call a "harbor" blue. There were blues coming out of the water all around us now, and Gaddis, beaming like a fanatic, was on to a fish. In the next half hour, we had a strike or a fish on almost every cast. We lost many because the blues slashed the line with their razor-sharp teeth. Still, we landed seven, and our forearms ached from the tension and excitement of taking them on light line. If we had had the time, we might have caught forty or fifty. Two-pound bluefish are not worth a brag in Long Island Sound or off the Jersey coast, but I can remember few times that were more exciting. The fish were a treat to come upon, they were more than a match for the tackle, the setting was splendid, and we were right on top of the school, drifting with the tide on mirror-smooth water. Later I discovered that Jack Garrett and Augie Berg of Ossining had at the very same time, taken five- and six-pound bluefish by casting dead spearing from the rocks at Senasqua. I have since seen large bluefish off Senasqua, but every time I have seen them I have been seining close to shore and the blues were just too far out to be reached by casting. These five- and six-pound blues do not seem to travel in schools, as do the snappers in the river. Apparently these larger fish are solitary travelers that have strayed up to Haverstraw Bay to look over the pickings.

I have found it impossible to keep bluefish alive in the aquarium. For all their nerve, they are a very nervous fish, and they succumb to shock upon capture. Once I did manage to keep an eight-inch snapper alive for two days, and I had the pleasure, if that is the word, of seeing him suddenly wheel around and chop a two-inch menhaden in half.

The late summer and early fall is the glory time of year for me at Senasqua, not only because of the marine forms, such as the bluefish and needlefish, but because of the southern and tropical fishes which come in. Thus far, I have taken the following:

MULLET (*Mugil sp.*) Small specimens up to four inches long have been seined on occasion. On the coast, mullet are common as far as New York City, but until the past few years none had ever been reported from the Hudson.

ROUGH SILVERSIDE (*Membras martinica*). In the summer of 1967, Dom Pirone and Dr. Ed Menhinick of the University of North Carolina took a number of this species which the doctor later identified. This is the first time the rough silversides has been reported from the Hudson. It is not common north of Virginia.

JACK CREVALLE (*Caranx hippos*). A gamefish of warm seas, the jack is usually associated with Florida waters. Yet these fish occur in the Hudson in numbers. In the late nineteenth century, Dr. Mearns took jacks at West Point (the specimens are in the American Museum of Natural History collection), and he reported that they occurred in the Highlands stretch of the river in years of drought. The 1936 state biological survey of the lower Hudson took one jack and listed the species as "rare." I seined a dozen jacks at Senasqua in two years, from as early as August 31 (1966) to as late as October 15 (1967), and specimens are now in the collections of the American Museum of Natural History and the Tropical Atlantic Biological Laboratory in Miami, operated by the U.S. Bureau of Commercial Fisheries.

Jacks are beautiful and lively fish in the aquarium. They are mostly gold in color and have a finely scaled, satin-like skin. Jacks of three inches or less have five dark, vertical bars on their sides. As the fish grow larger, these bars vanish, yet they reappear should the fish become excited. When excited, jacks may also make an audible grunt, similar to the "oink" of a pig. I have had them grunt in my hand when removed from the seine, and even after being placed in the aquarium they could be heard grunting twenty feet away.

Their streamlined bodies allow them to pivot quickly, and when feeding, they are the very spirit of speed and vigor. They will eat a variety of food, such as live and cut frozen spearing, grass and sand shrimp, small killies, sandworms, and crayfish. I once saw a six-inch jack grab a crayfish in a corner of the tank. The jack took in the crayfish claws first and then swam up and down like a man who had eaten a spoonful of hot mustard. Then it stopped momentarily, and spat out the clawing crayfish. The crayfish was spun around, and the jack then sucked it in tail first. For a period of five months, I was able to keep alive and enjoy four small jacks in my tank, which was replenished from time to time with water from the tap. They suddenly died from lack of oxygen when a late winter storm caused a day-long power failure. While alive, the jacks traveled as a school; they have a very strong schooling instinct. Seth Rosenbaum once made the mistake of putting a four-inch jack in an aquarium with a nine-inch kingfish. The jack adhered to its schooling instinct and shadowed the kingfish around the tank, to the latter's obvious discomfiture. "The kingfish did everything he could to shake off the jack," Seth said. "He did figure-eights, Immelmanns, and barrel rolls, but the jack stuck to him. It would have been easier to shake the Red Baron."

There are two different theories to account for the presence of jacks in the Hudson. The first theory is that of Dr. Frederick H. Berry of the Tropical Atlantic Biological Laboratory, an authority on the Carangidae, the family of fish to which jacks belong. He is of the opinion that the juvenile jack crevalle is carried north along the Coast as larva by the Gulf Stream and then "probably selectively inhabits inshore waters during the late juvenile stage."

This may be, but I toy with another idea. There may be a chance that jacks have become established year-round somewhere in the New York area. I say this because commercial fishermen on the Hudson tell me they sometimes take jacks in the spring during the shad run, and Rosenbaum has taken jacks in May in Shinnecock Inlet, Long Island.

If a number of southern terrestrial animals and plants—the opossum, fish crow, turkey vulture, etc.—can establish themselves in the Hudson Valley, why should not a species of fish be able to do the same in the river?

SILVER PERCH (*Bairdiella chrysura*). On October 2, 1967, I took a one-inch silver perch at Senasqua. This fish had never before been reported from the Hudson, and the specimen is now in the American Museum collection. Commercial fishermen say they sometimes catch silver perch up to five inches long in the fall, and although New York City is supposed to mark the northernmost range of this member of the drum family, I suspect that the Hudson gets them in fair numbers up to Peekskill.

MANGROVE SNAPPER OR GRAY SNAPPER (*Lutjanus griseus*). On September 30, 1967, I seined a one-inch mangrove snapper at Senasqua. This species was never before reported in the Hudson. I kept it alive for five days in a five-gallon aquarium filled with river water, but when it began to develop a fungus infection which I feared could obscure characteristics necessary for positive identification, I preserved it in a jar of formalin. C. Lavett Smith of the American Museum of Natural History identified the fish for me—I had thought it was a schoolmaster snapper—and the specimen is now in the museum collection. In the western hemisphere, the mangrove snapper ranges from Florida south to Brazil, and it is also found on the West African Coast.

Indeed, so far as I can determine, the mangrove snapper is now the only species of fish which has been taken from both the Hudson and Congo rivers.

11

THE TAPPAN ZEE

The Tappan Zee is almost nine miles long and a little more than two miles wide. It is bounded on the north by Croton Point and on the south by the Piermont Salt Marsh. Ecologically, it is akin to Haverstraw Bay, but because of its closer proximity to the Atlantic the Tappan Zee is more brackish. It probably is also more polluted. The Palisades Park takes up much of the west bank, but the east shore is heavily industrialized in places, and for a number of years various industries have been discharging their wastes directly into the river.

Besides the Penn Central and the Hudson Wire Company, the polluters include General Motors in Tarrytown ("When they're painting blue trucks, the river's blue," a worker once told me. "When they're painting red trucks, the river's red"); Anaconda Wire and Cable in Hastings, which discharges rinse water from tinning and pickling processes and wash water from its rod and rolling mills; and Refined Syrups & Sugars in Yonkers, which dumps in sugar wastes.

As unsavory as pollution might be in the Tappan Zee, this reach of the Hudson is still very much alive and not without interest. The Tappan Zee appears to have certain key ecological components, starting at the north with Croton Point and the Croton River.

Until now, I have largely omitted discussion of tributaries of the Hudson. The Battenkill, the Mohawk, Catskill Creek, Roundout Creek, the Esopus, the Walkill, the Roeliff Jansen Kill, the Sawkill, Wappinger Creek, Popolopen Creek, Peekskill Hollow Brook, all these streams have their attractions where they have not been despoiled by man. The Battenkill, in fact, is a celebrated trout stream, particularly in Vermont, where the famous tackle firm of Orvis posts a daily notice of stream conditions and fly hatches on the door of its store in Manchester. Yet there is a certain sameness, if that is the word, to these tributaries, and to discuss them at length would be to repeat a good part of what I have said about life in the upper Hudson. But the Croton River is different from the other tributaries. The Croton is unique. Thanks to the hand of man, it is now, in its lower reaches, only three and a half miles long. Unlike other tributaries, the lower Croton receives tidal salt water from the Hudson for a length of about a mile, and thus marine creatures, such as barnacles, blue crabs, mud crabs, and grass shrimp, are able to move into the Croton River and mingle with freshwater animals. The Croton is sort of a mini-estuary, a mini-Hudson, but with the important difference that it is much cleaner than the Hudson, and so what is obscured from sight by turbidity in the main river may be clearly observed in the Croton. And there are some unusual sights to see.

As intended by nature in post-glacial times, the Croton originally drained a watershed of 375 square miles in Westchester, Putnam, and Dutchess counties and a small sliver of western Connecticut. The unimpeded Croton ran with such volume that some early sailors are said to have mistaken it for the main stream of the Hudson. In 1842, the Croton was dammed six miles above its mouth to provide drinking water for Manhattan. This dam, only sixty feet high, checked part of the flow, which was diverted to Manhattan through the Croton Aqueduct, which parallels the Hudson down to Yonkers and serves nowadays as a trail for hikers. The dam blocked fishes from moving up the Croton, but water continued to pour into the lower Croton the year round, and the river remained viable in its final six-mile run to the Hudson. According to Everett Garrison of Ossining, who comes from old Hudson Valley Dutch stock and who makes what some anglers deem the finest split-bamboo fly rods in the world, this six-mile length of the lower Croton was one of the finest native brook trout streams in all North America. But the thirst of New York City grew, and in 1906 the huge New Croton Dam was finished. The New Croton Dam is three and a half miles upstream from the mouth of the Croton. It is 153 feet high, and instead of merely checking part of the flow, it chokes it off completely during the summer months. As a result of construction of the dam, the native brook trout were unable to survive, for much of the lower Croton dries up and the few holding pools that remain simmer in the summer sun. The old check dam built in 1842 lies buried in the enlarged and deepened reservoir near the Taconic Parkway bridge.

Even so, the Croton River comes to life each spring. In March, the level of the Croton Reservoir slowly begins to rise behind the Croton Dam, and suddenly water begins to thunder into the barren Croton below. The torrent bends trees that have taken root in the dry riverbed, and hundreds of carp that have sought refuge in the holding pools are battered to death on rocks and cast up on shore. The Croton roars over small dams, bounces over rapids, and glides through deep holes with waters almost as clear as those in the headwaters of the Hudson. It makes a run through a magnificent granite gorge lined with hemlocks, curves around a couple of islands, and then enters the Hudson at the marsh by the Penn Central bridge. Smelt and alewives running up the Hudson to spawn detect the outpouring of fresh water and swim up the Croton. In late March and early April, I like to hold onto a hemlock growing on a rock ledge and look down at the fishes swarming upstream. The alewives gather in a pool below the rapids, heading into the strong current. Suddenly several of them will dash forward and throw themselves into the white water. If they fail, they try again and again until they make it. They are so numerous that I have scrambled down the slope and caught them with my hands. Alewives do not need to feed on their spawning run. Their bodies are rich with fat stored at sea, but I have seen them chase tiny, silver-bodied flies and spoons, and someday perhaps I will succeed in catching them; I have hooked them only accidentally. All during April, alewives continue to jam into the Croton, and their pilgrimage soon attracts striped bass that have been slumbering on the bottom of the Hudson. Sometime in mid-April, stripers move into the Croton. Ravenous, they gorge themselves on the alewives, swallowing them whole. The bass chase the herring in towards shore, they attack from underneath in the pools, they surge after them in the rapids. A pool in the Croton is sometimes alive with swirling bass seeking their prey. I used to think the Hudson striper was a somewhat lazy fish, rather like a kingly, easy going lion, taking what fortune and the current swept its way with a minimum of exertion. But this is not the case in the Croton. After a long winter sleep, the bass are in a frenzy, and few obstacles seem to stop them. I have seen them in the white flume of the small dam at Black Rock on the Croton, swimming broadside to the current as easily and gracefully as terns in a high wind. Occasionally, a striper will arch its back, and with little effort vault the flume and swim upstream. Indeed, stripers go all the way to the foot of the New Croton Dam.

Besides entering the Croton to feed, stripers may come in to spawn. An eleven-pounder I took was a female with dark-green eggs and was only a day away from spawning. On June 23, 1968, Robert Hoebermann of Croton, an erstwhile trout fisherman, visited the tidal portion of the Croton, and in all likelihood he became one of the few persons in the Hudson Valley ever to witness the spawning of striped bass. He kindly wrote me an account of his observations, which I include here.

I arrived on the north shore of the Croton River at about 6:30 a. m. The air temperature was sixty-five to seventy degrees, wind calm, water surface calm, sky clear except for occasional large clouds. Water temperature unknown, but the water was reasonably clear with vision good with polaroids. The tide was running out and nearing low.

Fishing with spinning gear, I caught an eight-inch striped bass on a silver spoon and several white and yellow perch on a variety of lures. Action was relatively slow.

The tide was near low when at about a distance of fifty

yards upstream I heard what sounded like a large animal, such as a dog, fall into the river. I looked around and saw the river churning. The backs of several fish were visible out of the water almost on the near shore.

A few minutes later the same thing happened, followed by a series of noisy rises at midstream, and then more splashing and sightings at the base of a rock formation on the far shore.

The fish, an undetermined number of them at this point, then moved downstream on the far bank and continued the same noisy splashing activity under an overhanging bush directly across river from me.

Suddenly the activity stopped. But it began again about fifteen minutes later. By this time, I believe, the flood tide had started. The fish were now splashing in an area down stream about fifty yards at the point of a small island midstream and in a cutback on the far bank.

Then, in the water directly below me and not more than two feet away, I sighted a fish moving upstream. It was a striped bass about sixteen to twenty-four inches long. Two or three seconds later, it was followed by a school of similar size bass strung out in a long narrow school. There were about twenty-five stripers.

They were moving in a circular pattern clockwise in the river. They paid no attention to the small fish near the rock I was standing on, nor to any lure that I cast near them. In desperation, I even tried to snag a striper with a heavy spoon and came very close to doing so, but the stripers, rather than spooking, merely moved around my lure as if it were just a rock on the bottom.

The stripers continued to cruise the river, but with the exception of an occasional rise at the same point in the middle upstream, the surface action had stopped. I left the river at 9:45 a. m. The bass were still there

Hoebermann's observations coincide almost precisely with the classic account made by Chester Woodhull of striper spawning in the San Joaquin and Sacramento rivers in California. Unfortunately, like Woodhull, Hobermann did not have a plankton net at hand to collect eggs in verification. Perhaps stripers spawn not only in the Croton but in other tributaries of the Hudson. Everett Nack reports that stripers throng into Stockport Creek in the spring and may be caught in considerable numbers in the rapids below Columbiaville. I also know of striped bass caught in the spring in Catskill and Roundout creeks.

In late spring, when the current slows, I go snorkeling in the Croton with a face mask, flippers and a wet suit. I am able then to get a look at life in the river, an impossible thing to do in the murky Hudson. The trout seem to favor the fast water or cuts beneath the banks. Largemouth bass and sunfish prefer to lurk around large rocks, logs, and other obstructions. Of all the fishes, the sunnies are the least easily frightened; if I wiggle a finger, they will swim up to inspect it. The white perch travel in schools; I have seen as many as 150 of them, arranged in three ranks, slowly finning themselves over a gravel bar. The carp lumber in the shallows where the bottom is muddy, but they flee at the sight of me. Stripers less than twelve inches in length will come within three or four feet when I hold still, but the larger bass slip into the dark-green shadows of the depths. Inshore, there are schools of baby suckers and shiners, and where the river slows around a bend, pickerel lie in ambush in weedy shallows.

In late June or July, depending on the amount of runoff, water ceases flowing over the Croton Dam, and stretches of the Croton begin to dry up completely. The stripers retreat down to the tidal Croton, but not all of them make it. I once saw a five-pounder, covered with fungus, probably brought about by injury in an attempt to escape, slowly dying in the pool below the foot of the Croton Dam. It swam aimlessly in two feet of water, ignoring streamers and jigs cast its way.

As summer continues, the holding pools shrink in size. The Croton is dying. In the fall, I often visit the river. There is the sad spectacle of beleaguered fish penned in small pools, but a walk along the dry bed is not without interest. I can see where the force of water in ages past has thrust huge boulders downstream and sculpted rocks into bizarre shapes. Rattling around among the bare ribs of the river, I study the holes where bass lie in the spring, and on occasion I find an old lure caught on a rock or stuck in the side of a log.

Of course, the tidal Croton never dries up. Water sloshes back and forth from the Hudson, and fishes move in and out with the tide. Up until the 1920s, weakfish (*Cynoscion regalis*) used to come up the Hudson as far as the mouth of the Croton. Nowadays weakfish are very scarce even on the coast of Long Island and New Jersey. It appears that commercial fishermen working North Carolina waters have been taking baby weakfish as part of their catch of "industrial" fish to be ground up for fertilizer or catfood, and thus weakfish do not get a chance to grow and move north along the coast. Similarly, the spot (*Leiostomus xanthurus*), once a very popular fish in the Hudson, has not been seen in fifteen or twenty years. In fact, they are seldom found north of Norfolk, Virginia. In the Hudson Valley, where many people hold by tradition, spot are commonly called "Lafayettes," because there is said to have been a great run of them up the river when General Lafayette visited New York in 1824.

The marsh at the mouth of the Croton has been disfigured over the years. Part of it has been filled in for the new Route 9 bridge, and other acreage has succumbed to the Harmon railroad station parking lot. Then there are squishy deposits of oil from the Penn Central pipe in the bottom muds. Until ten or fifteen years ago, bald eagles still nested on the Ossining shore of the marsh. In fact, the nearby estate of the late Captain Joseph Patterson, publisher of the New York *Daily News*, was called Eagle Park. The principal vegation of the marsh is cattail (*Typha latifolia*) and common reed (*Phragmites communis*), neither particularly rich in food but both useful in stabilizing wetlands, absorbing runoff, and providing shelter for wildlife. In the tidal sloughs there are fiddler crabs (*Uca minax*), and so far as I have been able to determine, the Croton marsh marks the furthest penetration of this species up the Hudson. There are muskrats, mink, and snapping turtles, and birds often seen include the kingfisher (*Megaceryle alcyon*) and the great blue heron (*Ardea herodias*). For the past few years, anywhere from a half dozen to a dozen mute swans (*Cygnus olor*) have freqented the marsh, and I dread the day when they venture into the Central oil slick. They are often taken for the whistling swan (*Olor columbianus*) a rare bird in the region. The whistling swan is native to North America, while the mute swan is an importation from Europe first introduced into the Hudson Valley in 1910, probably as an ornamental bird for estate ponds. The mute swans stay as long as possible through the winter. In the cold weather, they have a knack for finding open water at spring holes in marshes or near the abutments of the Tappan Zee Bridge. In the fall, there are flights of ducks and geese near the mouth of the Croton, and they often settle down in the river.

Croton Point, which begins on the north shore of the mouth of the Croton River, is well known among bird watchers. The point rates three stars in *Enjoying Birds Around New York City*, a guide compiled by the Laboratory of Ornithology of Cornell. At Croton Point, while counting ducks in 1930, a fellow conservationist, William Vogt, gave Roger Tory Peterson the idea of writing his now-famous bird guide. In recent years Croton Point has lost much of its charm and some of its vitality; Westchester County has been using most of the marshland on the point as a dump, and where there was once lushness of life, there now is an enormous, hideous and stinking mountain of garbage, some of which washes into the river at high tide.

To the south along the east shore of the Tappan Zee, the Hudson is relatively shallow. These shoal waters run from one to eight feet deep for a width of between a mile to a quarter mile down to Tarrytown. Shaped like a pork chop, this shallow stretch is of great importance as a nursery and feeding ground for young striped bass, sturgeons, bluefish, and many other species. It is also vital to shellfish. The Tappan Zee is the only part of the Hudson where the softshell clam (*Mya arenaria*) has been found. The bottom hereabouts is carpeted with the shells, many ancient, some new. In the early 1950s, when seedbeds of the oyster (*Crassostrea virginica*) in Long Island Sound and Great South Bay became unproductive after a gigantic storm struck the area (and possibly also as the result of increasing pollution from the duck farms on the Island), Butler Flower of Bayville, Long Island, a leading oysterman, thought the brackish waters of the Tappan Zee might prove suitable. Flower, his two brothers, and a friendly competitor, G. Vanderborgh & Son of West Sayville, leased more than five thousand acres of river bottom from the state. They brought spawning oysters in from the Sound and placed them in the Hudson. Baby oysters, known as spat, "set" on bits and pieces of old

oyster shells on the bottom. After a year, the young oysters born
in the Tappan Zee were pumped from the Hudson and transferred to "growing" grounds in the Sound. After two years on the
growing grounds, they were again pumped up from the bottom
and placed on "fattening" grounds near Bayville, where they
stayed until ready for market. The Hudson-bred oysters did very
well, Flower says, but in the spring of 1957 "there was a lot of
snow up the river, and a slug of fresh water came down and
killed practically everything off." Since then the Tappan Zee beds
have not been used, but the Long Island oystermen, fearful of the
loss of native seedbeds, have continued to pay their lease money
to the state because they may want to try again some day.

The bottom of the Tappan Zee is composed of shells, mud, and
glacial rubble; bed rock lies five hundred feet further down,
which accounts for the curious curve in the Tappan Zee Bridge
between Tarrytown and Nyack. Until this bridge was finished
in 1955, bridges constructed across the lower Hudson were sus-
pended from the rocky shores on both sides of the river. The
Tappan Zee, however, is too wide for a suspension span, and so
the bridge was built on floating concrete caissons set in the mud
and in the form of an S to offset strain.

At present, about four hundred acres of the productive flats on
the east shore of the Tappan Zee are scheduled for obliteration.
The New York State Department of Transportation plans to fill in
a five-mile-long stretch of the Hudson between Ossining and Tarrytown for a four- to six-lane expressway. In some places, the fill
will reach thirteen hundred feet out into the river. Another super-
highway, a new Route 117, already under construction, will carry
traffic to and from the expressway. Both roads have caused an up-
roar. To start, the bills authorizing both were vague, but they
sailed through the closing sessions of the 1965 legislature in record
time. Before effective protest could be made, Governor Rockefeller signed them.

The new Route 117 runs through and along the northern portion of the Rockefeller family estate at Pocantico Hills. It is to
deflect traffic from the old 117, a winding country road that goes
through the estate near the governor's home. Critics have noted
that both the new 117, dubbed the Rockefeller Spur, and the
Hudson River Expressway will certainly increase the value of the

family lands by a great amount and possibly open the estate to extensive development. There is talk of a Rockefeller Center of the suburbs.

In May of 1968, as controversy continued, the state conservation department finally had to come up with a report of the likely ecological impact of the expressway on the Hudson. The department reported that in the area to be filled, fish and shellfish beds and wildlife habitat would be permanently lost. Moreover, inasmuch as the highwaymen planned to use 9.5 million cubic yards of fill for the expressway, excessive siltation could block spawning runs of shad, striped bass, sturgeon, herring, and other fishes for two or three years. The department allowed that such "blockage" could be "serious," but, forced to take its cue from the governor, the department did not object to the expressway. As a final touch, the state Hudson River Valley Commission held a hearing on the project. The commission had no authority to halt construction, but under the law it had to review the project and make a recommendation. In this instance, given the inflamed state of public opinion, an adverse finding would have killed the chances of the road. The HRVC heard a total of forty-three speakers, the great majority of them representing civic groups, and of these only two were definitely in favor of the expressway, much to the obvious discomfort of Alexander Aldrich, the executive director of the commission and the governor's cousin. Not long afterwards, the HRVC approved the expressway and announced it "found most persuasive the expert opinion of the Division of Fish and Game of the New York State Conservation Department." At present, the Hudson River Expressway is being contested in court fights by several parties, most notably the Citizens Committee for the Hudson, the National Association for the Advancement of Colored People, and the Sierra Club.

The most prominent natural feature of the Tappan Zee is the Palisades, a cliff of diabase rock that actually runs for a distance of fifty miles from Mt. Ivy, behind Haverstraw in Rockland County, south to Staten Island. The diabase rock sits on top of layers of sedimentary sandstones and shales laid down during the Triassic Period 225 to 193 million years ago, when much of the east was laced with streams, lakes, and marshes. These layers of sandstone and shales are known to geologists as the Triassic Lowlands, or Newark series, and the formation runs from Rockland County through eastern Pennsylvania down into Virginia. The battle of Gettysburg was fought on this formation. Seminary Ridge is composed of Triassic sandstone, while Big Round Top and Little Round Top are named after diabase knobs similar to the rock of the Palisades.

Sometime during the Triassic Period, magma oozed through a fault and solidified between the layers of sandstones and shales. Geologists estimate that the intrusion of magma, which hardened into diabase, was originally one thousand feet thick. However, years of erosion have worn away the cap of sandstones and shales and reduced the diabase of the Palisades to about half their original thickness.

The exposed face of the diabase is columnar in appearance. These columns were formed as the magma cooled and shrank. To the Indians, the Palisades were known as *weehawken* because the columns of rocks resembled "rows of trees." If the Palisades were placed on end, the columns of diabase would look like stairs, and so to quarrymen the rock is usually referred to as trap rock, from the Dutch word *trapp*, meaning "step." Whatever the name, the Palisades are an unusual geological formation, rivalled only by Fingal's Cave in Scotland and its continuation in Ireland, the Giant's Causeway.

Ever since the days of the Dutch, the tough diabase of Palisades and the layers of sandstone have been looked upon as fair game by quarrymen. The sandstones, which often contain hematite, giving the rock a striking color, were used during the nineteenth century for the building of the fashionable "brownstone" houses of Manhattan. But the main game always lay in the diabase rock. It was used as both a building stone and cheap ship ballast, and then it was employed in road construction after being broken up into gravel. A 1916 New York State Museum report, *The Quarry Materials of New York*, noted, "As a road metal it [the Palisades diabase] has long been recognized as the standard of quality." In the late nineteenth century, devastation of the Palisades grew, and the scars are still to be seen along the cliffs fronting the Tappan Zee. The outcry became voluminous, and in 1900 New Jersey and New York created the Palisades Interstate Park Commission to protect the ramparts. Thanks to gifts from

J. P. Morgan and John D. Rockefeller, Jr., among others, the commission owns much of the Palisades, but quarries still exist. Just north of Hook Mountain at Short Clove, the Palisades have been worked so thin that from behind they look like a stage set. Maxwell Anderson's verse play, *High Tor*, produced in 1936, is about the efforts of a company to acquire High Tor mountain, at 827 feet the highest point in the Palisades, from its owner, Van Dorn. In the play the company eventually succeeds, an ending which outraged Van Dorn's real-life prototype, Elmer Van Orden, who beat back the quarrymen. Van Orden's old homestead is now owned by Everett Crosby, who runs the High Tor Vineyards on the property.

On occasion, I like to use my boat to explore the rock beaches of the Palisades. This is not a practice I recommend to others, because rock slides do occur. I remember being at the south tip of Croton Point one day when I suddenly heard a tremendous roar, rather like that of an A-bomb exploding. Part of the face of Hook Mountain had given way, and the pall of dust hung in the air for half an hour. Even so, a visit to the beaches is usually rewarding. Directly opposite Croton Point, the Palisades overlie exposed sandstones and shales, and interesting fossils of worm trails are to be found in the latter. In point of fact, some very remarkable finds have been made in these strata. In 1910, part of the skeleton of a crocodile-like reptile, *Rutiodon manhattanensis*, was found along the riverbank near Fort Lee, New Jersey. Discoveries of fossil fish have been made in an old quarry at nearby North Bergen; there in 1960, three high school boys found the fossil of a gliding reptile, the earliest vertebrate to achieve aerial locomotion. It was named *Icarosaurus siefkeri*, after Icarus of Greek myth and Alfred Siefker, one of the youngsters who discovered it. Unhappily for fossil hunters, buildings now cover most of the North Bergen site.

Another key ecological unit of the Tappan Zee is the Piermont Salt Marsh, which stretches for almost two miles on the west shore from the village of Piermont south to the picturesque hamlet of Sneden's Landing. Whenever I ride the train to the city, I look for the marsh in the distance. In the summer, when the sky is blue and white puffs of clouds sail overhead, it seems to be most beautiful. The marsh grasses are a rich green line on the far shore, so richly green, in fact, that they look as though they were painted by a water colorist. Behind the marsh, by contrast, there is the dark leafy green of the trees atop the Palisades, with here and there a clearing for a house or estate.

The Piermont marsh throbs with life. The tidal creeks are awash with shrimp, fiddler crabs, killies, striped bass, and other fishes, and the bird life is equally profuse. Among the birds seen at one time or other are the green heron (*Butorides virescens*), American bittern, (*Botaurus lentiginosus*), least bittern (*Ixobrychus exilis*), clapper rail (*Rallus longirostris*), common gallinule (*Gallinula chloropus*), black-bellied plover (*Squatarola squatarola*), semipalmated sandpiper (*Ereunetes pusillus*), and Bonaparte's gull (*Larus philadelphia*). The marsh is known as the only place where the seaside sparrow (*Ammospiza maritima*) has nested away from the coast.

I have been to the Piermont marsh regrettably few times, and on each occasion either I forgot to bring some vital piece of collecting gear or else the tide was wrong. Given a good low tide in the early fall, I am certain that I could find any number of previously unreported species of fishes for the Hudson. One September day I went there by boat with C. Lavett Smith, Bill Harris of Museum Planning Inc., and Seth Rosenbaum. We were collecting for the new Hall of Ocean Life that the American Museum of Natural History was building, and although we did fairly well, gathering white perch, stripers, bluefish, and the usual mixture of Hudson fishes, we would have done better, I am certain, had not the tide been high. When the river is up to your neck only two feet from shore, it is difficult to collect with a seine. Still, we improvised. Just as the tide started ebbing, we stretched a seine across the mouth of a tidal creek. I rowed the boat a hundred yards upstream and then drifted down toward the net, whacking the water with an oar to scare fishes into it. We took one surprise, a mature female diamondback terrapin (*Malaclemys terrapin*), the gourmet's delight in the day of gas lamps and Lillian Russell. So far as I have been able to determine, the diamondback terrapin never before has been reported in the literature of the river. I brought her home for examination and then released her at Senasqua Beach, where she swam off. Ed Reilly at the state museum says that the terrapin is making an unpublicized comeback in New York coastal waters and probably could be found in the Hudson up to Poughkeepsie.

The plant life in the Piermont marsh is of great significance. Here the influence of the sea dominates, for many of the plants are halophytes or true saline species. Whatever knowledge I have of the flora is due not to my own study but to the patient investigations of J. Harry Lehr of Spring Valley, Rockland County. A mild-mannered officer of a local bank, Lehr moved to Rockland County from New York in 1937, and from 1940 to 1950 he raised mink. Always interested in natural history, he was curious about the vegetation of Rockland County, and in 1952 he purchased a copy of *Gray's Manual of Botany* and began educating himself. When he started investigating the local flora, the state museum listed about eight hundred species for Rockland County. Now Lehr has extended the list to more than twelve hundred species. When he discovers a new plant, he presses two specimens on herbarium sheets and deposits vouchers containing them at the New York Botanical Garden and Bear Mountain Museum. "As far as I know, the Piermont marsh contains the most northerly concentration of saline species in New York State," Lehr says. "There are four species of *Spartina*, swordgrass, at Piermont—*Spartina cynosuroides*, the giant cordgrass, *Spartina alterniflora*, *Spartina pectinata*, and *Spartina patens*, the smallest cordgrass. This is what farmers cut for salt-marsh hay. The Piermont salt marsh also marks the northernmost range in the state of *Distichlis spicata*, seashore saltgrass, and it is the site of the inland record for *Polygonum glaucum*, seabeach knotweed." At present, Lehr is carefully working his way along the west shore of the Hudson below the Palisades looking for plants hitherto unrecorded. Once I asked him to look at some plants in the Croton area, but he refused, exclaiming, "I don't have time other than for my own flora!"

12

THE HUDSON
AND THE HARBOR

New York Harbor, the product of the combined action of river and glacial erosion, is generally considered to be the finest natural port in the world. Sheltered from the open sea, it can be entered from either the Atlantic Ocean or Long Island Sound; it is deep and capacious, and it has a tidal fluctuation of only five feet. With 650 miles of navigable waterfront, it is the largest port in the world, and it handles approximately twenty-five thousand ships a year. Until 1960, the Port of New York handled more tonnage than any other in the world; now New York is second to Rotterdam, which derives much of its tonnage from supertankers carrying oil to Europe from the Middle East.

About one-fourth of the ships entering New York are tankers, and most of them are confined to the Arthur Kill and the Kill Van Kull, the waterways separating Staten Island from New Jersey and busier ship passages than the Panama Canal. The East River is largely given over to freighters, while the Hudson receives the great passenger liners. During Colonial times, the East River was the center of shipping, the lifeblood of the colony. In fact, before the Revolution, there were no ships or piers along the Hudson at all; shippers avoided the river because of the prevailing northwest winds and the threat of winter ice. According to Albion's *The Rise of New York Port,* on one day in 1836, a total of 921 vessels were tied up along East River wharves, while only 320, mostly sloops and little schooners were in the Hudson, and "of the square-rigged ships and brigs, the aristocrats of the sea lanes, 305 were moored in East River and only 39 in North River."

The Hudson did not start to come into its own until 1847, when Samuel Cunard, a Nova Scotian who had a mail subsidy from the British government, built a terminal at Jersey City. The Hudson offered much more turning room than did the East River for the large steamships that were being built. Cunard's entry into shipping had lasting results. Cunard ships were standardized, the crews were the best from the British merchant marine, and they were subjected to strict discipline. Speed was desirable, but the safety of a Cunard liner was paramount.

The excellence of the Cunard service rankled New Yorkers. With the help of a post-office subsidy, Edward Knight Collins set up the United States Mail Steamship Company, better known as the Collins line, to whip the Cunarders. American pride was at stake, and expense did not matter: Collins line ships were to be the fastest afloat. In 1851, the Collins liner *Baltic* crossed the Atlantic in the record time of nine days and eighteen hours. Other Collins liners strove to break that mark, and the line quickly fell into debt because the ships were devouring enormous amounts of coal and the excessive speeds caused a need for extensive repairs. There were also a couple of disasters. In 1854, the *Arctic* sank off Cape Race, Newfoundland, after ramming a French steamer in fog, and more than three hundred persons were lost, including Collins' wife, son, and daughter. In January, 1856, the *Pacific,* steaming from New York to Liverpool, disappeared without a trace, probably after striking an iceberg. The crew and forty-five passengers were lost. In 1858, the Collins line itself sank into financial ruin, and the American challenge from the Hudson, where Fulton had run his steamboat, was stilled.

At about the same time, the clipper trade was in a decline. During the 1840s and 1850s, New York dominated the clipper trade with China and California. Some of the best ships—the *Rainbow,* the *Sea Witch,* the *Samuel Russell,* and the *Comet*— were built in East River yards. True, Boston had Donald McKay, who built the famous *Flying Cloud,* but she was owned by New Yorkers and sailed out of New York. Moreover, McKay had spent time on the East River learning his craft. In 1853, a New York-built clipper, the *Hornet,* raced the *Flying Cloud* more than sixteen thousand miles from New York to San Francisco. The race was around Cape Horn, and when it was over, the *Hornet,* which had sailed a few hours ahead, had won by only forty minutes. The clipper trade succumbed for various reasons. For one, California became self-sufficient in producing its own food, and the clipper ships were built for speed, not heavy cargoes. For another, a clipper ship required dry docking every two years for repairs; so much sail weakened the hull. And finally, there was increasing competition from steamships.

Shipbuilding had existed on the East River since Dutch times, but the industry, which had set the standard for the rest of the world, was hurt by the collapse of the clipper trade. Furthermore, the East River builders were curiously stubborn and conservative in steamship design. Until the 1850s, they had rivalled the Scots on the Clyde, but then the New Yorkers clung to wooden sidewheelers while the Scots moved ahead to the screw propeller and iron hull. After the Civil War, the shipbuilding industry languished, and when it did revive later, the revival took place on the Delaware.

As larger ships came into use in the nineteenth century, one drawback to the harbor became obvious—the shallow bar off Sandy Hook caused by the deposit of sediments. The old main ship channel to the harbor had a depth of twenty-one feet; it was deepened to twenty-three feet in 1837 under the direction of Lieutenant R. T. Gedney, a naval officer. In 1860, when the *Great Eastern,* which drew thirty feet and was the biggest ship ever built, planned to call at New York, there was apprehension that she would not be able to "cross the bar" at Sandy Hook. A harbor pilot named Murphy was sent to Europe to make the trip to New

York aboard the *Great Eastern*. She reached the bar on June 28 and waited for high tide at 2 P.M. while the crew shifted cargo to place her on an even keel. The screw churned up mud, but the ship got across and passed through the Narrows to the Hudson as cannons were fired and thousands cheered. Ambrose Channel, the main entrance to the harbor now, is dredged to a depth of forty-five feet and is two thousand feet wide. Begun in 1899, it is named for John Wolfe Ambrose, an Irish immigrant who built most of the old Sixth Avenue and Second Avenue elevated train systems, operated the South Brooklyn ferry, and promoted port improvement.

Almost every ship entering or leaving the harbor takes a licensed pilot belonging to two organizations working as one, the United New York Sandy Hook Pilots Benevolent Association and the United New Jersey Sandy Hook Pilots Benevolent Association. There are 140 pilots in the two associations, with a sea company of 30 pilots waiting for ships on the pilot boat stationed near Sandy Hook. Pilots have been guiding vessels in and out of the harbor on a regular basis since 1694. For many years, there was a bitter rivalry between New York and New Jersey pilots, who raced to approaching ships to solicit business. Each side sought to have the fastest schooner, and the Jersey men won out for a time in 1841, when George Steers, a young ship designer, built them the speedy pilot boat *William G. Hagstaff*. Not to be outdone by the Jersey men, Captain Richard Brown had Steers build the *Mary Taylor* in 1849, and she defeated everything in sight. The fame of the pilot boats was such that the New York Yacht Club commissioned Steers to build a slightly larger version of the *Mary Taylor*. Steers produced the *America*, which sailed to England in 1851 and defeated the pick of the Royal Yacht Squadron in a race around the Isle of Wight, winning what is now known as the America's Cup. The skipper was Captain Richard Brown, who came back home to resume his post off Sandy Hook.

Piloting nowadays is not as romantic but just as exacting, and prospective pilots, almost always sons or nephews of licensed pilots, undergo a long apprenticeship. There is a network of channels to negotiate, and on most days the harbor cross-traffic of barges, freighters, ocean liners, tows, and pleasure boats is as maddening as a traffic tie-up in the garment district, with the difference that the pilot may be guiding a forty-eight-thousand-ton tanker loaded with volatile petrochemicals. To the uninitiated, the harbor tides are baffling. As Colonel Charles M. Duke of the Corps of Engineers once confessed, ". . . the interplay of alluvial and tidal currents in the lower Hudson defies mathematical analysis." The tides in the Hudson, which the pilots still refer to as the North River, run at a different time than those in the East River, which is actually a tidal strait. The tides in the East River run more swiftly than those in the Hudson, up to six knots per hour, and their force is such that many captains prefer not to dock except at slack water. The Sandy Hook pilots have jurisdiction up the Hudson to Yonkers; from there north, members of the Hudson River Pilots Association guide ships up and down the river.

Floating debris is often a menace to navigation. A stout piece of timber can cripple the propeller of an ocean liner. Jack Gelberman, chief of the New York Operations Division of the Corps of Engineers, which is responsible for keeping the harbor clear, says: "We have a lot of foreign dignitaries coming here, and I've honestly been ashamed to take them out into the harbor. Here in the greatest harbor in the world are two thousand hulks of old wooden vessels and one thousand tumbledown piers that, in a sense, are polluting our waterfront." Most of the hulks are hard aground on the Jersey side of the Hudson, running from Bayonne down into the Kill Van Kull and the Arthur Kill. The Corps has no authority to go behind pier and bulkhead lines, and Gelberman says, "If a man wants to pile up barges at his pier, I can't do a thing about it." A fair number of the hulks are wooden Erie Canal barges that date back to the 1850s. Pieces from the hulks and chunks of the piers break off and float around the harbor. Most of the debris eventually gathers in the Upper Bay north of the Narrows. To clear the harbor of flotsam, the Corps operates the *Driftmaster,* an aquatic carpet sweeper that starts out each morning in Gravesend Bay in Brooklyn and proceeds up the Hudson to 59th Street. Built like a catamaran on twin pontoons, the *Driftmaster* has an open bow and the vessel heads into the debris scooping it up in a net. Each year, the Corps collects and burns twenty-four thousand tons of debris. The oddest things have been found, among them a dead giraffe and a grand piano.

Occasionally, the *Driftmaster* scoops up a body, which the Corps turns over to the Harbor Precinct of the New York Police Department. On the average, the police, who operate eighteen patrol boats, recover one hundred bodies a year from the harbor. There seems to be no special pattern to where the bodies are found, and, contrary to popular impression, no bodies are found encased in cement. "Once it's loaded down, it stays down," a police officer says. "You won't find it unless you know exactly where to look for it. That's if they've done a good job, of course." Contrary to another impression, the bodies of few illegitimate infants are found. "They throw them down incinerators," the officer says. Bodies in the harbor are preyed upon by eels. Bill Brown, a state game warden on Staten Island, recalls: "I once saw a dead horse brought in on the beach, and there were eels coming out of every opening of the body. But it's all nature, no matter how vulgar it may seem." Interestingly, the discovery of the body of a murdered girl in the Hudson between Weehawken and Hoboken helped Edgar Allen Poe establish the detective story. In 1841, Mary Cecelia Rogers, a beautiful shopgirl, disappeared while crossing the river on a ferry. Her murderer was never discovered, and Poe, contemptuous of the efforts of the police, wrote "The Mystery of Marie Roget," in which he changed the setting from New York and the Hudson to Paris and the Seine.

Shoaling in the Hudson is another problem for the Corps. The river carries sediments in suspension downstream to Edgewater, New Jersey, just south of the George Washington Bridge. There the increasing salinity of the water moving in from the Atlantic is sufficient to cause a chemical reaction known as flocculation. Instead of remaining in suspension, the silt settles on the bottom of the Hudson near the west shore at the rate of four million cubic yards a year. In an effort to find a solution to the problem, the Corps has considered sealing off the Harlem River, another tidal strait, from the Hudson by means of a movable gate. The gate would open on the ebb tide to allow water to flow from the Hudson into the East River, and then it would close on the flood tide to prevent more saline water from going into the Hudson. Inasmuch as a gate on the Harlem River would solve only part of the problem at best, and since the Corps also foresaw all sorts of objections being raised, the idea has been put aside. In a further effort to cope with the shoaling and to get a picture of the overall workings of the tides and currents in the harbor, the Corps has constructed a hydraulic model of the Hudson as far north as Hyde Park. The model, 17,150 feet square, can duplicate a tidal cycle in eight minutes. It is located at the Corps' Waterway Experiment Station in Vicksburg, Mississippi.

Pending a feasible solution from model studies, the Corps dredges a five-mile stretch of the Hudson from Edgewater to Weehawken at a cost of five million dollars a year. The work is done by the largest dredge in the world, the *Essayons*, named after the Corps' French motto, "Let us strive." Built on the Delaware at a cost of $11.5 million and commissioned in 1950, the *Essayons* is 525 feet long, has accomodations for a crew of 147 officers and men, and is equipped with two huge pumps which suck up silt through two vacuum cleaner-like tubes that reach to the bottom of the river. The *Essayons* can carry more than eight thousand cubic yards of silt, and when filled to capacity, she carries the silt six and a half miles southeast of Ambrose Light and dumps it in the ocean through twenty-four trap doors in the bottom of her hoppers. The mission of the *Essayons* is to dredge the Hudson and the harbor, but she has been sent to Tampa Bay, the naval base at Guantanamo, and the Columbia River. After the Israeli-Egyptian war of 1956, the *Essayons* cleaned up the Suez Canal.

To mariners, the waters of the harbor are so filthy that New York is known ironically as a "clean port" because marine boring worms, which eat the wood in piers, are unable to live there. It is the opinion of David Wallace, the chief marine biologist in the state conservation department, that if Manhattan were not surrounded by salt water, which is inhibiting to most pathogenic bacteria, the island would be a ghost town. There is a story about a visiting Frenchman who made the Circle Line boat trip around Manhattan. Asked his impression of New York, he replied, "*Ma foi*, I think the people just have intercourse and eat oranges." Each day the West Side of Manhattan alone pours 175 million gallons of absolutely raw sewage into the Hudson. The sewage issues from skyscrapers, apartment houses, hospitals, gas stations, restaurants, theaters, public rest rooms, tenements, factories, and stores. It floats down the drains that gird the streets and empties straight into the Hudson, where the tides rock it back and forth. Sometimes sewage from the city is carried up into the Tappan Zee, but generally, the tidal action flushes it out to sea in six to ten days' time. Earle B. Phelps, Professor Emeritus of Sanitary Science at Columbia University, has written, semi-jocularly, in his otherwise serious treatise, *Stream Sanitation:* "Often homeward bound commuters, crowded on the front end of a ferry boat on a hot summer evening, enjoy the light spray of salt water carried aboard by the wind as the bow of the boat hits the passing waves. This is surely a situation where ignorance is bliss." In August, 1964, three small boys who ate a watermelon they fetched from the Hudson at 125th Street came down with typhoid fever. Anything raw out of the river offers perils, but fortunately the boys did not die.

For years, city, state, and federal officials have talked of cleaning up the harbor. In the fall of 1967, the Newtown Creek Sewage Treatment Plant went into operation on the East River, which has been even more of a man-made horror than the Hudson. The plant has the capacity to handle 310 million gallons of sewage a day coming from lower Manhattan, most of Brooklyn, and part of Queens, and city authorities are now working on a treatment plant for the West Side of Manhattan. This plant is to be built on landfill in the Hudson between 137th and 145th streets.

There is no question but that the Hudson is a mess as it flows past Manhattan. Coliform bacteria densities vary from 6,000 to 40,000/100 ml. If, instead of taking samples from mid-river, health authorities tested the water near sewer outlets, they would find the coliform count even higher. A microbiologist of my acquaintance, Dr. Emanuel Sorge, wrote his Ph.D. thesis at Fordham, *Physiological Studies of Algae Isolated From a Polluted Biotope*, after studying what is possibly the worst sewer outlet of all, the one at 172nd Street and Riverside Drive, just below the George Washington Bridge and the Little Red Light House of children's book fame. Directly at the discharge, Sorge found a coliform bacteria count of 10,000,000/100 ml, a record high for anywhere in the Hudson. This outlet is popularly known as the Medical Center sewer because it drains the discharge from nearby Columbia Presbyterian Medical Center. It also receives the sewage from a multitude of apartment houses and businesses.

Visually, the outlet is disgusting. A milky-white slick pours into the river, and on a cool day, vapors rise and small cloudlets scud along the shore.

Considering the amount of sewage discharged into the harbor, an astonishing variety of marine life is able to pass up and down the river. To be sure, the porpoises that frequented the harbor until the 1860s are rarely encountered; finicky animals, they doubtless have been kept away by the pollution. Yet at this point in time, at least, the dissolved oxygen content of the water is obviously sufficient for numerous species of fishes. For example, despite all the foulness pouring forth from the Medical Center outlet, striped bass have been known to crowd around the milky slick. According to Tony Mazza, the state game warden for Manhattan, a few hardy fishermen sometimes try their luck and/or intestinal fortitude by casting a plug or bucktail into the effluent. "I talked to a guy who reported the fishing could be pretty good," Mazza says. "He said the only trouble was the stuff he had to pick off the line after each cast." Elsewhere on the Hudson at theoretically less offensive outlets, fishermen often gather in good number. My seining friend, Seth Rosenbaum, grew up on the West Side and at an early age became a fan of the striper fishing at the Fifty-ninth Street sewer. Seth says: "Fifty-ninth street is warmwater fishing, and it is excellent in the winter. The sewer probably has some lines coming from factories that release warm water." In the early 1950s, Seth was part of a strange crowd that fished the Fifty-ninth Street outlet in mid-winter. One of the regulars, a Jay Thorpe executive, would appear before work in the morning wearing foul-weather gear over his cutaway. The assembled anglers each lowered bloodworms through the grate over the sewer. When a striped bass hit, the angler would haul it up to the grate for all to admire and then cut it loose. Seth now lives in Queens, but he says, "I still go down to Fifty-ninth Street once or twice a year, if a friend invites me."

Striper fishing at the Fifty-ninth Street outlet is best in the colder months, but the Seventy-second Street sewer outlet takes the palm during warmer weather. "Seventy-second street is straight sewage," Seth says, with all the finesse of a connoisseur. "Of course, a sewage outlet is not what most people think it is. It's mostly water coming out like a muddy stream. It is *not* sludge.

When I was a youngster and a big striper run was on at Seventy-second Street, you'd see thirty or forty people fishing from a walkway. The outlet was near an Italian neighborhood, and they're great fish eaters. You'd see old men fishing with drop lines on bells, and you'd see the old wooden sidewinder reels used at the turn of the century. They'd all be catching bass. There are two runs, one in the spring and one in the fall, and every once in a while in the summer there would be good runs of fish." When the runs are on, game warden Mazza puts in an appearance checking for illegal fish under sixteen inches. A favorite trick of lawbreakers fishing for the kitchen pot is to cut off the head and tail so that Mazza will not be able to measure size.

A long-time fishing acquaintance and friend of Seth's, Russ Fradkin, a Manhattan advertising man, is an avid fan of still another sewer outlet, that at Ninety-sixth Street. "It's bigger and better than Seventy-second Street," Fradkin says. "One day in mid-July, I ran down there at six in the morning and I made fifteen casts and had twelve bass on a bucktail. Sometimes you get shut out, but three or four weeks before that someone had fifteen keepers." The king of the sewer anglers is a sixty-two-year-old Jersey man called Bubbles who fishes with a friend called Pickles. Bubbles' last name is Syvarth, and he is called Bubbles, Fradkin says, "because he made a lure that bubbled when it went through the water." There are all sorts of legends about Bubbles. One has it that Bubbles has worked only once in his life, and that was when he took a job as a guard on a railroad barge in Hoboken so he could be near some good fishing in the Hudson. Bubbles laughs at such stories. "They say such things because I'm well known," he says. "I've even been credited with catching an electric eel. I'm retired, but I worked at plumbing. I've fished that river since I was able to walk. Take those bass at those outlets. There's just enough garbage and refuse coming out to bring in alewives, shiners, and millions and millions of spearing. I've tried everything, regular surf gear, plugs, tin, you name it. The fishing is marvelous! There's the sanitation pier at 130th. In the nighttime when it's lit up and the tide is going out, the fish gather. The biggest striper I've ever taken out of the outlets was fourteen pounds, two ounces; that was at Ninety-sixth Street. I'm not much of a fish eater, but my wife likes eels. She'd rather eat a

Hudson River eel than any. Sweet as butternuts, she says. Believe me, I catch eels. I caught a sturgeon once, hooked him in the tail end. I've seen porpoises going up the river and a blackfish whale."

Bubbles does not have a boat, but there are fishermen who troll in the harbor for stripers near the Statue of Liberty and Robbins Reef. Bass caught in the harbor have the reputation of tasting oily. Bill Brown, the Staten Island game warden, says that the bass caught near the Verrazano Bridge are less oily than those from Robbins Reef. Off the mouth of the harbor at Sandy Hook, the fish taste fine. Most of the Sheepshead Bay charter boats troll for stripers at Romer Shoals, a shallow ledge near Ambrose Channel. Stripers of forty pounds or more are frequently taken here during the spring and fall migrations.

Within sight from the Verrazano Bridge, bunker boats, assisted by airplane spotters, purse seine enormous schools of menhaden or "mossbunkers," drawn to the area by the rich pastures of plankton. Although menhaden are too naturally oily for human consumption, they are the favorite food of a number of fish, notably sharks and bluefish. On occasion, large blues will chase the menhaden up into the harbor. For example, this occurred in August, 1965, when a vast school of blues, with fish weighing from five to fifteen pounds each, pursued an even vaster school of menhaden through the Narrows and into the harbor. The bluefish penned the mossbunkers into a cove on the north side of the Navy pier at Bayonne, and for a month the blues stayed there, feeding voraciously, to the great joy of local anglers and the dismay of Jersey and Sheepshead Bay charter boat captains, who could not find a blue anywhere along the coast. One of the lucky anglers, Fred Walczyk, editor of the weekly *Angler's News*, published in Bayonne, went over to the pier every night after work with several cronies. "It got so boring trolling for them, and we were catching thirty in a night," Walczyk says, "that we gave up the boat and took to using freshwater rods and plugs from shore."

On rare occasions, a shark will enter the harbor and go up the Hudson. Back in the 1870s, Gilbert Ward of Cornwall, a famous oarsman of the period, struck a shark with an oar and captured it. From the description given to Dr. Mearns, the Highlands naturalist, it was one of the hammerheads. In 1881, several dusky sharks (*Carcharhinus obscurus*) were caught in the Hudson, one as far north as Peekskill. In 1952, a sand shark (*Carcharias taurus*) was reported taken at Peekskill, and in the summer of 1966, a dusky shark was reported dead on the shore near Newburgh. Off New York, between Long Island and New Jersey, the shark population is abundant. In August of 1962, John G. Casey, a Bureau of Sport Fisheries biologist, captured fifty-five sharks of twelve different species within a twenty-five-mile radius of Sandy Hook: the sand, dusky, mako (*Isurus oxyrinchus*), the blue (*Prionace glauca*), sandbar (*Carcharhinus milberti*), scalloped hammerhead (*Sphyrna lewini*), smooth hammerhead (*S. zygaena*), spiny dogfish (*Squalus acanthias*), smooth dogfish (*Mustelus canis*), tiger (*Galeocerdo cuvieri*), white (*Carcharodon carcharias*), and porbeagle (*Lamna nasus*). Several of these sharks, particularly the white, are feared as maneaters. In 1916 one white shark was credited with four fatal attacks on humans in New Jersey. Casey says that sharks are opportunistic feeders, and that they are attracted to the area by schools of menhaden, offal coming from the harbor, or garbage thrown overboard from ships. A twelve-foot long, eleven-hundred-pound tiger shark that Casey caught had half a sea-turtle shell and a side of bacon in its stomach.

Back in New York City, life is not quite so dramatic. Many of the wild places in the city that once teemed with wildlife a scant three hundred years ago have been buried under cement and steel. A few places remain: polluted Jamaica Bay, the ravaged Hackensack meadowlands in Jersey (slated for oblivion within the next decade), and Staten Island. With the completion of the Verrazano Bridge, Staten Island seems doomed to the march of development. Wildlife still persists, however, with the introduced pheasant the king of game. State law allows the pheasant to be hunted in season, but city law prohibits the discharge of firearms within the city limits. As a result, pheasant are still hunted on Staten Island; they are shot by cops out on a day off.

13

THE
HUDSON CANYON

Out beyond the Narrows and the Lower Bay and past where
Ambrose Light marks the approach to the harbor, the old channel
of the Hudson carves its way through the smooth slope of the
Continental Shelf. Before the last glacier retreated eleven thousand years ago, the Continental Shelf was above sea level, and
the Hudson of that ice age ran through the shelf for a distance of
120 miles before emptying into the Atlantic. Manhattan then was
a high inland ridge capped with ice, and the river was swift and
turbulent, fed by glacial melt and such tributaries as the Passaic,
Hackensack, and Raritan.

Now, near the approach to New York Harbor, the old channel
of the Hudson is smothered with silt; it does not start to become
discernible on charts until the "Mud Hole," just south of Ambrose
Light. The Mud Hole lives up to its name; it is a long gouge in

the surface of the shelf, and it abounds in fishes, such as silver hake and ling (*Urophycis chuss*), that like a muddy bottom. Bluefin tuna (*Thunnus thynnus*) are the most spectacular gamefish found in the area. Zane Grey, the western novelist and fishing fanatic, pioneered here for giant tuna before moving to California. "Once I hooked a tuna off Sandy Hook, out in the channel," he wrote in *Tales of Fishes*, "and as I was playing him the *Lusitania* bore down the channel. Like a mountain she loomed over us. Passengers waved down to us as the tuna bent my rod. The great ship passed on in a seething roar—passed on to her tragic fate. We rode the heavy swells she lifted—and my tuna got away." In September, 1933, Francis H. Low, fishing from a twenty-two-foot skiff in the steamer lane near Ambrose Light, caught a 705-pound bluefin tuna, the largest ever landed in American waters up to that time.

For years, the Mud Hole has served as a dumping ground for debris from New York City, and the rubble has inadvertently created new fishing grounds for black sea bass (*Centropristes striatus*) and scup (*Stenotomus chrysops*), species which like a broken bottom. There are, for instance, the "Doorknob," "New," or "Seagull Grounds," composed of the debris from East Side tenements razed for a housing project, and the "Subway Grounds," made of rock and cement blasted out of Manhattan island for the Eighth Avenue Subway.

Of course, even the sea has its limits as a dump. About two miles northeast of the Mud Hole, there is an area of approximately twenty square miles where no bottom life exists. It has been obliterated by sewage sludge barged out to sea and dumped for the last forty years by New York City and other municipalities. To the east of the Mud Hole is the so-called "Acid Grounds," a turbid, yellowish stain on the surface caused by the dumping of sulphuric acid-iron sulphate wastes from the National Lead Company titanium plant at Sayreville, New Jersey, on the Raritan River. Until 1948, National Lead, which mines titanium at Tahawus on the upper Hudson, simply dumped the wastes, sixty tons a day, directly into the Raritan. Now two barges make a daily trip to the Acid Grounds, where the wastes are dumped overboard, quickly buffered by the slightly alkaline sea water, and turned into finely divided iron floc or rust. The surface stain is usually noticeable to air travelers coming in to land at Kennedy Airport; depending on sea conditions, the Acid Grounds may cover as much as a thirty-square-mile area.

Without question, the creation of the Acid Grounds has altered conditions in the immediate area, but whether or not these alterations have been harmful is a matter of dispute. There are fishermen who maintain that the area has been despoiled, and there are others who insist that the fishing is excellent, particularly for large blues that appear to be attracted to the edge of the stain seeking baitfish which have taken refuge in the murk. To this, critics counter that there would be more blues in the area if were not for the wastes. Whatever the case, it is of some solace to know that marine biologists at the Sandy Hook Laboratory have started studying both the Acid Grounds and the sewage sludge deposits to the north. There is some apprehension that the sewage sludge is in part responsible for prompting recent outbreaks of a loathesome "red tide" along the Jersey coast in the late summer. The red tide is composed of microscopic dinoflagellates— *Glenodinium* and *Prorocentrum* are two which have been identified so far—which can flourish in warm polluted waters and drive swimmers from the surf by causing a burning sensation in the eyes, nose, ears, and throat. Annual outbreaks could prove ruinous to the Jersey resort business, the largest single industry in the state. Actually, the term red tide is a misnomer in this instance, for the water turns brown. The term originates with a far more virulent species of dinoflagellate, *Gymnodinium breves,* which has ravaged the west coast of Florida from time to time, causing enormous kills of fishes, porpoises, and turtles. The Sandy Hook scientists have made one interesting discovery so far. In October, 1968, Bob Wicklund of the lab placed one hundred sea bed drifters on the bottom of the Hudson channel about twenty miles out from shore. Sixty-three of the drifters have washed up on New York beaches so far; some of them were found within twelve days of release. In early 1969, salinity and temperature patterns indicated that the water on the bottom of the channel was "flowing" toward shore. Much more research is to be done, but it may be that the bottom of the channel is a sort of Hudson in reverse moving toward New York.

There are any number of shipwrecks in or near the Mud Hole,

and cod and pollock (*Pollachius virens*) gather around them. A couple of the better known wrecks littering the bottom are the *Ioannis P. Goulandris,* a 3,750-ton Greek freighter that sank in 128 feet of water nine miles off Long Branch, New Jersey, on December 1, 1942, after colliding with another ship, and the *Arundo,* a 5,163 ton Dutch freighter, torpedoed by a German submarine on April 28, 1942. The *Arundo* on the edge of the Mud Hole 140 feet down, fifteen miles off Belmar, New Jersey, carried a cargo of war material, and for years scuba divers have been salvaging souvenirs from her hulk. On New Year's Day, 1968, a party of scuba divers rented the *Black Hawk,* a fishing boat out of Belmar, to go down on the wreck. Only two divers, Bradley Ainsworth and Richard Miranda, decided to descend through the twenty-foot waves. Miranda reported:

> Our first view of the bottom was a great disappointment, because all we saw was a rolling plain of white sand with a few large cod and ling gliding along in search of food.
>
> We decided to conserve air by bouncing back up to the surface. In that way, we could let the skipper try again to pinpoint the wreck with his sounding devices and save us the trouble of maybe heading off in the wrong direction and using up our air.
>
> The skipper made another sounding and pointed us in the right direction. This time we had more luck. As we drifted down the first thing that came into sight was enough to make a man think he'd gone crazy.
>
> Sitting in the bottom in an upright position was a 1940 model steam engine with a cow catcher, bell, and all the trimmings. I learned later that the freighter had been laden with jeeps, trucks, and steam engines, as well as smaller supplies. This engine, with cod and ling drifting in and out of her cab windows, had apparently broken loose from the ship as it was going down. It was well crusted with marine life which added to the eerie sight.
>
> Within a few minutes, the whole picture began to come in clear, just as the image on a screen sharpens with an adjustment of the lens. Pieces of the freighter were strewn here and there. Samples of the cargo were waiting to be explored.

It looked like an abandoned wharf with the cargo laying around and the ship waiting to be untied and tugged out to open water.

But the scene was cast in another dimension with fish slipping in and out of the railings and gliding over the huge mass. Just as things seemed to be getting interesting, Brad signaled and pointed to his watch. At 140 feet, a diver can only stay safely at bottom for ten minutes without going through a decompression scale and we didn't have the air or daylight time for this, so we began to head for the surface.

After a brief struggle to get back onboard the *Black Hawk*, and a cheer from the spectators, we were inside the warm cabin munching on crackers again.

Perhaps the most unusual wreck of all is the remains of Texas Tower Number Four, which collapsed into the sea in January, 1961. Twenty-eight men went down with the tower, which now lies bent and twisted on the north rim of the old Hudson channel eighty-five miles off the Jersey coast.

As the channel nears the edge of the Continental Shelf, it widens to five miles and then suddenly slumps into the Atlantic depths. Here is the beginning of an underwater marvel, the Hudson Canyon, an enormous gorge that seemingly plunges forever downward to the sea floor. For years, the origin of the Hudson Canyon and other canyons along the shelf has been the subject of argument among geologists, with most contending that rivers had carved the canyons when the sea level was much lower during glacial times. Until 1930, when the United States Coast and Geodetic Survey undertook explorations of the shelf with an echo sounder, the Hudson Canyon was believed to be six thousand feet deep. The Survey discovered a depth of nine thousand feet, far greater than anyone had supposed. If the Hudson River had indeed carved such a canyon in the past, the level of the sea would have had to have been unbelievably low, and one geologist, Reginald A. Daly of Harvard, suggested that the canyons had been cut instead by turbidity currents, underwater currents carrying abrasive mineral particles in suspension. This suggestion was received with skepticism. Now, however, as the result of research in the late 1940s and 1950s by scientists at the Lamont Geological

Observatory of Columbia University, it appears Daly was correct.

Working from research vessels belonging to Lamont and the Woods Hole Oceanographic Institution, these scientists took extensive samples of sediments from the bottom of the Hudson Canyon by lowering a forty-foot pipe, or core, on a cable to the bottom. When the lower end of the core touched bottom, a triggering mechanism drove the core into the layers of sediment. The core was then retrieved and the sediments taken to Lamont at Palisades, New York, for study. In the laboratory, David B. Ericson and Goesta Wollin examined the sediments—shallow water shells, quartz sand grains, micas, felspars, glauconite, red and gray shale, flint, limestone, and ferromagnesian minerals—and concluded that they had been deposited not by river erosion but by turbidity currents. Moreover, Ericson and Wollin were able to deduce that these currents had been very active during the time of the last glacier. The rushing Hudson then carried a tremendous load of sediment, which it dumped at the river mouth on the edge of the shelf. The sediments piled up, and whenever the load became too great, they slid down the shelf, causing an underwater avalanche. As the avalanche reached bottom, it picked up speed and became "a great storm of mud, sand, gravel and water," as Ericson and Wollin write in their book, *The Deep and the Past*. Constant repetition of these underwater storms, or turbidity currents, gouged out the Hudson Canyon. In their work on the canyon, the scientists also found that it was much longer and deeper than previously known. It runs for 160 miles beyond the edge of the shelf and descends to a maximum depth of fifteen thousand feet before it finally disappears into an abyssal plain sloping toward Bermuda.

As fascinating as these findings may be, Ericson and Wollin's work on the sediments from the canyon region was really only a sideline of more important research. Core samples from the Hudson Canyon and other deep-sea stations around the world allowed them to make what they call, in *The Deep and the Past*, "the first complete record of the Pleistocene, the epoch which brought forth both ice and man." Previous estimates of the duration of the Pleistocene epoch had varied widely, from two hundred thousand to one million years, but now Ericson and Wollin write,

Our time scale dates the beginning of the Pleistocene at about 1,500,000 years ago. This date will necessitate a revision on the basic time scale of prehistoric events and particularly the rate of human development, past and future. We can now put the chronology of human evolution in order.

By our chronology we date the second ice age, during which the early men called *Pithecanthropus* appeared, as between 1,205,000 and 1,060,000 years ago, and the last interglacial, when *Homo sapiens* appeared, between 340,000 and 115,000 years ago. This time scale is in disagreement with a widely accepted chronology based on the ratio between oxygen isotopes in cores of sediment from the Atlantic and the Caribbean. According to it, the second ice age took place between 200,000 and 170,000 years ago and the last interglacial between 100,000 and 65,000 years ago. This greatly shortened timetable has met with skepticism among a few students of human evolution; they regard the implied rate of man's evolution as improbably rapid. Our chronology stretches out the span of the evolution of man and allows time for the slow accumulation of small changes which Darwin assumed to be the basis of evolution.

The geologic timetable worked out by the Lamont scientists has significant application in other fields, such as determining rates of erosion and of the building of mountains, and the time sequence of biological evolution in general. For instance, it was previously estimated that it took five hundred thousand years, a seemingly short span, for two distinct species of European elephants to develop from a common ancestor during the Pleistocene; now, by Ericson and Wollin's scale, it is apparent that this development took place over a period of almost 1,400,000 years.

The life forms in the Hudson Canyon itself have been studied on a few occasions, most notably by the late Dr. William Beebe, the triple-threat oceanographer, ornithologist, and writer, who was director of the Department of Tropical Research at the New York Zoological Society. Beebe's research on the Canyon took place in the late 1920s. He was a truly remarkable man who was able to leap, without noticeable pause, from pheasants to fishes, from scientific writing to popular books. It is a measure of his worth that when the first volume of his four-volume monograph *Pheasants: Their Lives and Homes* appeared, the National Academy of Sciences promptly awarded him the Daniel Giraud Elliot gold medal in recognition of his outstanding contribution to zoology for the year 1918.

For all his adventures the world over, Beebe was fascinated by the Hudson Canyon, or the Hudson Gorge, as he called it. He could not get over the idea that the weird creatures he found in the depths there were only one hundred miles from Broadway. Beebe's first trip was in 1925 aboard the four-hundred-ton steam yacht *Arcturus*, generously supplied to the New York Zoological Society by Henry D. Whiton, a member of the board of managers. In a grand gesture that smacks of the affluence of the 1920s, Whiton, newly elected to the board, approached Beebe on the very day of the doctor's return from an expedition to the Galapagos and said, "You seem tremendously interested in the Galapagos; if you ever want to go back there I will furnish the steamer if you can get someone else to provide the coal." Beebe quickly rounded up the millionaires who could supply the coal and on February 11 set off on a six-month trip to the Sargasso Sea, and the Cocos and Galapagos islands. Before steaming back to New York Harbor, the *Arcturus* halted over the Hudson Canyon, where Beebe established Station 113. The work done there in four days was among "the highlights of the expedition," so Beebe wrote in *The Arcturus Adventure*, a best-seller he turned out immediately upon his return.

The *Arcturus* began working the Canyon when the piano wire used for sounding reached a depth of three thousand feet. Beebe was thrilled when the wire touched bottom for it brought to his imagination "what the most marvelous piece of music conveys to the ear. It was a lost chord vibrant with all the wonder of past ages, before man or his kindred had begun to evolve." He ordered gear lowered. The first to descend was the otter trawl. Forty-feet long, it had a gaping mouth held open by two iron-bound boards. Then fine silk nets, each twenty feet long were lowered on a single cable, spaced every three hundred feet apart. As the *Arcturus* moved slowly through the water, the lowest of the nets trailed three thousand feet below. Beebe assumed he was over the deepest part of the Canyon, but later research has shown that he was off the target by miles.

For the next four days and nights, the *Arcturus* continued trawling, and Beebe never lacked for observation. Overhead petrels circled, and dusky sharks, seen on the surface waiting for garbage, were caught on hook and line. In the log, Beebe noted: ". . . we had a steak from one for lunch. Very good, not unlike swordfish but tougher and not so dry. Crew vastly disgusted at the idea, but cannot explain why." A young puppy on board tumbled overboard and drowned. A shark engulfed the pup, then spat him out. The dog had been treated with Glover's mange cure, and the taste was apparently repugnant. The most impressive sights were schools of small whales, "which rolled in a dignified elephantine manner through the waves and with huge sighs sent up spouts of mist."

Nothing was too obscure to escape Beebe's attention, from the small bits of sargassum weed that drifted by, often accompanied by small fishes or crabs seeking shelter underneath, to the insects that had flown out from land. Some thirty dragonflies, beetles, moths, and grasshoppers were collected. Beebe even took samples of surface drift. The list for the first day included one large wooden spigot, one rubber nipple from a baby's bottle, one empty milk of magnesia bottle, two cans, four cardboard milk bottle tops, one leg from a rubber doll, and one empty Gordon's gin bottle. The last, Beebe noted, might have come from the *Arcturus*, since all aboard were polishing off the liquor supply before landing in the America of prohibition.

The nets from the deep yielded largely three species of salpae, curious jelly-like creatures that claim very low and distant kinship with the vertebrates. One of the ship's officers exclaimed, "Well, I suppose you people would even eat that stuff!" Beebe thereupon ate one, but he confessed he got "no enjoyment from this bit of bravado—just a sensation of very salty, hard jelly."

On the evening of July 29, the *Arcturus* set out for the voyage home and docked after dawn on July 30 at Eighty-first Street and the Hudson. "Every ship on the way saluted us, from garbage scows to big ocean liners," Beebe wrote in his final entry in the log, "and as courtesy required that we answer every blast, we had barely enough steam to creep up to the pier."

But Beebe was not finished with the Hudson Canyon. In an

article in the *Bulletin* of the New York Zoological Society, he later wrote: "I had to spend most of the summer of 1928 in New York City, and yet I longed to be exploring on the edge of known things. How could I manage both at once? There came to mind a cartoon in which Skippy and his small friend stand for a long time gazing out to sea. Throughout three layers of cartoon strips not a word passed between the two urchins. At last, without turning his head, Skippy said, 'You know, that's only the top of it.' That cartoon set me thinking, and brought to mind the Hudson Gorge—silent, black, cold—with its sunken vastness filled with unknown forms of life."

With the help of L. F. V. Drake, president of the Salvage Process Corporation, Beebe borrowed a tug, the *Wheeler,* and on the evening of July 8, 1928, he set course for the Gorge. The tug arrived at eight the next morning. A winch lowered nets a half mile down, and for several hours the *Wheeler* crawled on the surface at a speed of two knots. With a wave from Beebe's hand, the engine stopped, and the winch began to reel in the nets. At length they came aboard, dripping and bulging with "pink treasure, glittering and gleaming, trembling with strange vitality, every spoonful a cosmos of hundreds of living beings." At the surface, the water temperature was 68° F., at five hundred fathoms down 40° and on the bottom 31°. Some of the fishes were so cold they were almost painful to touch. There was a dragonfish (*Chauliodus sloanei*), with a gaping mouth and long needle teeth on the lower jaw that fit through concealed holes in the head; a scarlet shrimp, *Acanthepyra,* which ejects a blazing phosphorescent cloud to befuddle its enemies; and a species of *Stylophthalmus,* which Beebe called the "strangest of living fish," for it has a bill like a duck, eyes on the tops of long stalks, and a pale, thread-like body lined with what looked like "scores of glowing portholes." There were several species of fishes that hitherto had been found only in such distant places as the Gulf of Guinea, off Panama, and in the Pacific. Two fishes were completely unknown to science. One, a deep-water relative of the herring, Beebe named *Bathytroctes drakei,* in honor of the helpful Mr. Drake; the other a small, transparent, ribless, balloon-skinned creature related to the angler fish, Beebe called *Haplophryne hudsonius* for the Canyon.

After only a day at sea, the *Wheeler* headed back for New York. Beebe thought of the lines from Kipling:

"The wrecks dissolve above us; their dust drops down from afar—
Down to the dark, the utter dark, where the blind white sea-snakes are.
There is no sound, no echo of sound, in the deserts of the deep,
On the great grey level plains of ooze where the shell-burred cables creep."

All told, Beebe considered his findings aboard the *Wheeler* so important that he formally named the jaunt the Eleventh Expedition of the Department of Tropical Research of the New York Zoological Society. Although he planned to make a comprehensive survey of the Canyon, he never did so, but he had found so much about which to be enthused that he wrote, "Long after the last animal and insect from the heart of Africa and New Guinea has [sic] been collected and named, and the north and south poles have been crossed and recrossed with tourist planes, strange fish and other creatures will still be brought to light within a day's motorboat run of New York City."

Almost thirty years passed before another man, Finn Magnus, decided to explore the Hudson Canyon. Magnus is a sports fisherman, a beefy, inventive Norwegian in his late fifties who emigrated to the United States when he was seventeen. In the early 1950s, Magnus made a fortune manufacturing plastic harmonicas, and he added to his riches by inventing a small, portable, plastic organ with numbered keys that would enable any musical illiterate to play a tune in ten minutes. Given ample money and time, Magnus decided to turn to the sea for relaxation. He brought a forty-foot Matthews cruiser and navigation charts. After some study of the charts—Magnus is not the sort of man to do things on impulse—he reasoned that the Hudson Canyon looked promising, and so he lassoed on extra gasoline tanks and embarked one morning in August, 1957, amid jeers that he was "just a crazy Norwegian."

What Magnus discovered was some crazy big-game fishing. He was so excited over the prospects that he sold his boat and spent one hundred thousand dollars on a new one specially designed to make the hundred-mile trip from Brielle, N.J., in four and a half hours. The new boat, 47½-feet-long and named *Magnus,* is powered by two 235-horsepower diesel engines and has a cruising range of six hundred miles. The *Magnus* is equipped with radar, Loran, a depth finder, a direction finder, an automatic pilot, a fish finder, a ship-to-shore telephone, a permanent thermometer for surface temperatures, a graph depth thermometer for readings to 450 feet, fishing tackle galore, and a small portable plastic organ on which Magnus thumps out *Home on the Range* and *You are My Sunshine* during starlit nights over the Canyon.

Magnus has found a tremendous variety of life in the area, and he attributes this to the diversity of currents and the rugged terrain below. There are giant leatherback turtles (*Dermochelys sp.*) weighing upwards of one thousand pounds, killer whales (*Grampus orca*), blackfish whales (*Globicephala melaena*), sharks, and schools of porpoises that can seemingly make the water boil for miles around. Most of all, there are fishes, some of which are not supposed to be in the area at all. "I believe the Canyon is the most fabulous fishing spot in the world," Magnus says. False albacore (*Euthynnus alletteratus*) are so plentiful as to be pests. One day Magnus caught seventeen in self-defense. "I didn't want to catch any more," he says. "I wanted to get away from them." There are white marlin (*Makaira albida*); blue marlin (*M. nigricans*), very rare north of Cape Hatteras; five-hundred-pound bluefin tuna; yellowfin tuna (*Thunnus albacares*), ordinarily found in warmer waters; and multitudes of dolphin (*Coryphaena hippurus*) and bluefish. There are times when Magnus likes to fish deep. He has caught lancet fish (*Alepisaurus ferox*), eel-shaped monstrosities with great spiny, sail-like dorsal fins and alligator mouths with sharp teeth an inch long. There are tilefish (*Lopholatilus chamaeleonticeps*) by the ton, and Magnus has caught some weighing up to thirty pounds. The tilefish has a strange history. It is present off the East Coast in enormous numbers, but commercial fishermen did not even suspect its existence until 1879. Then, in 1882, disaster struck; an estimated billion and a half tilefish were found dead on the surface. Study revealed that the species is a bottom dweller, winter or summer. The kill was caused, in all likelihood, by a temporary flooding of the bottom zone by abnormally cold water from which the tilefish could not escape. The tilefish began to come back, and by 1915, the government was seeking to popularize it for the market. It is both delicious and nutritious, but there never has been a strong demand for it.

Magnus has taken numerous temperature readings at the Canyon, and he has found wide variations. Within one five-hundred-foot section, there was a difference of 27°. The Gulf Stream flows to the east, but there are times, Magnus says, when it veers toward land. A pale blue, it snakes into the indigo waters of the Canyon, jumping the surface temperature by as much as 10°. It carries small strange fishes by the thousands, and flying fish ordinarily not found in these northern waters fill the air with frightened leaps. Sometimes, under the stress of a meander, a chunk of the Gulf Stream will break off, so to speak, and warm-water fishes will be taken inshore. Such meanders perhaps play a role in distributing juvenile tropical fishes along the northeast coast and up the Hudson.

As a result of his extensive fishing of the Canyon, with its myriad of unusual fishes, Magnus has come up with a theory of his own on fish migration. In essence, he believes that adult fishes do not migrate by instinct or by what might be termed free will, but are moved from place to place in the sea because they live in blocks of water that are in turn moved by pressures, currents, and changing conditions in the ocean. He has done up a mimeographed brochure supporting his theory and sent it to marine biologists and oceanographers. A few have raised their eyebrows heavenward at his theorizing, but all agree that he has made some unusual observations, and, after all, it is difficult to knock the trapper who has the skins on the wall.

Frank Mather III, an associate scientist at Woods Hole who has corresponded with Magnus, says: "We're getting quite excited about the Hudson Canyon. There is absolutely no doubt that large predatory fish are concentrated there in unusually large numbers." Mather says that in the fall commercial fishermen, mostly from Nova Scotia, go there for swordfish (*Xiphias gladius*) in such numbers as to pose a traffic problem. "The Canadians learned about it from the Norwegians," says Mather, "who accidentally found swordfish there while fishing for sharks." A decade ago commercial swordfishing was a chancy business. Now commercial fishermen catch the swordfish not by harpooning, the traditional practice, but by longlining. Long, multihooked lines are baited and strung from floating barrels. Swordfish either take the swinging bait or foul themselves on the hooks in the attempt. Inasmuch as a single longline may extend for ten miles or more and contain several thousand hooks, it is little wonder that a ship may haul in as many as one hundred swordfish in a day, more than a crew used to harpoon in an entire season. Now sports fishermen fear that the species may be wiped out along the Atlantic Coast.

Starting in 1963, foreign fishing vessels, particularly ships from the Soviet Union, began converging on the Hudson Canyon in the winter and spring months. On one April day in 1966, a U.S. Coast Guard reconaissance plane counted thirty-nine Soviet ships, mostly stern trawlers, in the area. In the main, the Soviet ships concentrated on silver hake, ling, scup, and fluke, all fishes which, in a sense, are biologically American, although they do frequent offshore waters of from fifty to one hundred fathoms from late December until mid-April, when inshore temperatures are low. As the Soviet take rose to a high of two hundred thousand tons, the American commercial catch slumped to an abnormal low of twenty thousand, while the sport fisheries also tumbled. In November of 1967, the U.S. State Department negotiated the first of what appears to be a series of agreements with the Soviet Union. The Soviets agreed to restrict their operations in certain areas, and in exchange the U.S. permitted them to transfer catches to factory ships off Long Island and New Jersey and to fish a sixty-square mile area within nine miles of the Long Island coast. The agreement prompted a roar of protest ("Opens Door for Reds," ran one headline), and perhaps predictably, the Hudson Canyon, like the Hudson River, knows little peace.

14

THE FUTURE
OF THE RIVER

I have two visions of the Hudson River as it will appear to the next generation.

The first is that of a clean and wholesome river from the Adirondacks down to the harbor; a wild, unfettered stream in its forested mountain headwaters; productive tidewater from Troy south. Useful for both navigation and drinking water, the Hudson will be a river toward which millions of people can turn with pride and expectation. In recreation alone, the Hudson will be worth billions to the communities along its banks.

The second vision is not pleasant. Dammed and strangled in the Adirondacks to serve as a draw-down reservoir, the upper river trickles to the estuary. Overloaded with sewage and industrial wastes and cooked by cooling water from power plants, the lower Hudson is bereft of the larger forms of life except for a few stray catfish or carp in isolated "zones of recovery." At night, the mountains of the Highlands thrum to the noise of pumped storage plants sucking part of the river uphill. Discovery of a dead sturgeon or a striped bass along the shore is cause for excitement and a front-page story in the *Times* on the wonder of it all. Here and there, between the transmission towers and stacks, a few breathtaking views of the valley landscape are still to be seen, if you look quickly while speeding behind a truck over a six-lane highway built on filled-in river bottom. In essence, the valley is jammed with senseless sprawl, and the river is a gutted ditch, an aquatic Appalachia, a squalid monument to greed.

Neither vision is exaggerated. Anyone who doubts the latter is invited to visit Verplanck and look at the hellish plants that have sprung up at Tomkins Cove and Indian Point in the past few years. What was once a great river scene has been scarred by industrial ugliness. Multiply this ten or twenty times and that is the sort of Hudson some would foist upon us.

As might be expected, I opt for a productive and enjoyable Hudson. The means to achieve this are within reach, provided certain measures are adopted as either state or federal policy. If it were within my power to establish a program for the Hudson (or any other river, where the same points are applicable) I have several suggestions. If these points appear to be conflicting or redundant, they are purposely so, for I wish to cover any contingency that may arise. Experience on the river has taught me this the hard way.

To start, I would make it a point of state principle and policy that the Hudson be considered first from an ecological point of view. It is not a river that God made for power companies or pulp mill owners. The Hudson is a living, natural system, and any industrialist who wishes to utilize this resource should have to prove that he will do no harm whatsoever to the ecological or aesthetic vitality of the river.

There should be prompt and vigorous enforcement of anti-pollution laws.

The state should outlaw the use of chlorinated hydrocarbon pesticides.

Marshlands, wetlands, mouths of tributaries, and shallow waters in the Hudson (and elsewhere in the state) should be declared inviolate. These are among the most productive areas of the river, and using them as garbage dumps or as fill areas for highways, airports, factories, housing developments, and the like is insane. There is no question but that such a law can be passed and enforced against would-be ravagers of the environment. The Commonwealth of Massachusetts, not ordinarily thought of as being in the vanguard of decent governmental practices, has had the sense to enact a law protecting coastal marshes from despoliation. When a "developer" sought to buck the law, a court upheld it, finding: "Broad Marsh is a 'salt marsh' necessary to preserve and protect marine fisheries. . . . Property is acquired by private citizens with the tacit understanding that it shall not be used to the detriment of the public, and the legislature is authorized to take action to prevent such detrimental use." In accordance with the law, owners of marshland who seek financial compensation may have it set by a court. Thus far, no one has applied.

The state should sponsor an ecological survey of the Hudson and other watersheds in the state, and these surveys should enumerate and describe areas of critical importance. Governor Rockefeller pledged such a survey in his 1966 campaign for reelection, but he has done nothing to date. This survey should list all ponds, wetlands, parks, wildlife preserves, lakes, streams, open spaces, and other natural resources, along with information about their productivity or uniqueness. (Local governments should do the same. The village of Croton and the town of Cortlandt should move to protect the lower Croton River.) This information could be mapped and computerized. Thus an industry seeking a location on the river would be directed toward areas that are not of great significance and away from areas that are. Readily available information of this sort is essential, not only for industry or recreation or for educational or scientific use, but to the people as a whole if they have any wish to shape a desirable future.

One would expect that the colleges and universities would have done considerable research on the Hudson—the river is a great laboratory open to all for firsthand inspection. But thus far the schools along the Hudson have done next to nothing. New York University has made a start, and some of the research is valuable, but the studies underway involve only a handful of graduate students. Life in and along the Hudson should be a part of the curriculum of undergraduates at Columbia, NYU, Vassar, Bard, Union, the various community colleges, and West Point (especially for cadets entering the Corps of Engineers). Their contributions are almost nil. Vassar offers a course on the river, and I have been out in the early fall when the girls from Poughkeepsie made their annual yacht trip upstream. These girls should have been *in* the river, up to their necks in muck, tagging shad or gathering fungus growth from a sewage outlet. Perhaps colleges and universities ought to band together for a cooperative study center on the Hudson. At this writing, Dr. James Melville of Mercy College, a new Roman Catholic college directly on the river at Dobbs Ferry, is proposing to establish an ecological research center for study of the Hudson. Local school systems could get involved in the river. A great deal could be done on the high school level. For example, it would be quite easy to position an underwater television camera and other monitors in the mouth of the Croton River or any clear tributary. Biology students need only turn on a receiving set to see what fishes are moving upstream or spawning, what insects are hatching, or how a crab scurries along the bottom in its natural environment. There are all sorts of educational possibilities.

For example, what about a floating laboratory for school systems? This is being done right now in the Pacific for ten thousand youngsters in Orange County, California. According to Ronald B. Linsky, director of the Marine Science Floating Laboratory Program for the Orange County Schools, the *Fury II*, a sixty-five-foot, twin-diesel sport-fishing vessel has been outfitted for marine studies. Several dozen youngsters, ranging from seventh-graders to high school seniors, spend a day at sea aboard the *Fury II*. The first thing they do is to assist in the collection of live bait, anchovies in this case, which serve as the basis for teaching specimen identification. The students help identify all fishes taken on board, and at the end of a month, all specimens and data collected are sent to various institutions and universities interested in the coast. The youngsters also become familiar with scientific instruments, help retrieve a seventy-five-foot balloon-trawl net laid over the stern, and learn the rudiments of navigation in the wheel house. Linsky writes: "We think we accomplish four things by going to sea: (1) we encourage students to consider the marine sciences as a career; (2) we stimulate anew the interest in science which falls off considerably after the junior high years; (3) we illustrate to young people that science can be an exciting experience in this last frontier of inner space; and (4) we help young people gain a better appreciation of an environment too often taken for granted in maritime communities."

There should be a Hudson River Valley Commission involving the federal government and the states of New York and New Jersey. The present state commission is a bad joke. In 1966, Congress passed a bill introduced by Representative Richard Ottinger calling for the establishment of a federal-state commission. In approving the Ottinger Bill, Congress gave its consent to the states of New York and New Jersey (and also to Vermont, Massachusetts, and Connecticut, if they wished to participate) to negotiate with each other and with the federal government for purposes of entering into a compact on the Hudson River basin. According to the act, consideration should be specifically given to:

(a) the need to encourage all beneficial uses of the lands and waters of the Hudson Riverway including, but not limited to, commercial, industrial, and other economic development consistent with the preservation and rehabilitation of the natural, scenic, historical, and recreational resources of the Hudson Riverway;

(b) the need to encourage and support local and State autonomy and initiative in planning and action to develop, preserve, and restore the land and waters of the Hudson Riverway, insofar as such planning and action is consistent with comprehensive development, preservation, and restoration of the natural, scenic, historic, and recreation resources of the Hudson Riverway;

(c) the need to abate water pollution, protect clean water, and develop the water resources of the Hudson Riverway for beneficial use;

(d) the need to preserve, enhance, and rehabilitate the scenic beauty of the Hudson Riverway;

(e) the need to preserve, enhance, and develop archeological and historic sites, shrines, or structures along the Hudson Riverway; and

(f) the need to protect and enhance the fish and wildlife and other natural resources of the Hudson Riverway.

At present, negotiations on the compact have bogged down because of Governor Rockefeller's refusal to cooperate, and what eventually will be agreed upon, if anything at all, is anyone's guess. However, a federal-state compact is a necessity; as I noted earlier, a number of federal agencies already have jurisdiction over much of the Hudson, and these agencies, which include the Federal Power Commission, the Atomic Energy Commission, and the Corps of Engineers, have been in the vanguard of the despoilers. A new and more powerful body is needed to subjugate them and such wayward state agencies as the Department of Transportation, the Water Resources Commission, the Public Service Commission, and the Atomic and Space Development Authority. If it were within my power to do so, I would see to it that the executive director of a federal-state commission was a naturalist or conservationist of stature, on the order of David Sive of the Sierra Club; Roland Clement or Charles Callison of the National Audubon Society; Richard Pough of the Nature Conservancy; Rod Vandivert of Scenic Hudson; John Clark of the Sandy Hook laboratory; Professors Edward Raney or Alfred Eipper of Cornell, Harry Darbee, the Catskill angler and flytier; or Dr. James Alexander and Dominick Pirone of the Hudson River Fishermen's Association. I have seen enough of engineers in such sensitive posts. We have been engineered to death.

Whatever naturalist or conservationist is the director, I would like to see him out on the river the length of the year, nailing polluters on the spot, telling highwaymen they cannot build the road here but over there, talking to schoolchildren, telling anglers where the stripers or sturgeon are running—in essence, giving a sense of time, place, and purpose to people who live in or visit the valley. In my mind's eye, I imagine the job to be somewhat like an expanded version of the role played by the late William James Lunn, river keeper for the Houghton Club on the Test, the most famous British trout stream. For almost fifty years, Lunn worked on the river, restocking it with aquatic insects, cutting weed, hatching trout. There is a marvelous photograph of him, elderly and bewhiskered, tweezers in hand, sorting out insects, in the biography by John Waller Hills. So, I like to imagine, will appear the river keeper of the Hudson in future years, a no-nonsense naturalist, with the idiosyncrasies, migrations, and workings of the Hudson engrained in his mind. We need someone like this on the Hudson and on every major river in the country.

There is one thing that New York State could do. This is a simple step that I suggested earlier—to put the tidal river under the jurisdiction of its marine biologists. Given state neglect of the Hudson, imaginative deeds are stifled. Let me give an example. It would be easy to seine five thousand striped bass of from three to ten pounds each from the river and stock them in the Croton Reservoir. This artificial lake has never been managed, and it is overpopulated with hordes of tiny pan fishes. As a result the lake is only lightly fished. The stripers undoubtedly would wax fat on a diet of stunted sunnies and perch. The introduction of stripers would certainly stimulate a very active sport fishery, to the benefit of local communities. At present, various inland states, such as Oklahoma and West Virginia, are trying to get striped bass going in some of their larger lakes, and it seems a pity that New York State, which has an abundant striper population right at hand in the Hudson, has not made even a token experiment.

There are similar ways of improving the lot of the commercial fisherman. The wholesale price of striped bass fluctuates wildly, depending on the size of the catch. In spring and fall, when there are heavy shipments from the Chesapeake, the price may be as low as fifteen or twenty cents a pound for a striper "in the round," the unscaled, ungutted fish. That is the price for the most desirable stripers, the so-called "chicken" bass of from two to six pounds that are in demand by housewives. However, stripers from the Hudson often do not command the full market price. They are supposed to taste of oil, and so the few wholesale dealers who will buy bass from the river offer only half the going price, say ten cents instead of twenty cents a pound. Thus four thousand pounds of bass from the Hudson would fetch only four hundred dollars. However, if these same four thousand pounds of bass were transported alive to a clean freshwater pond and held there until late December or January, when bass are scarce in the market, they would lose any off-taste and would be worth anywhere from $1.50 to $2.00 a pound. Instead of getting four hundred dollars, a commercial fisherman would get anywhere from six thousand to eight thousand dollars. Expenses would be minimal, inasmuch as the metabolism of the striped bass slows in colder weather and the fish does not actively feed.

Much the same might be done with other edible species, such as sturgeon, white perch, carp, or eels. For instance, eels are so scarce in Europe that some American and Canadian fishermen are finding it profitable to air-express them to London and Paris. Bait fish are another possibility. I am dismayed whenever I read in the local paper about men being laid off at the Harmon yards by the Penn Central. If I were fired from my job tomorrow, I think I could make a living, or at least scratch out the semblance of one, just seining bait from the Hudson.

There are times when threats to the river—dams, dredging projects, pollution, power plants, etc.—seem so overwhelming that I am tempted to throw up my hands in surrender. But this would be a betrayal of trust, and nothing positive will ever be accomplished if people despair or bow to the supposedly inevitable. Fortunately, there are a number of organizations interested in the river, such as the Scenic Hudson Preservation Conference, the Hudson River Conservation Society, and the Adirondack Hudson River Association that people may join. The organization that seems the most basic in its approach is the Hudson River Fishermen's Association, formed in 1966. The aims of the HRFA, to quote from the papers of incorporation, are to "encourage the rational use of the aquatic resources of the Hudson River and its tributaries. The Association will gather, study and disseminate information about the ecology of the Hudson watershed, particularly in regard to the life histories and needs of fishes; endeavor to protect the spawning and nursery grounds of desirable sports and commercial fishes; and assist in efforts to abate pollution." In less than three years, membership has jumped from ten to three hundred, despite scant publicity, and the members, who pay dues of three dollars a year, include sports fishermen, commercial fishermen, bait and tackle dealers, biologists, and just plain folks who are fed up with abuse of the river. The HRFA literally has a grass roots membership; Richie Garrett, the president, is the superintendent of St. Augustine's Cemetery in Ossining. As Richie says, "Fellas, I'm the last guy to let you down." Among the members are a number of persons previously mentioned in this book: Ace Lent, Charlie White, Henry Gourdine, and Everett Nack. Dom Pirone, Dr. James Alexander, Ric Riccardi, Art Glowka, Dan Salzberg, Bob Hoebermann, and myself are on the board of directors. Jim Alexander also is Scientific Advisor. Other scientist members are Dr. Malcolm Hair of Adelphi College, Dr. Emmanual Sorge, and Jim's wife, Betty, a specialist in algae. When a problem arises we can usually get an expert opinion. Irving Younger, a former assistant United States attorney and a professor at New York University Law School, served as counsel until he became a judge.

Three or four times a year, depending on funds, the HRFA mails a bulletin to members on what fish are biting and where, what polluters have been bagged, and other news of interest. Twice a year, the HRFA holds open meetings at a former one-room schoolhouse, now the Parker-Bale American Legion Post in Crotonville, just to the north of Ossining. The sessions are lively. A typical meeting is like a cross between a seminar at Woods Hole and an old Duffy's Tavern program. I remember one meeting when Representative Ottinger spoke on federal legislation on the Hudson. After he finished speaking he was free to leave, but the exchange was so lively on this and other questions that he remained until the end, well after midnight. No one pulls any punches. At another meeting, the late Jack Garrett, Richie's brother, asked for the floor. "We've heard all about the scientific names of fish," he began, "but what I want to know is, do we have jurisdiction over the Harlem River? I'm working on an apartment house going up at Riverdale, and every day when I sit down for lunch on the sixteenth floor, I look down and what do I see but a lot of crap coming out of a pipe on the Harlem River. Excuse me, lady, but I want to throw up. Now who's putting this crud through that pipe, and what can we do to stop it?"

The meetings can be very moving. I have seen factory workers stand up and put their jobs on the line by reporting their own employers as polluters. "Don't check on the company during the day," one man said. "They keep the stuff downstairs and let it out after midnight." In other instances, pollution has been stopped by members within factories. This was the case at a large plant near Yonkers, which regularly released oil wastes into the Hudson. A new member who had learned of the anti-pollution laws marched into the front office and announced the men would no longer dump the oil into the river. "It's detrimental to marine life!" he shouted. "It's against federal law!" The startled plant manager said the dumping would cease. At another plant there was a spill of heavy lubricating oil. Instead of cleaning it up, the management ordered workers to shovel the oil into a brook flowing into the river. Richie Garrett learned of this almost immediately when a member working at the plant snuck away to a phone.

Perhaps the most heartening thing about the HRFA to me is to see the love and concern that members have for the Hudson, and their awareness that they can fight for the river and beat the power companies, the polluters, and the garbage dumpers. And the more people who realize this, the sooner the river will be saved. I have seen this most vividly with members from Crotonville. Thanks to Richie Garrett and his wife, Gloria, the HRFA must have forty to fifty members in this small hillside hamlet overlooking the lower Croton River. The Croton and its marshes and the shores of the Hudson mean a great deal to the hardworking people of Crotonville. This is their Grand Banks, Riviera, and Chesapeake Bay rolled into one. Most Crotonvillers are Irish and German who came up from Hell's Kitchen in Manhattan at the turn of the century. At first, they lived in bungalows on Croton Point, but then they were evicted by Westchester County as squatters. A real estate promoter then sold them plots in what is now Crotonville, and they settled down there during the Depression years. They helped one another build houses, and after a house was built it was topped with an American flag and there was a giant beer bust. The youngsters fished, hunted, and trapped in the marshes. In the spring, they and their fathers knew where the smelt ran and the trout lurked. On a summer day, the boys rode a fifty-pound snapping turtle with its mouth held shut by a wire bridle. Several of the men took to commercial fishing, and boys helped to haul nets. Joe Schmidt grew a beard and looked like the fisherman on the cod liver oil label. An old German, he netted and sold killifish for live bait. I was exploring the Croton marshes one summer day when Richie Garrett started to tell me about Joe. We moved along talking until we came to the abutment of the old bridge that had been torn down when the new state highway was built. Richie said that old Joe used to keep his killies in live boxes right near the bridge. Then one day, Richie went on, Joe dropped dead. He was found floating face down in the water on top of his killie boxes. Richie took a deep breath, and then he said, half to me and half to the wind that swayed the reeds, "God Almighty, what a beautiful way to die."

Bibliography

I have not arranged the bibliography chapter by chapter, but instead I have grouped books and articles under various general headings for the convenience of the reader who is interested in pursuing a particular subject. Some titles could fall under either one of two headings, so the reader who is interested in, say, the forest composition of the Highlands, is advised to check under "Vegetation" and then "Hudson Highlands."

HUDSON RIVER HISTORY.

The best-known study is Carl Carmer's *The Hudson* (New York, 1939), part of The Rivers of America series and still in print. It has an excellent bibliography. Other works of a similar nature are Benson J. Lossing, *The Hudson, from the Wilderness to the Sea* (New York, 1866), scarce and costly, but crammed with information by a careful observer who traveled and sketched his way from the Adirondacks to the harbor; Edgar Mayhew Bacon, *The Hudson River from Ocean to Source* (New York, 1902), helpful for its literary associations and map, of the river from Manhattan to Troy; Wallace Bruce, *The Hudson* (New York, 1907), an excellent guide; Clifton Johnson, *The Picturesque Hudson* (New York, 1909); Nelson Greene, editor, *History of the Valley of the Hudson, River of Destiny* (Chicago, 1931), a great catchall of five volumes, of which the first two are valuable for historical notes, and the other three are puffs of local personages; and Paul Wilstach, *Hudson River Landings* (Indianapolis, 1933). Illustrated books are Henry Collins Brown, *The Lordly Hudson* (New York, 1937); Croswell Bowen, *Great River of the Mountains: The Hudson* (New York, 1941); and John Reed, *The Hudson River Valley* (New York, 1960). Also of use are David Lear Buckman, *Old Steamboat Days on the Hudson River* (New York, 1907);

Bibliography

William E. Verplanck and Moses W. Collyer, *The Sloops of the Hudson* (New York, 1908); Harold Donaldson Eberlein, *The Manors and Historic Homes of the Hudson Valley* (Philadelphia, 1924); and David Maldwyn Ellis, *Landlords and Farmers in the Hudson-Mohawk Region, 1790–1850* (Ithaca, N.Y., 1946).

INDIANS.

William A. Ritchie, state archeologist, has written a three-part study, *Indian History of New York State,* published by the New York State Museum and Science Service in the 1960s. Separate papers deal with "Pre-Iroquoian Cultures," "The Iroquoian Tribes," and "The Algonkian Tribes." Ritchie also wrote *The Archeology of New York State* (New York, 1965). Alanson Skinner, assistant curator of anthropology at the American Museum of Natural History, wrote a helpful little book, *The Indians of Greater New York* (Cedar Rapids, Iowa, 1915). A most valuable reference is E. M. Ruttenber's *History of the Indian Tribes of Hudson's River* (Albany, 1872). William Beauchamp wrote a number of pioneering studies for the New York State Museum, and two I have relied upon are *Aboriginal Place Names of New York* (Albany, 1907) and *A History of the New York Iroquois* (Albany, 1905). See also George T. Hunt, *The Wars of the Iroquois* (Madison, Wis., 1960) and Edmund Wilson, *Apologies to the Iroquois* (New York, 1960), which includes Joseph Mitchell's study, "The Mohawks in High Steel." A standard reference work is Frederick Webb Hodge, editor, *Handbook of American Indians North of Mexico* (Washington, 1912), published in two volumes as Bulletin 30, Bureau of American Ethnology, Smithsonian Institution. *The Bulletin* of the New York State Archeological Association occasionally contains papers dealing with the Hudson River. See Walter S. Newman, "Holocene History of the Lower Hudson River Estuary," *The Bulletin,* No. 38, 1966, and "Late Pleistocene History of the Lower Hudson River Estuary," No. 40, 1967, and Louis A. Brennan, "A Six-Thousand-Year-Old Midden of Virginia Oyster Shell at Croton Point," No. 29, 1963. Brennan also wrote, "A Beginning in Chronology for the Croton River Area," *The Pennsylvania Archaeologist,* Vol. 32, Nos. 3–4, 1963. The Hudson River Valley Commission has published a brief report, *The Hudson Archeological Sites* (n.p., n.d.).

COLONIAL TIMES.

Accounts of the early days by Juet, Van der Donck, de Vries, et al., are to be found in *Collections of the New-York Historical Society,*

Second Series, Volume I (New York, 1841) and J. Franklin Jameson, editor, *Narratives of New Netherland,* 1609–1664 (New York, 1909). John Bakeless, *The Eyes of Discovery* (Philadelphia, 1950), is a superb account of America as seen by the first explorers. It was reprinted by Dover in 1961. Dover also has reprinted Peter Kalm, *Travels in North America* (New York, 1964) in two volumes. Ralph H. Smith's paper on the native vegetation and land use, "Definition of Game Range Divisions in New York," appeared in the July, 1955, issue of *New York Fish and Game Journal,* which is published by the state conservation department. See also E. B. O'Callaghan, editor, *Documents Relative to the Colonial History of the State of New-York* (Albany, 1856), Vol. I, and Maud Wilder Goodwin, *Dutch and English on the Hudson* (New Haven, 1919).

ART, AESTHETICS, AND CONSERVATION.

Thomas Cole and the Hudson River School figure at length in James Thomas Flexner, *That Wilder Image* (Boston, 1962). Cole and other Hudson River admirers also figure in Hans Huth, *Nature and the American* (Berkeley and Los Angeles, 1957), an account of the development of the conservation movement in the United States, and in Roderick Nash, *Wilderness and the American Mind* (New Haven and London, 1967). Farida Wiley edited the anthology *John Burroughs' America, Selections from the Writings of the Hudson River Naturalist* (New York, 1951). Clara Barrus wrote a two-volume study, *The Life and Letters of John Burroughs* (Boston and New York, 1925), and Elizabeth Burroughs Kelley wrote *John Burroughs: Naturalist* (New York, 1959).

NATURAL HISTORY SURVEY.

In the nineteenth century, the state published thirty volumes, many with magnificent color plates, on the natural history of New York. Volumes of special value are John Torrey, *A Flora of the State of New-York* (Albany, 1843) in two volumes, and the five by James E. DeKay, who wrote *Zoology of New-York, or New-York Fauna* (Albany, 1842–1844), which deal with mammalia, reptiles and amphibia, fishes, mollusca and crustacea, and birds. Other publications in this series were on the agriculture, minerology, geology, and paleontology of New York. The run of paleontological works were written by James Hall, who labored, most lovingly, at the task from 1847 to 1894.

Bibliography

GEOLOGY AND GEOGRAPHY.

John H. Thompson, editor, *Geography of New York State* (Syracuse, 1966) is a most helpful work, as is *New York, A Guide to the Empire State* (New York, 1940), compiled by workers of the Writers' Program of the Work Projects Administration. The New York State Museum has published a number of geological studies, and those I have consulted include William J. Miller, *The Geological History of New York State* (Albany, 1914); Robert Balk, *Geology of the Newcomb Quadrangle* (Albany, 1932); Winifred Goldring, *Geology of the Coxsackie Quadrangle, New York* (Albany, 1943); Rudolf Ruedemann, John H. Cook, and David H. Newland, *Geology of the Catskill and Kaaterskill Quadrangles* (Albany, 1942); C. E. Gordon, *Geology of the Poughkeepsie Quadrangle* (Albany, 1911); and Charles P. Berkey and Marion Rice, *Geology of the West Point Quadrangle, N.Y.* (Albany, 1921). Christopher J. Schuberth has written a most informative study, *The Geology of New York City and Environs* (Garden City, N.Y., 1968). The natural terrain of Manhattan was explored by George Everett Hill and George E. Waring, Jr. in "Old Wells and Water-Courses on the Island of Manhattan," Parts I and II, *Half Moon Series Papers on Historic New York* (New York, 1897). Recently, the Hudson River Valley Commission published *The Hudson Mineral Resources* (n.p., n.d.) by John G. Broughton, James F. Davis, and John H. Johnsen.

VEGETATION.

E. Lucy Braun, *The Deciduous Forests of Eastern North America* (Philadelphia, 1950) is valuable, but for the specialist. Maurice Brooks writes extensively about plant life in layman's language in *The Appalachians* (Boston, 1965). Norman Taylor wrote "Native Trees of the Hudson River Valley," *Bulletin of the New York Botanical Garden*, No. 23, 1909. William F. Fox wrote a thorough account, "History of the Lumber Industry in the State of New York," *Sixth Annual Report of the Forest, Fish and Game Commission* (Albany, 1901), from which I have copied the hammer marks used on logs in the upper Hudson. See also A. B. Recknagel, *The Forests of New York State* (New York, 1923). Ulysses Prentiss Hedrick, *A History of Agriculture in the State of New York* (Albany, 1933), is, in good part, about land use and the changing social scene.

Homer D. House, *Wild Flowers of New York* (Albany, 1919), was published originally in two volumes by the New York State Museum and then reprinted as a single volume, with minor changes, by the Macmillan Company, New York, in 1934, under the title of *Wild Flowers*. House also compiled the *Bibliography of the Botany of New York State, 1751–1940* (Albany, 1942), published in two parts by the state museum. In this, he cited titles by region, including the Hudson River Valley. More recently, Frank E. Egler wrote, "A Cartographic Guide to Selected Regional Vegetational Literature—Where Plant Communities have been described. Part I. Northeastern United States," in *Sarracenia*, No. 1, August, 1959. A basic study is William L. Bray, "The Development of the Vegetation of New York State," *Bulletin New York State College of Forestry at Syracuse University*, Vol. XVI, No. 2, November, 1915.

Rogers McVaugh, *Flora of the Columbia County Area, New York* (Albany, 1958), published by the state museum in two parts, has much to say about native flora and the introduction of foreign plants. H. A. Haring, *Our Catskill Mountains* (New York, 1931), deals with hemlock and tanbark peeling and other subjects related to the Catskills. See also Edith Adelaide Roberts and Helen Wilkinson Reynolds, *The Role of Plant Life in the History of Dutchess County* (n.p., but presumably Poughkeepsie, 1938).

STREAM AND ESTUARINE LIFE.

Three essential volumes for any serious student of the Hudson were edited by Dr. Emmeline Moore of the New York State Conservation Department, a most vigorous lady who supervised investigations of all the watersheds in the state during the 1920s and 1930s. The three volumes are *A Biological Survey of the Upper Hudson Watershed* (Albany, 1933); *A Biological Survey of the Mohawk-Hudson Watershed* (Albany, 1935); and *A Biological Survey of the Lower Hudson Watershed* (Albany, 1937). Much of the information is now out of date, but the surveys nonetheless contain many valuable papers.

For later investigations, see Alistair W. McCrone, "The Hudson River Estuary," *Geographical Review*, April, 1966, pp. 175–189, and *Hudson River Ecology*, papers from a symposium held on October 4–5, 1966, at Tuxedo, New York, and published by the Hudson River Valley Commission. The Hudson River Valley Commission also has published *The Hudson Fish & Wildlife* and *The Hudson Biological Resources*. Dr. Gwyneth Parry Howells edited *Ecological Survey of the Hudson River*, Progress Report Number 3, September 30, 1968, for the Institute of Environmental Medicine, New York University

Medical Center. It has some interesting papers for the specialist.

Readers interested in general stream or pond life should see David G. Frey, editor, *Limnology in North America* (Madison, Wis., 1963); Paul Welch, *Limnology* (2nd. ed., New York, 1952); James G. Needham and J. T. Lloyd, *The Life of Inland Waters* (3rd ed., Ithaca, N.Y., 1937); Kathleen E. Carpenter, *Life in Inland Waters with Especial Reference to Animals* (New York, 1928); Anne Haven Morgan, *Field Book of Ponds and Streams* (New York, 1930); T. T. Macan and E. B. Worthington, *Life in Lakes and Rivers* (London, 1951); Robert E. Coker, *Streams, Lakes, Ponds* (Chapel Hill, 1954); Elsie B. Klots, *The New Field Book of Freshwater Life* (New York, 1966); and John Bardach, *Downstream, a Natural History of the River* (New York, Evanston, and London, 1964).

For estuarine life, see George A. Lauff, editor, *Conference on Estuaries, Jekyll Island, 1964* (Washington, 1967), a massive collection of papers published by the American Association for the Advancement of Science; Lionel A. Walford, *Living Resources of the Sea* (New York, 1958); George K. Reid, *Ecology of Inland Waters and Estuaries* (New York, 1961); *A Symposium on Estuarine Fisheries*, Special Publication No. 3 of the American Fisheries Society (n.p., 1966); John Clark, *Fish and Man, Conflict in the Atlantic Estuaries* (Highlands, N.J., 1967), Special Publication Number 5 of the American Littoral Society; J. Green, *The Biology of Estuarine Animals* (Seattle and London, 1968); Eugene P. Odum, "The Role of Tidal Marshes in Estuarine Production," *The New York State Conservationist,* June–July, 1961; H. F. Udell, J. Zarudsky, T. E. Doheny, and P. R. Burkholder, "Productivity and Nutrient Values of Plants growing in the Salt Marshes of the Town of Hempstead, Long Island," *Bulletin of the Torrey Botanical Club,* January–February, 1969; Robert Livingstone, Jr., *A Preliminary Bibliography with KWIC Index on the Ecology of Estuaries and Coastal Areas of the Eastern United States,* U. S. Fish and Wildlife Service, Special Scientific Report—Fisheries No. 507 (Washington, 1965). John Brooks wrote a two-part article on the Hackensack marshes, "The Meadows," in *The New Yorker,* March 9 and 16, 1957.

AQUATIC INSECTS AND INVERTEBRATES.

Studies cited above generally offer information on aquatic insects or invertebrates, but there are more specialized works. A standard reference is Robert W. Pennak, *Fresh-Water Invertebrates of the United States* (New York, 1953). The *first* edition of Ward and Whipple is to be preferred to the present expensive edition when it comes to life histories, so see Henry Baldwin Ward and George Chandler Whipple, *Fresh-Water Biology* (New York, 1918). A handy work for the field is James G. and Paul R. Needham, *A Guide to the Study of Fresh-Water Biology* (5th ed., revised and enlarged, San Francisco, 1966). Of special relevance to the Hudson are Ephraim Porter Felt et al., *Aquatic Insects in New York State* (Albany, 1903); James G. Needham and Cornelius Betten, *Aquatic Insects in the Adirondacks* (Albany, 1901); Cornelius Betten et al., *The Caddis Flies or Trichoptera of New York State* (Albany, 1934); C. L. Metcalf and W. E. Sanderson, *Black Flies in the Adirondacks* (Albany, 1932); Alan Stone and Hugo A. Jamnback, *The Black Flies of New York State* (Albany, 1955); and D. L. Collins, "Flies—Real and Artificial," *The New York State Conservationist,* April–May, 1956. See also Harold Hinsdill Smedley, *Fly Patterns and Their Origins,* (4th ed., revised and enlarged, Muskegon, Mich., 1950); Justin W. Leonard and Fannie A. Leonard, *Mayflies of Michigan Trout Streams* (Bloomfield Hills, Mich., 1962); Ernest G. Schweibert, Jr., *Matching the Hatch* (New York, 1955); and Ralph B. Swain, *The Insect Guide* (Garden City, N.Y., 1948), a handy pocket volume for the field.

Philip Garman, "The Odonata or Dragonflies of Connecticut," *State Geological and Natural History Survey Bulletin* No. 39 (Hartford, Conn., 1927) is the best and least expensive guide for the northeastern enthusiast. The authoritative guide for the whole continent is James G. Needham and Minter J. Westfall, Jr., *Dragonflies of North America* (Berkeley and Los Angeles, 1955). The best modern survey of the ecology of Odonata on a worldwide basis is Philip S. Corbet, *A Biology of Dragonflies* (London, 1962).

For oysters in the Hudson, see Al Bromley, "The Oyster and the Brothers Flower," *The New York State Conservationist,* December–January, 1953–54. Other books are Frederick C. Paulmier, *Higher Crustacea of New York City* (Albany, 1905); Morris K. Jacobson and William K. Emerson, *Shells of the New York City Area* (Larchmont, N.Y., 1961); Carleton Ray and Elgin Ciampi, *The Underwater Guide to Marine Life* (New York, 1956); Roy Waldo Miner, *Field Book of Seashore Life* (New York, 1950); and C. M. Yonge, *The Sea Shore* (revised ed., London, 1966).

FISHES.

Tarleton H. Bean, *Fishes of New York* (Albany, 1903) is the latest statewide work. Fred Mather wrote several interesting books, *Memo-*

Bibliography

randa Relating to Adirondack Fishes (Albany, 1886); *Men I Have Fished with* (New York, 1897); and *My Angling Friends* (New York, 1901). Mather introduced the brown trout to the United States, and I suspect, although I have not been able to prove the point, that the first plantings were made in a Hudson tributary, the Sacandaga. For trout, see Paul R. Needham, *Trout Streams* (Ithaca, N.Y., 1940), a scarce study well worth revision and reprinting, and W. E. Frost and M. E. Brown, *The Trout* (London, 1967), one of the finest life histories I have ever read.

The question of whether Atlantic salmon were native to the Hudson is dealt with by several authorities, most recently by Anthony Netboy, *The Atlantic Salmon* (Boston, 1968), the first study to deal with this species in all the rivers and countries where it has been a great resource. Edwin C. Kent also examines the question of salmon in the Hudson in *The Isle of Long Ago* (New York, 1933), as does Charles Eliot Goodspeed in *Angling in America* (Boston, 1939). For an account of salmon stocking, see Fred Mather, "Salmon in the Hudson River," *Transactions of the American Fisheries Society*, 1889, pp. 39–65. Also of interest is A. Nelson Cheney, "The Hudson River as a Salmon Stream," *Proceedings and Papers of the National Fishery Congress* (Washington, 1898), pp. 247–251.

Carl L. Hubbs and Reeve M. Bailey wrote *The Small-Mouthed Bass* (Bloomfield Hills, Mich., 1938), while Dr. James A. Henshall authored the classic *Book of the Black Bass* (New ed., revised and extended, Cincinnati, 1904). George Bennett, "Largemouth Bass in Ridge Lake, Coles County, Illinois," *Bulletin of the Illinois Natural History Survey*, Vol. 26, Article 2, November, 1954, is an outstanding paper on the ecology of this fish.

For shad, see Romeo Mansueti and Haven Kolb, *A Historical Review of the Shad Fisheries of North America*, Publication No. 97, Chesapeake Biological Laboratory, Solomons, Md., December, 1953; Gerald B. Talbot, "Factors Associated with Fluctuations in Abundance of Hudson River Shad," *Fishery Bulletin 101*, Vol. 56 (Washington, 1954); and Gerald B. Talbot and James E. Sykes, "Atlantic Coast Migrations of American Shad," *Fishery Bulletin 142*, Vol. 58 (Washington, 1958). Seth Green's account of planting Hudson shad in California is in "Fish-Culture," *Report of the Commissioner of Agriculture* (Washington, 1873), pp. 248–274. See also Livingston Stone, "Report of Operations in California in 1873," *Report of the Commissioner for 1873–4 and 1874–5, United States Commission of Fish and Fisheries* (Washington, 1876), Part III, pp. 377–429, and H. M. Smith, "A Review of the History and Results of the Attempts to

Acclimate Fish and Other Water Animals in the Pacific States," *Bulletin of the United States Fish Commission, 1895* (Washington, 1896), pp. 379–472. George Laycock deals with carp and other imported wildlife in *The Alien Animals* (Garden City, N.Y., 1966).

For sturgeon, see J. A. Ryder, "The Sturgeons and Sturgeon Industries of the Eastern Coast of the United States," *Bulletin of the United States Fish Commission, 1888* (Washington, 1890), pp. 231–288; Vadim D. Vladykov and John R. Greeley, "Order Acipenseroidei," *Fishes of the Western North Atlantic* (New Haven, 1963), Part Three, pp. 24–60; and G. V. Nikol'skii, *Special Ichthyology* (2nd. revised and enlarged ed., Jerusalem, 1961), an English translation from the Russian. L. Zenkevitch, *Biology of the Seas of the U.S.S.R.* (London, 1963), another translation from the Russian, offers detailed information on the Black Sea, the Sea of Azov, and the Caspian Sea.

Striped bass literature is voluminous. The basic work is Edward C. Raney, Ernest F. Tresselt, Edgar H. Hollis, V. D. Vladykov, and D. H. Wallace, "The Striped Bass," *Bulletin of the Bingham Oceanographic Collection*, Peabody Museum of Natural History, Yale University, Vol. XIV, Article 1, December, 1952. Raney's paper "The Life History of the Striped Bass," is the major study in this volume. See also Daniel Merriman, "Studies on the Striped Bass (*Roccus saxatilis*) of the Atlantic Coast," *Fishery Bulletin of the Fish and Wildlife Service*, Vol. 50 (Washington, 1941); Edward C. Raney and Donald P. de Sylva, "Racial Investigations of the Striped Bass," *The Journal of Wildlife Management*, Vol. 17, No. 4, October, 1953, pp. 495–509; Romeo J. Mansueti, "Effects of Civilization on Striped Bass and other Estuarine Biota in Chesapeake Bay and Tributaries," *Proceedings of the Gulf and Caribbean Fisheries Institute*, Fourteenth Annual Session, November, 1961, pp. 110–136; Warren F. Rathjen and Lewis C. Miller, "Aspects of the Early Life History of the Striped Bass (*Roccus saxatilis*) in the Hudson River," *New York Fish and Game Journal*, January, 1957, pp. 43–60; Walter S. Murawski, "Comparative Study of Populations of the Striped Bass, *Roccus saxatilis* (Walbaum), based on Laterial-line Scale Counts" (Master's thesis, Cornell University Library); Irwin M. Alperin, "Dispersal, Migration and Origins of Striped Bass from Great South Bay, Long Island," *New York Fish and Game Journal*, January, 1966, pp. 79–112; Richard H. Schaefer, "Size, Age Composition and Migration of Striped Bass from the Surf Waters of Long Island," *New York Fish and Game Journal*, January, 1968, pp. 1–51; John Clark, "Seasonal Movements of Striped Bass Contingents of Long Island Sound and the New York Bight," *Transactions of the American Fisheries Society*, October, 1968,

Bibliography

pp. 320–343; Arthur Glowka, "Stripers in the Hudson," *Outdoor Life*, August, 1964; and Mark Sosin, "New Facts about Hudson Stripers," *Sportfishing*, February, 1968. The Sport Fishing Institute in Washington, D.C., has published *A Bibliography of the Striped Bass*, revised in 1967 by William H. Massman.

Descriptions and life histories of striped bass, alewives, sturgeons, tomcod, and other species in the estuarine Hudson are to be found in Henry B. Bigelow and William C. Schroeder, *Fishes of the Gulf of Maine, Fishery Bulletin 74* (Washington, 1953), a truly great work. Two books of interest are John Treadwell Nichols, *Fishes of the Vicinity of New York City* (New York, 1918) and J. T. Nichols and C. M. Breder, Jr., *The Marine Fishes of New York and Southern New England* (New York, 1927). For tropical strays, see Irwin M. Alperin and Richard H. Schaefer, "Marine Fishes New or Uncommon to Long Island, New York," *New York Fish and Game Journal*, January, 1965, pp. 1–16, and Seth Rosenbaum, "Collecting for a Salt Water Aquarium," *Underwater Naturalist*, Winter, 1968, pp. 33–37.

BIRDS.

Elon Howard Eaton, *Birds of New York* (Albany, 1910 and 1912) was published in two volumes by the state museum. I have relied a good deal on John Bull, *Birds of the New York Area* (New York and Evanston, 1964). Robert S. Arbib, Jr., Olin Sewall Pettingill, Jr., and Sally Hoyt Spofford wrote the useful *Enjoying Birds Around New York City* (Cambridge, Mass., 1966). In 1959, the Rockland Audubon Society in West Nyack, New York, published *Birds of Rockland County and the Hudson Highlands*. For life histories of North American birds, see the studies by Arthur Cleveland Bent and collaborators, originally published by the Smithsonian Institution and reprinted by Dover. The Bent life histories are indispensable for anyone seriously interested in birds. In 1947, the New York State Conservation Department published the thorough work *The Ruffed Grouse*, by Gardiner Bump, Robert W. Darrow, Frank C. Edminster, and Walter F. Crissey. J. D. Summers-Smith, a British ornithologist, has written *The House Sparrow* (London, 1963). Dillon Ripley, *A Paddling of Ducks* (New York, 1957), is a charming book on aviculture from which I have drawn my account of the comeback of the wood duck.

POLLUTION.

The literature on pollution in the Hudson and elsewhere is voluminous. The state and federal governments have issued a number of studies. The United States Department of Health, Education, and Welfare published *Report on Pollution of the Hudson River and Its Tributaries* in September, 1965, and then, in two volumes, *Proceedings—Conference in the matter of Pollution of the interstate Waters of the Hudson River and Its Tributaries—New York and New Jersey,* the transcript of a hearing held on September 28, 29, and 30, 1965. The New York State Department of Health has published several useful volumes, for example, *Lower Hudson River, From Mouth to Northern Westchester-Rockland County Lines,* Lower Hudson River Drainage Basic Survey Series Report No. 9, 1960; *Drainage Basins of Streams: Entering the Hudson River in Albany, Columbia, Greene and Rensselaer Counties,* Lower Hudson River Drainage Basin Survey Series Report No. 11, 1962; *Upper Hudson River Drainage Basin, Except Hoosic River Drainage Basin,* Upper Hudson River Drainage Basin Survey Series Report No. 2, 1963. See also Earle B. Phelps, *Stream Sanitation* (New York, 1944) and Edwin L. Cooper, editor, *A Symposium on Water Quality Criteria to Protect Aquatic Life,* Special Publication No. 4 of the American Fisheries Society, 1967. For the reader who wonders what oil or excessive nitrogen or phosphorus does to water quality or animal life, I recommend Kenneth M. Mackenthun and William Marcus Ingram, *Biological Associated Problems in Freshwater Environments, Their Identification, Investigation and Control,* published by the Federal Water Pollution Control Administration, the Department of the Interior. Copies may be procured, at $1.25 each, from the Superintendent of Documents, U.S. Government Printing Office, Washington, D.C. 20402.

Ever since Rachel Carson sounded the alarm in *Silent Spring* (Boston, 1962), there has been a great public concern about pesticides, especially DDT and the chlorinated hydrocarbons. Dr. Charles F. Wurster, who has conducted important research on the problem, has written a most useful review, with a bibliography, "Chlorinated Hydrocarbon Insecticides and the World Ecosystem," for *Biological Conservation* (Elsevier, in press). See also Robert L. Rudd, *Pesticides and the Living Landscape* (Madison, Wis., 1964), a detailed study with a bibliography.

Spokesmen for some utilities may claim that little is known about thermal pollution; however, two extensive bibliographies have been issued: Edward C. Raney and Bruce W. Menzel, *Heated Effluents and Effects on Aquatic Life with Emphasis on Fishes,* Philadelphia Electric Company and Ichthyological Associates, Bulletin No. 1, July 7, 1967, and V. S. Kennedy and Joseph Mihursky, *Bibliography on the Effects of Temperature in the Aquatic Environment,* Contribution

No. 326, May, 1967, University of Maryland, Natural Resources Institute. The Kennnedy-Mihurksy bibliography was reprinted in *Thermal Pollution—1968*, Part 1, Hearings before the Subcommittee on Air and Water Pollution of the Committee on Public Works, United States Senate, Ninetieth Congress, Second Session (Washington, 1968). A Part 2 was also published (Washington, 1968), and both volumes are most useful. The best review of the overall problem to date is John R. Clark, "Thermal Pollution and Aquatic Life," *Scientific American*, March, 1969. Immodestly I cite my own article, "The Nukes Are in Hot Water," *Sports Illustrated*, January 20, 1969. The Citizens Committee to Save Cayuga Lake has recently published two pamphlets, with bibliographical references: "Thermal Pollution of Cayuga Lake by a Proposed Power Plant" and "Radioactivity and a Proposed Power Plant on Cayuga Lake." Both were largely written by scientists at Cornell University, spearheaded by Dr. Alfred W. Eipper. Dangers of radiation and nuclear accidents are investigated by Sheldon Novick, *The Careless Atom* (Boston, 1969). See also Dr. Malcolm L. Peterson, "Environmental Contamination from Nuclear Reactors," *Scientist and Citizen*, November, 1965, pp. 1–11.

ADIRONDACKS.

Alfred L. Donaldson's two volume study, *A History of the Adirondacks* (New York, 1921), is the basic reference on the mountains. See also William Chapman White, *Adirondack Country* (New York and Boston, 1954), a delightful and informative book. Harold K. Hochschild's labor of love, *Township 34*, was privately published in 1952, but the Adirondack Museum at Blue Mountain Lake has published some chapters in paperbound form, e. g., *Lumberjacks and Rivermen in the Central Adirondacks, 1850–1950* (Blue Mountain Lake, 1962) and *The MacIntyre Mine—from Failure to Fortune* (Blue Mountain Lake, 1962). See also William L. Wessels, *Adirondack Profiles* (3rd ed., Lake George, N.Y., 1961). For information on Mount Marcy, see "Plants and Animals of Mount Marcy, New York," by Charles C. Adams, George P. Burns, T. L. Hankinson, Barrington Moore, and Norman Taylor, *Ecology*, Volume 1, Numbers 2, 3, and 4, 1920, and Howard E. Woodin, "Establishment of a Permanent Vegetational Transect above Timberline on Mt. Marcy, N.Y.," *Ecology*, Vol. 40, No. 2, April, 1959. There are any number of studies on Adirondack wildlife, but those I found valuable include W. J. Hamilton, Jr., and Arthur H. Cook, "The Biology and Management of the Fisher in New York," *New York Fish and Game Journal*, January, 1955; Madison Grant, "Moose," *Seventh Report of the Forest, Fish and Game Commission* (Albany, 1902); and Harry V. Radford, "History of the Adirondack Beaver," *Annual Reports of the Forest, Fish and Game Commissioner for 1904–1905–1906* (Albany, 1907). Radford also wrote *Adirondack Murray: A Biographical Appreciation.* (New York, 1905). Verplanck Colvin covered a multitude of subjects—"Geodetic and trigonometrical measurements, magnetic variation, hydrography, river surveys, levelling and barometric-hypsometry, meteorology, rainfall, botany, zoology and geology"—in his yearly reports to the legislature. The Colvin quotation in Chapter Four on the grandeur of the mountains may be found on pages 66 through 67 of Colvin's *Seventh Annual Report on the Topographical Survey of the Adirondack Region of New York* (Albany, 1880). For a succinct account of the geology of the region see Y. W. Isachsen, "Geological History of the Adirondack Mountains," *The Conservationist,* June–July, 1962. The reader interested in the Adirondacks should see *Adirondack Bibliography* (Gabriels, N.Y., 1958), compiled by the Bibliography Committee of the Adirondack Mountain Club.

HUDSON HIGHLANDS.

Researchers at the Black Rock Forest have published various studies in issues of *The Black Rock Forest Bulletin.* See Hugh M. Raup, "Botanical Studies in the Black Rock Forest," *Bulletin,* No. 7; C. S. Denny, "Glacial Geology of the Black Rock Forest, *Bulletin,* No. 8; Henry H. Tryon, "Practical Forestry in the Hudson Highlands," *Bulletin,* No. 12; and Henry H. Tryon and Raymond P. Finn, "Twenty-Year Progress Report, 1928–1948," *Bulletin,* No. 14. Lawrence J. Crockett edited "Some Contributions to the Floristics, Plant Ecology, and Geology of the Hudson Highlands Section of the Lower Hudson Valley," *Sarracenia,* No. 11, June, 1967. Some of the papers of note are A. W. McCrone, "An Introduction to the Geologic Setting of the Newburgh-Hudson Highlands Sector of the Lower Hudson Valley," J. H. Lehr, "The Marshes at Piermont" and "The Plants of Iona Island," John Nicholas, "Vegetation of Sterling Forest since the Last Ice Age," and Suzanne Keatinge, "The Major Plant Communities of Sterling Forest." Essential to any study of the Hudson or the Highlands are the reports by Dr. Edgar A. Mearns, "Birds of the Hudson Highlands," the *Bulletin of the Essex Institute,* 1878–1881, and "A Study of the Vertebrate Fauna of the Hudson Highlands, with Observations on the Mollusca, Crustacea, Lepidoptera, and the Flora of the Region," *Bulletin American Museum of Natural History*, Vol. X, 1898. See also C. W. Severinghaus and C. P. Brown, "History of the Whitetailed Deer in New York," *New York Fish and Game Journal*, July, 1956. The Appalachian Mountain Club issued *In the Hudson Highlands* (New York, 1945), edited by "Solvitur Ambulando," which contains a number of essays on such diverse subjects as the Catskill Aqueduct, the Jackson Whites, the West Shore Railroad, and the Appalachian Trail. The U.S. Government Printing Office published two key records involving the Storm King power controversy: *Anadromous Fish—1965*, Hearings before the Subcommittee on Fisheries and Wildlife Conservation of the Committee on Merchant Marine and Fisheries, House of Representatives, Eighty-ninth Congress, First Session, on Hudson River Spawning Grounds, May 10 and 11, 1965, Serial No. 89–9 (Washington, 1965), and *Hudson Highlands National Scenic Riverway*, Hearings before the Subcommittee on National Parks and Recreation of the Committee on Interior and Insular Affairs, Eighty-ninth Congress, First Session, July 24 and 25, 1965 (Washington, 1965), Serial No. 14.

NEW YORK CITY AND THE HARBOR.

See *New York City Guide* (Revised ed., New York, 1939) by the Guilds' Committee for Federal Writers' Publications, Inc.; *A Maritime History of New York* (Garden City, N.Y., 1941) compiled by the Workers of the Writers' Program of the Work Projects Administration; Robert Greenhalgh Albion, *The Rise of New York Port* (New York, 1939); Joseph Mitchell, *The Bottom of the Harbor* (Boston and Toronto, 1959); and Charles Edward Russell, *From Sandy Hook to 62°* (New York, 1929), an account of the harbor pilots. For natural history, see William Beebe, *Unseen Life in New York as a Naturalist Sees It* (New York and Boston, 1953) and John Kieran, *A Natural History of New York City* (Boston, 1959). For a comparison of life in big cities, see R. S. R. Fitter, *London's Natural History* (London, 1945). Mabel Abbott, *The Life of William T. Davis* (Ithaca, N. Y., 1949) is a pleasant biography of the Staten Island naturalist whose special interest was the seventeen-year locust. Any New Yorker seeking to explore the countryside near the city should have a copy of *New York Walk Book* (3rd ed., New York, 1951) by Raymond H. Torrey, Frank Place, Jr., and Robert L. Dickinson. This excellent guide is published by the American Geographical Society under the sponsorship of the New York-New Jersey Trail Conference.

HUDSON CHANNEL-HUDSON CANYON.

The literature is scanty; however, relevant works are Bostwick H. Ketchum, Alfred C. Redfield, and John C. Ayers, "The Oceanography of the New York Bight," *Papers in Physical Oceanography and Meteorology* published by the Massachusetts Institute of Technology and Woods Hole Oceanographic Institution (Cambridge and Woods Hole, Mass.), Vol. XII, No. 1, August, 1951; Walter and Richard Krotee, *Shipwrecks off the New Jersey Coast* (Philadelphia, 1966); William Beebe, *The Arcturus Adventure* (New York, 1926); "Fishing a Mile Down in Hudson Gorge," *Bulletin New York Zoological Society*, Vol. XXXII, No. 2, March–April, 1929; "Deep-Sea Fish of the Hudson Gorge," *Zoologica*, Vol. XII, No. 1, April 30, 1929; "Haplophryne Hudsonius," *Zoologica*, Vol. XII, No. 2, April 30, 1929; and David B. Ericson and Goesta Wollin, *The Deep and the Past* (New York, 1964).

INDEX

Index

Index

Index

Index

Index

Nack, Everett, 116–19, 121, 236
Narrows, 20, 29, 30, 33, 34, 38, 67, 140, 248, 249, 257
National Audubon Society, 171, 276
Nature Conservancy, Inc., 157, 170, 276
Needham, Paul R., 39
Needlefish (*Strongylura marina*), 22, 224–25
Newburgh, 19, 21, 22, 52, 60, 65, 66, 105, 216; Bay, 146
New Jersey, 16, 17, 23, 27, 41, 85, 93, 101, 107, 132, 133, 162, 174, 178, 194, 237, 245, 275
New York Aquarium, 199, 200, 213, 221
New York City, 16, 17, 19, 22, 51, 53, 54, 55–56, 57, 60, 63, 65, 229, 256, 258; water supply, 59, 108, 156, 173, 215, 232; *see also* Manhattan Island
New York Harbor, 98, 99, 140, 159, 257; bodies found in, 250; clipper trade, 247; debris, 249–50; pilots, 248–49; pollution, 215–53; sewer fishing, 253–55; shipbuilding, 247; ship traffic, 245–47; tides, 249, 251
New York Harbor Act (1888), 97, 98, 99, 102
New York State Barge Canal, 88, 94, 119
New York State Conservation Department, 23, 33, 101, 129, 137, 158, 160, 168, 240
New York State Museum, 42, 66, 70, 103, 241
New York Zoological Society, 263, 264, 266, 267

Olmsted, Frederick Law, 60
Opposum (*Didelphis marsupialis virginiana*), 128
Ossining, 28, 67, 102, 121, 129, 130, 148, 152, 187, 237
Ottinger, Richard, 99, 101, 103, 161, 163, 164, 167, 174, 275, 279

Pagano, Jimmy, 149
Palisades, 17, 19, 27, 51, 62, 104, 209, 243; fossils (*Icarosaurus siefkeri*, *Rutiodon manhattanensis*), 242; geology of, 240–41; Interstate Park, 125, 155, 173, 231, 241; quarries, 241–42
Patterson, Captain Joseph, 148, 237
Paul, Weiss, Rifkind, Wharton and Garrison, 168
Paulding, James Kirke, 59
Pauw, Michael, 48
Pearson, Arthur, 178
Peck, Charles H., 70
Peek, Jan, 49
Peekskill, 21, 22, 24, 49, 56, 66, 73, 86–87, 128, 147, 152, 174, 182, 187, 196, 229, 256; Bay, 182; Hollow Brook, 232
Penn Central, 98, 99, 101, 103, 150, 206, 231, 237, 278
Peppermint (*Mentha piperita*), 66
Perch, silver (*Bairdiella chrysura*), 229; white (*Morone americanus*), 22, 38, 149, 218, 220, 236, 278; yellow (*Perca flavescens*), 22, 73, 215
Perlmutter, Alfred, 158–59, 165, 169
Peterson, Malcolm, 179
Peterson, Roger Tory, 238
Pheasant, ring-necked (*Phasianus colchicus*), 67
Phelps, Earle B., 252
Phelps, Orson Schofield, 81
Philipse, Frederick, 48
Pickerel, 223, 236; chain (*Esox niger*), 73
Piermont Salt Marsh, 231, 242–44

Pike (*Esox lucius*), 20, 73
Pinweed (*Lechea racemulosa*), 125
Pipefish, 223–24
Pirone, Dominick, 103, 158, 160, 161, 166, 167–68, 177, 178, 211, 221–22, 227, 276, 279
Plover, black-bellied (*Squatarola squatarola*), 243; golden (*Pluvialis dominica*), 120
Poe, Edgar Allan, 250
Pollock (*Pollachius virens*), 260
Pollution, 16, 23, 33, 38, 39, 67, 117, 153, 184, 211, 272, 275, 278; anti-pollution enforcement, question of, 98–104, 272–73; of canalized Hudson, 93–95; coliform bacteria densities, 96, 252; companies contributing to, 71, 72, 93–94, 102, 105–6, 117, 177, 179, 184, 231, 258; dragonflies, damselflies and, 93; effect on animal life, 103–4; legislation restricting, 97–98; of Mohawk River, 94; oil, 91, 98, 101–2, 103, 149–51, 237, 279–80; pathogenic organisms, 94, 95–96; pesticides, 103; and plankton, 208; radionuclides, 178–80; sewage, 21–22, 94, 95, 96, 208, 251–53, 258, 259; and shad production, 112–13; standards of, 96–97; of the Tappan Zee, 213–32; thermal, 174–78; *see also* Albany Pool
Pomeroy, R. Watson, 161, 162, 164, 165
Pondshiners, 106-7
Porpoises, 253, 255, 268
Pough, Richard, 276
Poughkeepsie, 21, 25, 42, 56, 105, 108, 161, 224, 274
Powley, Howard, 147–48
Prickly pear (*Opuntia humifusa*), 19
Punkies (*Culicoides biguttatus*), 74, 75
Purple loosestrife (*Lythrum salicaria*), 66

Quail, bobwhite (*Colinus virginianus*), 63
Queen Anne's lace (*Daucus carota*), 66
Quill Gordon (*Epeorus pleuralis*, *Iron fraudator*), 76
Quincy, Mrs. Josiah, 51

Rabbit, cottontail (*Sylvilagus floridanus*), 63
Raccoon (*Procyon lotor lotor*), 127
Radford, Harry, 86
Rail, clapper (*Rallus longirostris*), 243
Rambova, Natasha, 83
Raney, Edward C., 137, 138, 139, 166, 276
Rasieres, Isaack de, 36, 38–39, 43
Rathjen, Warren F., 137–38, 159, 162, 164–65, 168
Rattail maggots, 94
Rattlesnake, timber (*Crotalus horridus horridus*), 128
Reed, common (*Phragmites communis*), 237
Reilly, Ed, 87, 103, 127, 243
Revolution, American, 54, 55, 56, 65, 83, 107, 246
Riccardi, Ric, 91, 177, 279
Ritchie, William A., 42, 44
Roach, *see* shiner, golden
Robinson, Henry, 89
Rockefeller, John D., Jr., 242
Rockefeller, Laurance, 163
Rockefeller, Nelson A., 162–64, 180, 273, 276
Rockefeller, William, 82
Rockefellers, the, 239–40
Rogers, Mary Cecilia, 250

Index

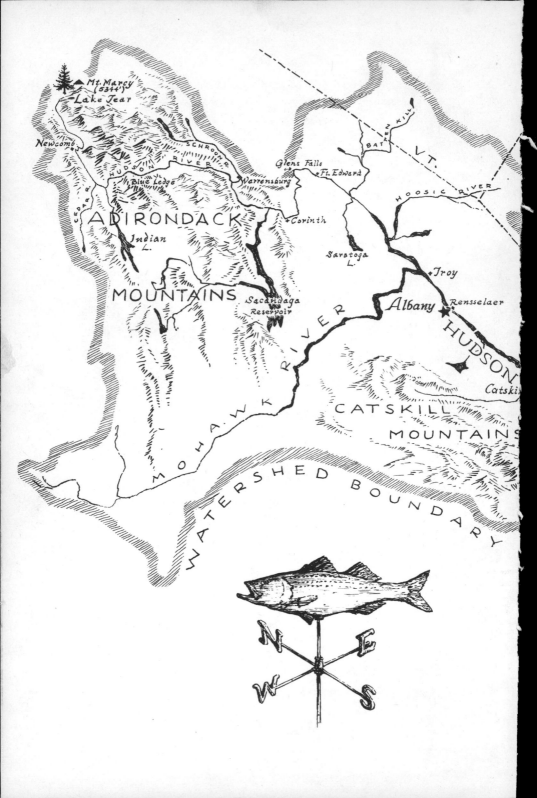